CLIFFS

TEXAS ACADEMIC SKILLS PROGRAM™

PREPARATION GUIDE

by

Jerry Bobrow, Ph.D.

Contributing Authors

Robert Dixon-Kolar, M.S.Ed.

Peter Z Orton, M.Ed.

Consultant

Merritt L. Weisinger, J.D.

ACKNOWLEDGMENTS

My loving thanks to my wife, Susan, and my children, Jennifer Lynn 11, Adam Michael 8, and Jonathan Matthew 4, for their patience and support in this project.

My sincere thanks to Michele Spence of Cliffs Notes for final editing and careful attention to the production process.

Jerry Bobrow

I would like to thank the following authors and companies for permission to reprint excerpts from their materials:

"The Ultimate Teaching Machine" by R. J. Heathorn from *Punch*.

"Professor on Trial" from *Son of the Great Society,* copyright 1966 by Art Buchwald, publisher G. P. Putnam's Sons.

"How Dictionaries Are Made" from *Language in Thought and Action,* copyright 1964 by S. I. Hayakawa, publisher Harcourt, Brace and World, Inc.

From the Los Angeles Times:
"Casseroles" by Rose Dosti, March 1989.
"Holy Matrimony!" by Beth Ann Krier, March 1989.
"Window Tints Put Value, Law in the Shade" by Ralph Vertabedian, March 1989.

ISBN 0-8220-2042-4

CONTENTS

Part I: INTRODUCTION

PART II: ANALYSIS OF EXAM AREAS

- **Ability Tested** • **Basic Skills Necessary** •
  • **Directions** • **Analysis** •
  • **Suggested Approach with Samples** •

- **Ability Tested** • **Basic Skills Necessary** •
  • **Directions** • **Analysis** •
  • **Suggested Approach with Samples** •

- **Ability Tested** • **Basic Skills Necessary** •
  • **Directions** • **Analysis** •
  • **Suggested Approach with Samples** •

PART III: PRACTICE-REVIEW-ANALYZE-PRACTICE
Two Full-Length Practice Tests

PREFACE

Getting a good score on the TASP is important to you. Since the TASP requires you to use some basic skills you may not have used recently, thorough preparation is the key to doing your best. This makes your study time more important than ever. You must use it effectively.

Test preparation experts and instructors have developed this *Cliffs TASP Preparation Guide*. It is thorough, direct, concise, and easy to use. The materials, techniques, and strategies have been carefully researched and tested and are presently used in college and teachers' association preparation programs throughout the country.

This guide is divided into three parts:

Part I: Introduction—a general description of the exam, recent format, questions commonly asked, and basic overall strategies.

Part II: Analysis of Exam Areas—focuses on ability tested, basic skills necessary, directions, analysis, suggested approaches with samples, and additional tips.

Part III: Practice-Review-Analyze-Practice—two complete, full-length practice tests with answers and in-depth explanations.

Each practice test is followed by analysis charts to assist you in evaluating your progress. This guide is not meant to substitute for comprehensive courses, but if you follow the Study Guide Checklist and study regularly, you should get the best TASP preparation possible.

STUDY GUIDE CHECKLIST

- ____ 1. Read the TASP Information Bulletin.
- ____ 2. Become familiar with the Test Format, page 3.
- ____ 3. Familiarize yourself with the answers to Questions Commonly Asked about the TASP, page 4.
- ____ 4. Learn the techniques of Three Successful Overall Approaches, page 8.
- ____ 5. Carefully read Part II, Analysis of Exam Areas, beginning on page 13.
- ____ 6. Take Practice Test 1, section by section (review answers after each section), page 109.
- ____ 7. Check your answers and analyze your results, page 173.
- ____ 8. Fill out the Tally Sheet for Questions Missed to pinpoint your mistakes, page 174.
- ____ 9. While referring to each item of Practice Test 1, study *all* the Answers and Explanations that begin on page 177.
- ____ 10. Review necessary basic skills, formulas, and grammar given in Part II of this book. (For additional review refer to *Cliffs Math Review for Standardized Tests* and *Cliffs Verbal Review for Standardized Tests*.)
- ____ 11. Take Practice Test 2, page 205.
- ____ 12. Check your answers and analyze your results, page 273.
- ____ 13. Fill out the Tally Sheet for Questions Missed to pinpoint your mistakes, page 274.
- ____ 14. While referring to each item of Practice Test 2, study *all* the Answers and Explanations that begin on page 277.
- ____ 15. Again, selectively review materials as needed.
- ____ 16. Carefully reread Part II, Analysis of Exam Areas, beginning on page 13.
- ____ 17. Go over Final Preparation on page 303.

Part I: Introduction

FORMAT OF THE TASP

Subject Area	Approximate Number of Questions
Reading (8 to 10 passages, 300–750 words each)	40–50 multiple choice
Mathematics	40–50 multiple choice
Writing I	40–50 multiple choice
Writing II	1 essay of 300–600 words

Scoring

All questions (except the essay) are multiple choice—four answer choices. Your score is based on the number of correct answers that you have. There is no "penalty" (points deducted) for wrong answers. One score is provided for each of the three areas.

GENERAL DESCRIPTION

The TASP measures proficiencies in three areas: reading, mathematics, and writing. The test is based upon the theory that all students attending college and all prospective teachers seeking certification ought to be able to use basic skills in these three areas.

QUESTIONS COMMONLY ASKED
ABOUT THE TASP

Q: WHO ADMINISTERS THE TASP?

A: The TASP is administered by National Evaluation Systems, Inc., with guidelines drawn up by the Texas Higher Education Coordinating Board and the Texas State Board of Education.

Q: WHO NEEDS TO PASS THE TASP?

A: The TASP is required of students entering or enrolled in (or transferring to) a college-level degree program in a Texas public institution and teacher education students at any public or private institution in Texas. You may need to take the exam if you are already a college student who has not earned at least three semester credit hours before fall 1989. Candidates for Texas teaching certificates may also need to take the exam. *It is important that you check with the institution you plan to attend to see if you must take the test.*

Q: DO I NEED THE TASP FOR STUDENT TEACHING?

A: You may need to pass the TASP for enrollment in a state-approved teacher education program. Check with the teacher certification office at your campus.

Q: WHEN AND WHERE IS THE TASP GIVEN?

A: The TASP is administered statewide five times each year. You can obtain dates and test locations by consulting the *TASP Test Registration Bulletin,* available free from National Evaluation Systems, Inc., P.O. Box 140347, Austin, Texas 78714-0347— (512) 926-0743.

Q: HOW MUCH DOES THE TASP COST?

A: The TASP costs $24. However, additional charges may be made for late registration, changes of registration, additional score reports, etc. Consult the free *TASP Test Registration Bulletin* for complete fee information.

Q: DO I HAVE TO PAY AGAIN IF I REPEAT THE TEST?

A: Yes. You must pay the test fee each time you register to take the TASP, even if you take only one section of the test.

Q: WHAT MATERIALS SHOULD I BRING TO THE TEST?

A: Bring your admission ticket, two forms of personal identification (at least one with a recent photograph), several sharpened Number 2 pencils with good erasers, and a recent, recognizable photo of yourself to be left with your testing materials. No calculators, calculator watches, dictionaries, briefcases, food, or other aids will be permitted in the test center.

Q: WHAT IS ON THE TASP?

A: The exam consists of three parts: Reading (passages of approximately 300 to 750 words each followed by multiple-choice questions based on the content of each passage, for a total of 40 to 50 questions); Mathematics (40 to 50 multiple-choice questions requiring knowledge of arithmetic, algebra, and geometry); and Writing (40 to 50 multiple-choice questions testing various writing skills and a writing exercise of approximately 300 to 600 words).

Q: HOW LONG IS THE TASP?

A: Four hours. However, if you need additional time, another hour will be provided.

Q: WHAT ARE THE PASSING SCORES REQUIRED FOR THE THREE SECTIONS?

A: The passing scores for the TASP are set by the Texas Higher Education Coordinating Board and the State Board of Education and are subject to change. Check with your educational institution for current requirements.

Q: WHEN WILL I GET MY SCORE REPORT?

A: Your test scores will be mailed to you about three to five weeks after you take the TASP and will show the results of each section of your test.

Q: MAY I TAKE THE TASP MORE THAN ONCE?

A: Yes. You may take the complete TASP, or any part(s) of it, as many times as you like. You must, however, pay the entire fee each time you register to take the test.

Q: DO I NEED TO TAKE ALL THREE PARTS OF THE TEST?

A: You must *pass* all three parts of the test. However, if you pass any part of the exam at one administration, you may then take only the sections you have not as yet passed. Thus, you do not necessarily have to pass *all* sections in one administration; you can obtain passing scores on the individual sections in separate administrations.

Q: SHOULD I GUESS ON THE TEST?

A: Yes! Since there is no penalty for guessing, *guess* if you have to. If possible, first try to eliminate some of the choices to increase your chances of guessing the right answer. But don't leave any of the answer spaces blank.

Q: SUPPOSE I DO TERRIBLY ON THE TEST. MAY I CANCEL MY TASP SCORE?

A: Yes, you may cancel the scores of one or more of the sections on your TASP, but only if you notify the test authorities in writing, postmarked within seven days after the test administration. Once you request your score(s) canceled, you won't be able to have that score(s) reported at a later date. Consult the free TASP bulletin for complete instructions about canceling scores.

Q: MAY I WRITE ON THE TEST?

A: Yes! Since scratch paper will not be provided, you must do all your work *in* the test booklet. Your answer sheet, however, must have no marks on it other than your personal information (name, registration number, etc.) and your answers.

Q: HOW SHOULD I PREPARE FOR THE TASP?

A: Understanding and practicing test-taking skills will be helpful. Reviewing subject matter in arithmetic, algebra, and geometry, as well as practicing reading and writing skills, will be particularly effective. Some schools offer preparation programs to assist you in attaining a passing score. Check with local educational institutions for information.

Q: WHAT IF I CANNOT AFFORD TO TAKE THE TASP?

A: Financial assistance may be available for eligible students. Contact the financial aid office of your university.

Q: MAY I CANCEL OR CHANGE MY TEST DATE OR TEST CENTER?

A: Yes. Procedures for canceling or changing test date or center are detailed in the free *TASP Test Registration Bulletin,* or call (512) 926-0743.

Q: HOW DO I REGISTER OR GET MORE INFORMATION?

A: Information is available from TASP Test, National Evaluation Systems, Inc., P.O. Box 140347, Austin, Texas 78714-0347— (512) 926-0743.

TAKING THE TASP: THREE SUCCESSFUL OVERALL APPROACHES

I. The "Plus-Minus" System

Some candidates who take the TASP don't get their best possible score because they spend too must time on difficult questions. Don't let this happen to you. Since every question within each section is worth the same amount, use the following system:

1. Carefully answer all the easy questions first.

2. When you come to a question that seems "impossible" to answer, mark a large minus sign ("−") next to it on your test booklet.

3. Then mark a "guess" answer on your answer sheet and move on to the next question.

4. When you come to a question that seems solvable but appears quite time consuming, mark a large plus sign ("+") next to that question in your test booklet and register a guess answer on your answer sheet. Then move on to the next question.

   After working all the easy questions, your booklet should look something like this:

1.
2.
+3.
4.
−5.
6.
−7.
8.
etc.

5. After working all the easy problems, go back and work your "+" problems. Change your "guess" on your answer sheet, if necessary, for the problems you are able to work.

6. When you finish your "+" (time-consuming) problems, you may wish to now try those "impossible" questions. Test takers sometimes find that something later on in the test may "trigger" their memory of how to do an earlier, difficult question. Or, having worked a number of problems, you may now be more "up to speed" and find that that "impossible" question isn't as impossible as you previously thought.

7. When you finish answering all the questions on the test, you may wish to review all the questions to make sure that you haven't made any careless mistakes. Remember, you do not have to erase the +'s and −'s in your test booklet.

Why Fill In Guesses?

Some test takers choose to leave blanks for the difficult or time-consuming questions and fill them in later when they go back to them. This may cause problems if the test taker is not careful.

Sometimes a test taker may skip a question, leave a blank on the answer sheet, and then carelessly put the answer to the *next* question in the space left blank (for the previous question).

This guide encourages you to *always fill in a guess answer* when you skip a question. You can erase and change your guess answer later when you eventually work the problem.

II. The Elimination Strategy

Take advantage of being allowed to mark in your testing booklet. As you eliminate an answer choice from consideration, make sure to mark it out in your question booklet:

(A)

?(B)

(C)

?(D)

Notice that some choices are marked with question marks, signifying that they may be possible answers. This technique will help you avoid reconsidering those choices you have already eliminated. It helps you narrow down your possible answers.

Again, these marks on your test booklet do not have to be erased.

III. Avoiding "Misreads"

Sometimes a question may have different answers depending upon what is asked. For example,

If $6y + 3x = 14$, what is the value of y?

The question may instead have asked, "what is the value of x?"
Or

If $3x + x = 20 + 4$, what is the value of x + 2?

Notice that this question doesn't ask for the value of x, but rather the value of x + 2.

Or

All of the following statements are true except . . .

Or

Which of the expressions used in the first
paragraph do not help develop the main idea?

Notice that the words *except* and *not* change the above question significantly. It is easy to miss these small and sometimes subtle distinctions in questions.

To avoid "misreading" a question (and therefore answering it incorrectly), simply *circle* what you must answer in the question. For example, do you have to find x or x + 2? Are you looking for what is true or the *exception* to what is true? To help you avoid misreads, mark the questions in your test booklet in this way:

If $6y + 3x = 14$, what is the value of y?

If $3x + x = 20 + 4$, what is the value of x + 2?

All of the following statements are true except . . .

Which of the expressions used in the first
paragraph do not help develop the main idea?

And, once again, these circles in your question booklet do not have to be erased.

Part II: Analysis of Exam Areas

This section is designed to introduce you to each TASP area by carefully reviewing the

1. Ability Tested
2. Basic Skills Necessary
3. Directions
4. Analysis of Directions
5. Suggested Approach with Samples

INTRODUCTION TO THE READING SECTION

The reading section consists of 8 to 10 passages, each from 300 to 750 words in length. Each passage is followed by several multiple-choice questions based on its content.

Ability Tested

This section tests your ability to understand the content of the passages and includes any of the following:

- main idea
- supporting ideas
- specific details
- author's purpose and point of view
- relationships of ideas presented
- inferences that can be drawn from the passage
- intended audience
- meanings of words used in the passage

No outside knowledge is necessary; all questions can be answered on the basis of what is stated or implied in the passage.

Basic Skills Necessary

Understanding, interpreting, and analyzing passages are the important skills for this section. The technique of *actively* reading (marking a passage) is helpful.

Directions

Several questions follow each of the passages in this section. Using only the stated or implied information given in the passage, answer the questions by choosing the best answer from among the four choices given.

Analysis of Directions

Answer all the questions for one passage before moving on to the next one. If you don't know an answer, take an educated guess on your answer sheet.

Use only the information given or implied in a passage. Do not use outside information, even if it seems more accurate than the given information.

Suggested Approaches with Samples

Two strategies that may improve your reading comprehension are *prereading the questions* and *marking the passage*. Readers who use these strategies tend to score higher on reading tests than readers who don't.

Prereading the questions: Before reading the passage, read each question for that passage—but do *not* read the four answer choices for each question. As you preread the questions, circle the most important word or phrase. For example,

1. The author's argument in favor of freedom of speech may be best expressed in which of the following ways?
   (A) If every speaker is not free, no speaker is.
   (B) Speech keeps us free from the animal kingdom.
   (C) As we think, so do we speak.
   (D) The Bill of Rights ensures free speech.

The most important part of a question is usually the most concrete and specific part. In the example above, you might circle "freedom of speech." The question parts that you circle will be those you'll tend to remember when you read the passage. In this case, you would most likely notice and pay close attention to "freedom of speech" when it occurs in the passage. Prereading therefore helps you focus on the parts of the passage that contain the answers.

Note, however, that when you preread the question, you do *not* read the four answer choices.

Marking the passage: After prereading the questions, read and mark the passage. Mark those spots that contain information relevant to the questions that you've read and remember. (Don't worry if you don't remember all the questions.) In addition, mark other important ideas and details. But most important, *try not to overmark.* If you get carried away and mark much more than a few marks per paragraph, too much of the passage will be marked and nothing will stand out.

Marking the passage helps to keep you actively engaged in looking for important concepts, and it helps you "organize" the passage should you need to refer back to its content.

Elimination strategy: After you've preread the questions and read and marked the passage, read and answer each question carefully, using the elimination strategy (explained in Part I), crossing out the obviously wrong choices.

SAMPLE PASSAGE 1

Questions 1 through 5 are based on the following passage.

SURPRISE WEDDINGS

1   It was, by all appearances, an innocent, if lavish, fiftieth birthday celebration. Black tie. Elegant invitation. The patio outside the Beverly Hills Hotel Polo Lounge. Guests flying in from New York and Hawaii.

2   But suddenly, after the expected birthday toasts, the honoree watched her boyfriend commandeer the microphone, drop to one knee, and announce to the crowd, "Susan, there's something I've been meaning to ask you. I love you madly. Will you marry me?"

3   "Everybody screamed," recalls Susan Lane, his intended. "They thought, 'Oh my God, how fabulous! This is an engagement party.' So then I took the microphone—we'd rehearsed this—and I said, 'I don't believe in long engagements. What did you have in mind?' He said, 'OK, big shot, you're putting me on the spot. How about *now?*'"

4   Thus, Lee Wertheimer, co-owner of a Los Angeles janitorial and parking service firm, and Susan Lane, a bridal gown designer/manufacturer, hopped aboard a fast-spreading, late '80s trend: surprise weddings.

5   According to Lane, once she accepted the proposal, Wertheimer instantly moved in for the matrimonial kill. "He got up and yelled, 'Reverend!' The Reverend—Connie Pujaney—was hiding in the bushes with my bouquet!"

6   "She called the family forward. People were still screaming, carrying on like you wouldn't believe. They were saying things like, 'Are you sure?' They had some champagne. Then she started the ceremony. We have it on video. They panned around and people's mouths were just wide open."

7   Pop weddings such as the Wertheimer-Lane extravaganza of last July have taken place at restaurants, the beach, country clubs, and even a bowling alley, where the blissful couple posed beneath a beer sign just after the service.

8   "Within the last year, they [surprise weddings] have come up more and more. It's snowballing," reports Kevin Ray, owner of the Bent Willow flower shop in North Hollywood. "Actually, I love them, because you're not dealing with crazy brides changing their minds. It's a lot easier and more fun."

9   Occasionally the nuptial equivalent of a sly Penn and Teller magic comedy act, the ceremonies are typically staged by those who say they want to avoid the hassles of traditional weddings in which many family members aid in the planning, sometimes disastrously.

10   As Lane puts it, "No one's telling you that your Aunt Millie should be invited or that your fat cousin in Iowa needs to be a bridesmaid."

1. Which of these phrases best defines the word *commandeer* as it is used in paragraph 2?
    (A) adjust the volume
    (B) take over for use
    (C) remove from a holder
    (D) grip with both hands

While choices (C) and (D) may fit within the context of the passage, choice (B) best defines the word *commandeer* as it is used here. It expresses the idea that the boyfriend has suddenly and surprisingly taken control of the microphone—*and* also the ceremony—and is about to alter the expected schedule of events.

2. The main idea of the passage is best expressed by which of the following?
   (A) Surprise weddings involve minimal planning and no input from participants.
   (B) The popularity of surprise weddings has been fueled by professional wedding designers eager to attract impulsive buyers.
   (C) A surprise wedding generally begins as a birthday party at which an unsuspecting bride-to-be receives a wedding proposal.
   (D) Current fashion may forgo traditional marriage planning in favor of weddings built around an element of surprise.

Choice (A) is only partially correct according to the passage: while surprise weddings may involve minimal planning, they do, in fact, require significant input from participants (hiring the reverend, arranging the "birthday" ceremony, etc.). Choice (B) is also incorrect: nothing in the passage indicates that professional wedding designers desire to attract "impulsive" buyers. Choice (C) is not necessarily true: while the surprise wedding on *this* occasion happened to be a birthday, nothing in the passage indicates that surprise weddings *generally* begin as birthday parties. Even if this were so, it still would not be the main idea of the passage, merely a secondary idea. Choice (D) is the main idea of the passage, that surprise weddings are a new late-1980s trend.

3. When the owner of the flower shop states that he loves surprise weddings, his comment most likely relates to
   (A) weddings in which the intended bride is the one to be surprised.
   (B) how brides-to-be are more definite about their flower choices when planning a surprise wedding.
   (C) how family members help the bride-to-be make a positive decision about what flowers to buy.
   (D) how his business has "snowballed" to the point that he needs to work only with customers who are emotionally stable.

The exact phrase this question refers to is this comment by the owner of the flower shop: "Actually, I love them, because you're not dealing with crazy brides changing their minds. It's a lot easier and more fun." This indicates choice (B), that brides-to-be are more definite about their flower choices when planning a surprise wedding.

4. Based on information in the passage, which of these is the *least* likely location for a surprise wedding?
   (A) a mountain resort
   (B) a ski lodge
   (C) a church
   (D) a baseball park

Since the important element of a surprise wedding is surprise, the least likely location for a surprise wedding would be where one might expect a wedding to take place. Therefore a church, choice (C), would be the least likely location for a surprise wedding.

5. Which of these pairs of topics best shows the content organization of the passage?
   (A)   I. Account of an engagement party
         II. Plans for the surprise wedding
   (B)   I. Traditional versus surprise weddings
         II. The traditional wedding's enduring popularity
   (C)   I. Criticisms of traditional weddings
         II. The pleasures and pitfalls of surprise weddings
   (D)   I. Account of a surprise wedding
         II. Surprise weddings as a rising trend

Choice (D) best shows the organization of the content of the passage. The first part of the passage relates an account of what first seemed to be a birthday party, but was, in effect, a surprise wedding. The latter part of the passage concerns surprise weddings in general and how more and more couples are planning them (a rising trend).

SAMPLE PASSAGE 2

Questions 6 through 10 are based on the following passage.

PLAINS INDIANS AND THE SETTLEMENT OF THE WEST

1   The railroads played a key role in the settlement of the West. They provided relatively easy access to the region for the first time, and they also actively recruited farmers to settle there (the Santa Fe Railroad, for example, brought 10,000 German Mennonites to Kansas). The railroads are criticized for their part in settling the West too rapidly, with its resultant economic unrest. (After the Civil War the vast Great Plains area was settled all at once). Of course there were abuses connected with building and operating the railroads, but it must be pointed out that they performed a useful service in extending the frontier and helping to achieve national unity.

2   The real tragedy of the rapid settlement of the Great Plains was the shameful way in which the American Indians were treated. Threatened with the destruction of their whole mode of life, the Indians fought back savagely against the white man's final thrust. Justice was almost entirely on the Indians' side. The land was clearly theirs; frequently their title was legally certified by a treaty negotiated with the federal government. The Indians, however, lacked the military force and the political power to protect this right. Not only did white men encroach upon the Indians' hunting grounds, but they rapidly destroyed the Indians' principal means of subsistence—the buffalo. It has been estimated that some 15 million buffalo roamed the plains in the 1860s. By 1869 the railroads had cut the herd in half, and by 1875 the southern herd was all but eliminated. By the middle of the 1880s the northern herd was also a thing of the past. Particularly galling to the Indians was the fact that the white man frequently killed the buffalo merely for sport, leaving the valuable carcass to rot in the sun.

3   The plains Indians were considerably different from the Indians encountered by the English colonists on the Atlantic coast. Mounted on horses descended from those brought by the Spanish to Mexico many years before, typical plains Indians were fierce warriors who could shoot arrows with surprising accuracy

while galloping at top speed. Although they quickly adapted themselves to the use of the rifle, the Indians were not equal to the firepower of the United States army and thus were doomed to defeat.

4   Theoretically, at least, the government tried to be fair to the Indians, but all too often the Indian agents were either too indifferent or corrupt to carry out the government's promises conscientiously. The army frequently ignored the Indian Bureau and failed to coordinate its policies with the civilians who were nominally in charge of Indian affairs. The settlers hated and feared the Indians and wanted them exterminated. This barbaric attitude is certainly not excusable, but it is understandable in the context of the times. Many pioneers had seen their wives, children, and close friends brutally murdered by the Indians and had come to believe in the old frontier dictum that "the only good Indian is a dead Indian." In retrospect the bloody Indian wars appear to have been inevitable, but the fact remains that the Indians' lands were unjustly taken from them.

6. The phrase *encroach upon* in paragraph 2 is best defined as which of the following?
   (A) to use military force against
   (B) to build settlements on
   (C) to trespass upon
   (D) to fence in

The context of paragraph 2 makes clear that white men invaded the property of the Indians. The passage states, "Justice was almost entirely on the Indians' side. The land was clearly theirs." This idea of invading someone else's property is best represented by choice (C), to trespass upon.

7. The main idea of the passage is best expressed by which of the following?
   (A) Rapid settlement of the West led to unjust and barbaric treatment of the American Indian nation.
   (B) The Indians did not have the military or political power to protect their rights.
   (C) The railroads made possible the rapid settlement of the vast Great Plains region.
   (D) The U.S. military often ignored Indian land treaties.

Choices (B), (C), and (D) are true statements, but each serves only to *support* the main idea, expressed in choice (A), that Indians were victims of the rapid settlement of the West.

8. According to the passage, for what reason did pioneer settlers want the Indians exterminated?
   (A) The plains Indians could shoot arrows from horseback with surprising accuracy.
   (B) The Indians had killed off the entire southern herd of buffalo.
   (C) Corrupt Indian agents would not fulfill the government's promises.
   (D) Many pioneers saw their family members and friends murdered by Indians.

The claim made by choice (D) is found explicitly in paragraph 4. Choice (B) distorts the fact that white men were killing off the buffalo. Choices (A) and (C) are true statements but have no bearing on why pioneer settlers wanted the Indians exterminated.

9. The author's most probable intent in writing the passage is to
   (A) outline the railroad's role in the settlement of the Great Plains.
   (B) describe the treatment of Indians during the settlement of the Great Plains.
   (C) persuade the reader that present-day Native Americans deserve restitution for their ancestors' harsh treatment.
   (D) explain the relationship between the U.S. army and the Bureau of Indian Affairs.

Choice (A) identifies the concern of the first paragraph, not the entire selection. Choice (D) identifies an issue covered only in paragraph 4. Choice (C) deals with a concern not dealt with by the author. Choice (B) best represents the writer's aim to characterize how Indians were treated in the late 1800s.

10. Which of the following groups of topics best shows the content organization of the passage?

(A) I.   Differences between the plains Indians and the Atlantic Indians
     II. The white settlers' barbaric attitudes toward the Indians
     III. The settlement of the Great Plains after the Civil War

(B) I.   The railroad's recruitment of farmers
     II. The Indians' right to their land
     III. The government's attempt to be fair
     IV. The inevitable onset of the Indian wars

(C) I.   The role of the railroad in westward expansion
     II. The shameful treatment of the plains Indians
     III. The plains Indians as skilled warriors
     IV. Reasons underlying the Indian wars

(D) I.   Railroads as cause of economic unrest
     II. The disappearance of the buffalo
     III. The plains Indians as warriors on horseback

Choice (C) lists the key topics in the passage: the railroad's role in settling the West, the savage treatment of Indians, the warrior skills of Indians, and reasons that the Indian wars were inevitable. Choice (A) omits the important role of the railroad in its list. Choice (B) notes the railroad but deals only with the supporting fact that farmers were recruited to settle in new western regions.

INTRODUCTION TO THE MATHEMATICS SECTION

The mathematics section of the TASP contains approximately 40 multiple-choice questions.

Ability Tested

This part of the exam tests your ability to use your knowledge of mathematics and your reasoning ability to perform mathematical operations and solve problems.

Basic Skills Necessary

This section requires competence in high school arithmetic, algebra I, and intuitive geometry. Skills in approximating, comparing, evaluating, and problem solving are also necessary. No knowledge of advanced mathematics is necessary.

Directions

Solve each problem in this section by using the information given and your own mathematical calculations. Then select the one correct answer of the four choices given.

Following are some mathematical symbols and formulas for reference during your exam.

Analysis of Directions

This test is designed to give you plenty of time to complete each section. But you should still skip problems that give you difficulty and return to them later if you have time.

There is no penalty for guessing, so you should not leave any blanks. If you don't know the answer to a problem but you can size it up to get a general range for your answer, you may be able to eliminate one or more of the answer choices. This will increase your odds of guessing the correct answer. But even if you cannot eliminate any of the possible choices, take a guess because there is no penalty for wrong answers.

Be sure that your answers on your answer sheet correspond to the proper numbers on your question sheet. Placing one answer in the incorrect number on the answer sheet could possibly shift all of your answers to the incorrect spots. Be careful of this!

Certain terms, definitions, and formulas are given, similar to those following. Be familiar with the terms and definitions and know how to use the formulas. You should be comfortable with this information before you enter the exam.

MATHEMATICAL SYMBOLS AND FORMULAS

Common Math Symbols

Symbol References:

$=$ is equal to	$\geq$ is greater than or equal to
$\neq$ is not equal to	$\leq$ is less than or equal to
$>$ is greater than	$\parallel$ is parallel to
$<$ is less than	$\perp$ is perpendicular to

Math Formulas

Triangle
$$\text{Perimeter} = s_1 + s_2 + s_3$$
$$\text{Area} = \tfrac{1}{2}bh$$

Square
$$\text{Perimeter} = 4s$$
$$\text{Area} = s \cdot s, \text{ or } s^2$$

Rectangle
$$\text{Perimeter} = 2(b + h), \text{ or } 2b + 2h$$
$$\text{Area} = bh, \text{ or } lw$$

Parallelogram
$$\text{Perimeter} = 2(l + w), \text{ or } 2l + 2w$$
$$\text{Area} = bh$$

Trapezoid
$$\text{Perimeter} = b_1 + b_2 + s_1 + s_2$$
$$\text{Area} = \tfrac{1}{2}h(b_1 + b_2), \text{ or } h\left(\frac{b_1 + b_2}{2}\right)$$

Circle
$$\text{Circumference} = 2\pi r, \text{ or } \pi d$$
$$\text{Area} = \pi r^2$$

Pythagorean theorem (for right triangles) $a^2 + b^2 = c^2$

The sum of the squares of the legs of a right triangle equals the square of the hypotenuse.

Cube
$$\text{Volume} = s \cdot s \cdot s = s^3$$
$$\text{Surface area} = s \cdot s \cdot 6$$

Rectangular Prism
$$\text{Volume} = l \cdot w \cdot h$$
$$\text{Surface area} = 2(lw) + 2(lh) + 2(wh)$$

Suggested Approach with Samples

Here are a number of different approaches which can be helpful in attacking many types of mathematics problems. Of course, these strategies will not work on *all* the problems, but if you become familiar with them, you'll find they'll be helpful in answering quite a few questions.

MARK KEY WORDS

Circling and/or underlining key words in each question is an effective test-taking technique. Many times you may be misled because you may overlook a key word in a problem. By circling or underlining these key words, you'll help yourself focus on what you are being asked to find. Remember, you are allowed to mark and write on your testing booklet. Take advantage of this opportunity. *For example:*

1. In the following number, which digit is in the thousandths place?

$$6574.12398$$

(A) 2
(B) 3
(C) 5
(D) 9

The key word here is *thousandths*. By circling it you will be paying closer attention to it. This is the kind of question which, under time pressure and testing pressure, may often be misread. It may be easily misread as *thousands* place. Hopefully, your circling the important words will minimize the possibility of misreading. Your completed question may look like this after you mark the important words or terms:

1. In the following number, which (digit) is in the (thousandths) place?

$$6574.12398$$

(A) 2
(B) 3
(C) 5
(D) 9

2. If 3 yards of ribbon cost \$2.97, what is the price per foot?
    (A) \$ .33
    (B) \$ .99
    (C) \$2.94
    (D) \$3.00

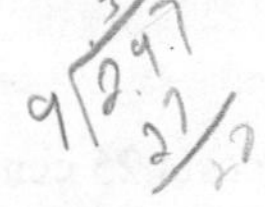

The key word here is *foot*. Dividing \$2.97 by 3 will tell you only the price per *yard*. Notice that \$ .99 is one of the choices, (B). You must still divide by 3 (since there are 3 feet per yard) to find the cost per foot. \$ .99 divided by 3 is \$ .33, which is choice (A). Therefore, it would be very helpful to circle the words *price per foot* in the problem.

3. If $3x + 1 = 16$, what is the value of $x - 4$?
    (A) 19
    (B) 16
    (C) 5
    (D) 1

The key words here are *find the value of x − 4*. Therefore circle *x − 4*. Note that solving the original equation will tell only the value of x:

$$3x + 1 = 16$$
$$3x = 16 - 1$$
$$3x = 15$$
$$x = 5$$

Here again, notice that 5 is one of the choices, (C). But the question asks for the value of $x - 4$, not just x. To continue, replace x with 5 and solve:

$$x - 4 =$$
$$5 - 4 = 1$$

The correct answer choice is (D).

4. Together a bat and ball cost \$1.25. The bat costs 25 cents more than the ball. What is the cost of the bat?
    (A) \$ .25
    (B) \$ .50
    (C) \$ .75
    (D) \$1.00

The key words here are *cost of the bat,* so circle those words. If we solve this algebraically,

$$x = \text{ball}$$
$$x + .25 = \text{bat (costs 25 cents more than the ball)}$$

Together they cost $1.25.

$$(x + .25) + x = 1.25$$
$$2x + .25 = 1.25$$
$$2x = 1.25 - .25$$
$$2x = 1.00$$
$$x = .50$$

But this is the cost of the *ball.* Notice that $ .50 is one of the choices, (B). Since x = .50, then x + .25 = .75. Therefore, the bat costs $ .75, which is choice (C). *Always answer the question that is being asked.* Circling the key word or words will help you do that.

5. What is the value of r in the following equation?

(A) $r = \dfrac{-6 - 11}{5 - 4}$

(B) $r = \dfrac{6 - 11}{5 + 4}$

(C) $r = \dfrac{-6 + 11}{5 - 4}$

(D) $r = \dfrac{6 + 11}{5 + 4}$

Notice that even though the question asks for the value of r, the answer choices do not simply give a value.

Solve for r: $4r - 6 = 5r - 11$

Bring 5r from the right side of the equation to the left side by changing its sign:

$$4r - 6 = 5r - 11$$
$$4r - 6 - 5r = -11$$

Combine r's: $-r - 6 = -11$

Bring -6 to the other side in the same way:

$$-r = -11 + 6$$
$$-r = -5$$
$$r = 5$$

By simplifying each of the answer choices, you will see that choice (C) solves as r = 5:

$$\frac{-6 + 11}{5 - 4} = \frac{5}{1}$$

You may have spotted that each answer choice actually shows the possible steps you would use to solve for x. First, subtract 4r from each side (5 − 4 on the right side). Then, add +11 to each side (−6 + 11 on the left side). Finally, divide through by whatever number is in front of the "r" (divide by 5 − 4). This leaves

$$\frac{-6 + 11}{5 - 4}$$

PULL OUT INFORMATION

Pulling information out of the wording of a word problem can make the problem more workable for you. Pull out the given facts and identify which of those facts will help you to work the problem. Not all facts will always be needed to work out the problem. *For example:*

1. Bill is 10 years older than his sister. If Bill was 25 years of age in 1983, in what year could he have been born?
   (A) 1948
   (B) 1953
   (C) 1958
   (D) 1963

The key words here are *in what year* and *could he have been born.* Thus the solution is simple: 1983 − 25 = 1958, answer (C). Notice that you pulled out the information *25 years of age* and *in 1983.* The fact about Bill's age in comparison to his sister's age was not needed, however, and was not pulled out.

2. John is 18 years old. He works for his father for ¾ of the year, and he works for his brother for the rest of the year. What is the ratio of the time John spends working for his brother to the time he spends working for his father per year?

(A) ¼
(B) ⅓
(C) ¾
(D) 4⁄3

The key word *rest* points to the answer:

$$1 - \tfrac{3}{4} =$$

$\tfrac{4}{4} - \tfrac{3}{4} = \tfrac{1}{4}$ (the part of the year John works for his brother)

Also, a key idea is the way in which the ratio is to be written. The problem becomes that of finding the ratio of ¼ to ¾.

$$\frac{\frac{1}{4}}{\frac{3}{4}} = \frac{1}{4} \div \frac{3}{4} = \frac{1}{\underset{1}{\cancel{4}}} \times \frac{\overset{1}{\cancel{4}}}{3} = \frac{1}{3}$$

Therefore, the answer is choice (B). Note that here John's age is not needed to solve the problem.

PLUG IN NUMBERS

When a problem involving variables (unknowns, or letters) seems difficult and confusing, simply replace those variables with numbers. Simple numbers will make the arithmetic easier for you to do. Usually problems using numbers are easier to understand. Be sure to make logical substitutions. Use a positive number, a negative number, or zero when applicable to get the full picture. *For example:*

1. If x is a positive integer in the equation $2x = y$, then y must be
   (A) a positive even integer
   (B) a negative even integer
   (C) zero
   (D) a positive odd integer

At first glance, this problem appears quite complex. But let's plug in some numbers and see what happens. For instance, first plug in 1 (the simplest positive integer) for x:

$$2x = y$$
$$2(1) = y$$
$$2 = y$$

Now try 2:

$$2x = y$$
$$2(2) = y$$
$$4 = y$$

Try it again. No matter what positive integer is plugged in for x, y will always be positive and even. Therefore, the answer is (A).

2. If a, b, and c are all positive whole numbers greater than 1 such that a < b < c, which of the following is the largest quantity?
    (A) a(b + c)
    (B) ab + c
    (C) ac + b
    (D) they are all equal

Substitute 2, 3, and 4 for a, b, and c, respectively.

a(b + c) =	ab + c =	ac + b =
2(3 + 4) =	2(3) + 4 =	2(4) + 3 =
2(7) = 14	6 + 4 = 10	8 + 3 = 11

Since 2, 3, and 4 meet the conditions stated in the problem and choice (A) produces the largest numerical value, it will consistently be the largest quantity. Therefore, a(b + c) is the correct answer, (A).

WORK FROM THE ANSWERS

At times, the solution to a problem will be obvious to you. At other times, it may be helpful to work from the answers. If a direct approach is not obvious to you, try working from the answers. This technique is even more efficient when some of the answer choices are easily eliminated. *For example:*

1. Barney can mow the lawn in 5 hours, and Fred can mow the lawn in 4 hours. How long will it take them to mow the lawn together?
    (A) 5 hours
    (B) 4½ hours
    (C) 4 hours
    (D) 2⁴⁄₉ hours

You may never have worked a problem like this, or perhaps you have worked one but do not remember the procedure required to find the answer. If this is the case, try working from the answers. Since Fred can mow the lawn in 4 hours by himself, it will take less than 4 hours if Barney helps him. Therefore, choices (A), (B), and (C) are not reasonable. Thus, the correct answer—by working from the answers and eliminating the incorrect ones—is (D).

2. Find the counting number that is less than 15 and when divided by 3 has a remainder of 1, but when divided by 4 has a remainder of 2.
   (A) 5
   (B) 8
   (C) 10
   (D) 12

By working from the answers, you can eliminate wrong answer choices. For instance, (B) and (D) can be immediately eliminated because they are divisible by 4, leaving no remainder. Choice (A) can also be eliminated because it leaves a remainder of 1 when divided by 4. Therefore, the correct answer is (C): 10 leaves a remainder of 1 when divided by 3 and a remainder of 2 when divided by 4.

APPROXIMATE

If a problem involves calculations with numbers that seem tedious and time consuming, round off or approximate those numbers. Replace those numbers with whole numbers that are easier to work with. Find the answer choice that is closest to your approximated answer. *For example:*

1. The value for $(.889 \times 55)/9.97$ to the nearest tenth is
   (A) 49.1
   (B) 17.7
   (C) 4.9
   (D) 4.63

Before starting any computations, take a glance at the answers to see how far apart they are. Notice that the only close answers are (C) and (D), but (D) is not a possible choice, since it is to the nearest hundredth, not tenth. Now, making some quick approximations, .889 $\simeq$ 1 and 9.97 $\simeq$ 10, leaving the problem in this form:

$$\frac{1 \times 55}{10} = \frac{55}{10} = 5.5$$

The closest answer is (C); therefore, it is the correct answer. Notice that choice (A) is not reasonable.

2. The value of $\sqrt{7194/187}$ is approximately
   (A)   6
   (B)   9
   (C) 18
   (D) 35

Round off both numbers to the hundreds place. The problem then becomes

$$\sqrt{\frac{7200}{200}}$$

This is much easier to work. By dividing, the problem now becomes

$$\sqrt{36} =$$
$$= 6$$

The closest answer choice is the exact value of choice (A).

3. Give the closest approximation for $19\frac{3}{8} \div 3\frac{7}{8}$.
   (A)   5
   (B)   8
   (C) 57
   (D) 80

Realizing that your answer choices are not close together in value, you should *estimate* this problem: $19\frac{3}{8}$ is nearly 20, and $3\frac{7}{8}$ is nearly 4. So 20 divided by 4 = 5. The answer is (A).

MAKE COMPARISONS

At times, questions will require you to compare the sizes of several decimals or of several fractions. If decimals are being compared, make sure that the numbers being compared have the same number of digits. (Remember, zeros to the right of a decimal point can be

inserted or eliminated without changing the value of the number.)
For example:

1. Put these in order from smallest to largest: .6, .16, .66⅔, .58
   (A) .6, .16, .66⅔, .58
   (B) .58, .16, .6, .66⅔
   (C) .16, .58, .6, .66⅔
   (D) .66⅔, .6, .58, .16

Rewrite .6 as .60. Now all of the decimals have the same number of digits: .60, .16, .66⅔, .58. Treating these as though the decimal point were not there (this can be done only when all the numbers have the same number of digits to the right of the decimal), the order is as follows: .16, .58, .60, .66⅔. The correct answer is (C). Remember to circle *smallest to largest* in the question.

2. Put these in order from smallest to largest: ⅝, ¾, ⅔
   (A) ⅔, ¾, ⅝
   (B) ⅔, ⅝, ¾
   (C) ⅝, ⅔, ¾
   (D) ¾, ⅝, ⅔

Using common denominators, we find

$$\frac{5}{8} = \frac{15}{24}$$
$$\frac{3}{4} = \frac{18}{24}$$
$$\frac{2}{3} = \frac{16}{24}$$

Therefore, the order becomes ⅝, ⅔, ¾.

Using decimal equivalents:

$$\frac{5}{8} = .625$$
$$\frac{3}{4} = .75 \text{ or } .750$$
$$\frac{2}{3} = .66\frac{2}{3} \text{ or } .666\frac{2}{3}$$

The order again becomes ⅝, ⅔, ¾. The answer is (C).

3. Of the following, which is the largest?
   (A) ⅜
   (B) 5/9
   (C) 6/13
   (D) 7/15

You should be able to immediately realize that choices (A), (C), and (D) are each less than one half (3 out of 8, 6 out of 13, and 7 out of 15), whereas choice (B) is greater than one half (5 out of 9). The answer is (B).

PERFORM THE OPERATIONS INDICATED

If the problem asks you to perform the operations indicated, or to simplify, be careful not to make simple mistakes. *For example:*

1. Do the following operations.

$$5 - 2(8 + 3)$$

   (A)   33
   (B)   14
   (C) −17
   (D) −18

The answer is (C). If multiplication, addition, parentheses, etc., are all contained in one problem, the order of operations is as follows: (1) parentheses, then (2) powers and square roots, then (3) multiplication and division, whichever comes first, left to right, then (4) addition and subtraction, whichever comes first, left to right. Therefore,

$$5 - 2(8 + 3) =$$
$$5 - 2(11) =$$
$$5 - 22 = -17$$

2. $\dfrac{18 \times 10^9}{3 \times 10^5} =$

   (A) 6×10^4
   (B) 6×10^{14}
   (C) 15×10^4
   (D) 15×10^{14}

The answer is (A). To quickly divide numbers in scientific notation, simply divide the first numbers, and then subtract the powers of ten to get the second number. So

$$\frac{18 \times 10^9}{3 \times 10^5} = 6 \times 10^4$$

3. $\dfrac{18x + 6}{3} =$

(A) $6x + 6$
(B) $18x + 2$
(C) $6x + 2$
(D) $18x + 9$

The answer is (C). Dividing the numerator by the denominator:

$$\frac{18x + 2}{3} = \frac{18x}{3} + \frac{6}{3} = 6x + 2$$

4. Simplify.

$$\frac{12 \times 0.08}{0.4}$$

(A) 480
(B) 24
(C) 2.4
(D) 0.060

The answer is (C). First multiply both the top and bottom by 100 to clear the fractions:

$$\frac{12 \times 0.08}{0.4}$$

$$\frac{12 \times 0.08 \times 100}{0.4 \times 100} = \frac{12 \times 8}{40} = \frac{96}{40} = 2^{16}\!/_{40} = 2^4\!/_{10}$$

The answer is 2.4, choice (C). You could also have worked this problem by first canceling:

$$\frac{12 \times 0.08^2}{0.4_1} = \frac{12 \times 0.02}{0.1}$$

and then multiplying:

$$\frac{.24}{0.1} = 2.4$$

5. If the quadratic equation $6y^2 - 16y - 6$ is factored into two terms, one of the factors is

   (A) $(2y - 3)$
   (B) $(2y - 6)$
   (C) $(y + 2)$
   (D) $(y - 6)$

The answer is (B). To factor $6y^2 - 16y - 6$, use the double parentheses method, (   ) (   ). Factoring the first terms, $6y^2$ gives $1y \times 6y$ or $2y \times 3y$. These are the choices for the first part of each set of parentheses. Factoring the last terms, -6 gives -1×6, $6 \times -1, 2 \times -3,$ or 3×-2 as the choices for the second part of each set of parentheses. Using trial and error, you will see that $(2y - 6)$ and $(3y + 1)$ are each factors.

MARK DIAGRAMS

When a figure is included with the problem, mark the given facts on the diagram. This will help you visualize all the facts that have been given. *For example:*

1. If each square in the figure that follows has a side of length 1, what is the perimeter?

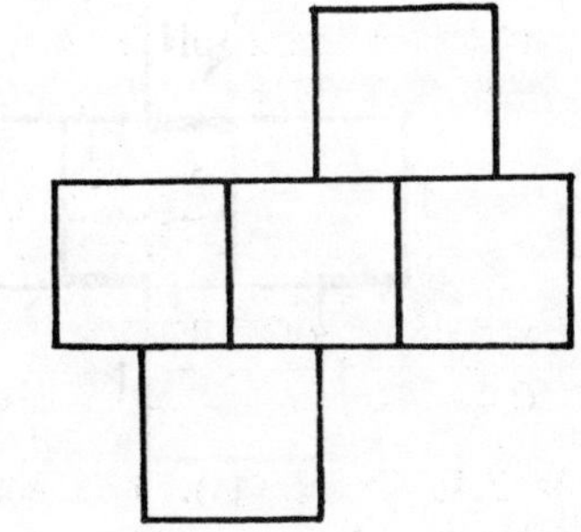

   (A) 8
   (B) 12
   (C) 14
   (D) 16

Mark the known facts:

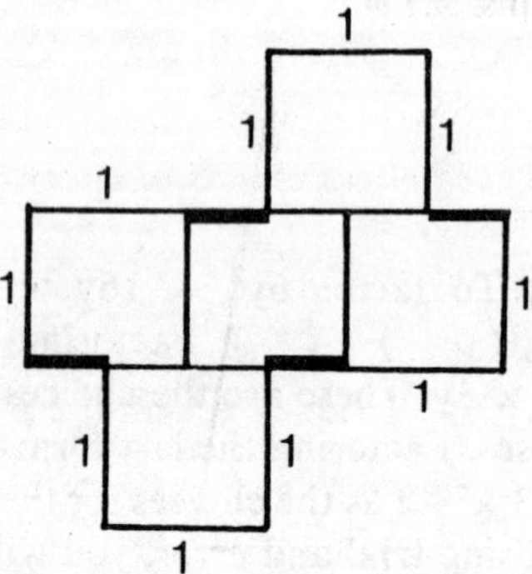

We now have a calculation for the perimeter: 10 *plus* the darkened parts. Now look carefully at the top two darkened parts. They will add up to 1. (Notice how the top square may slide over to illustrate that fact.)

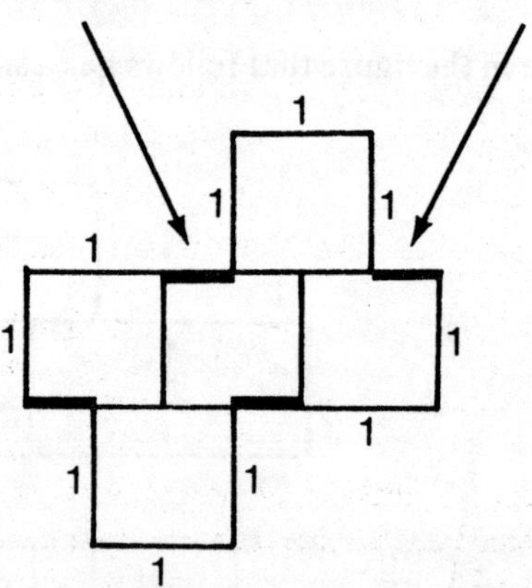

The same is true for the bottom darkened parts. They will add to 1. Thus, the total perimeter is 10 + 2, or 12, choice (B).

2. The perimeter of the following isosceles triangle is 42″. The two equal sides are each three times as long as the third side. What are the lengths of each side?

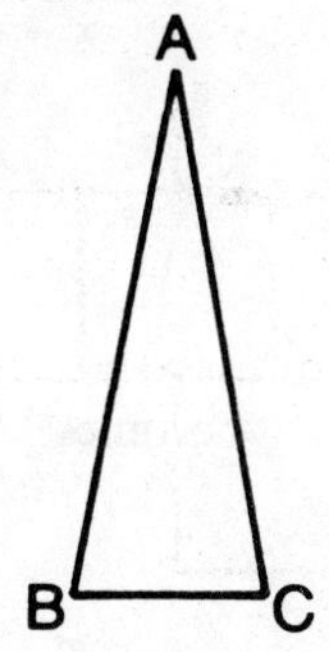

$\triangle ABC$ is isosceles

$\overline{AB} = \overline{AC}$

(A) 21, 21, 21
(B) 6, 6, 18
(C) 18, 21, 3
(D) 18, 18, 6

Mark the equal sides on the diagram:

$\overline{AB}$ and $\overline{AC}$ are each three times as long as $\overline{BC}$:

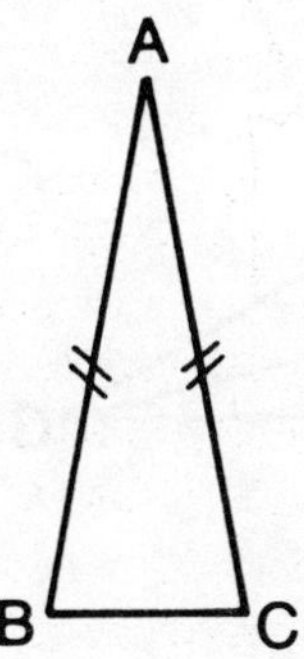

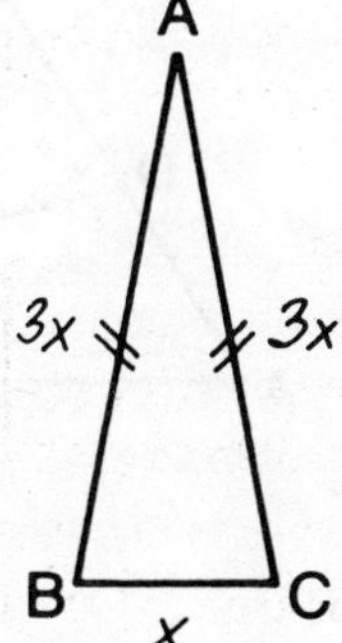

The equation for perimeter is

$$3x + 3x + x = 42$$
$$7x = 42$$
$$x = 6$$

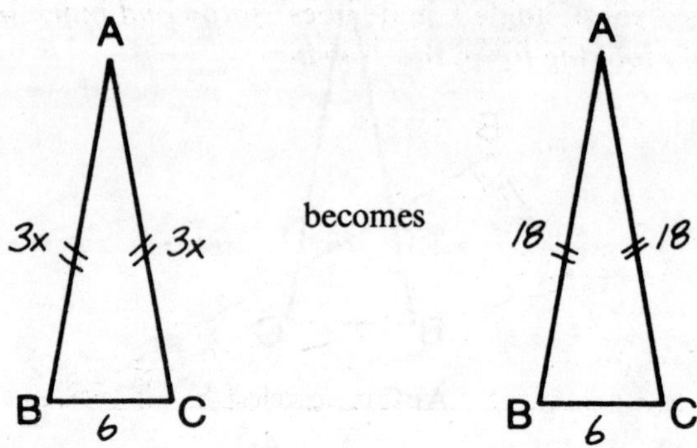

The answer is (D). Note: This problem could have been solved by working from the answers given.

3. In the triangle below, CD is an angle bisector, angle ACD is 30°, and angle ABC is a right angle. What is the measurement of angle x in degrees?

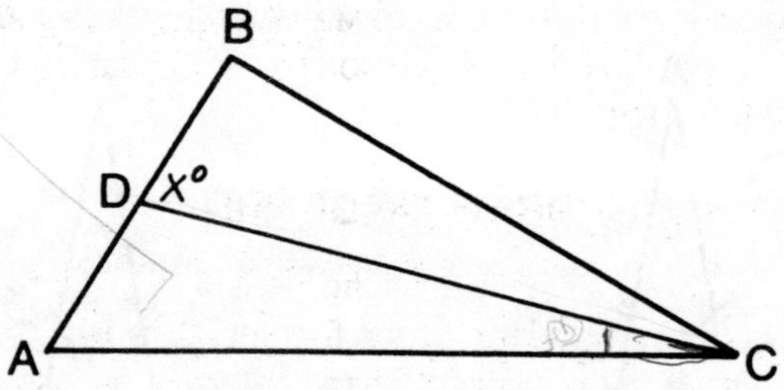

(A) 30°
(B) 45°
(C) 60°
(D) 75°

You should have read the problem and marked as follows:

In the triangle below, CD is an angle bisector (*stop and mark in the drawing*), angle ACD is 30° (*stop and mark in the drawing*), and angle ABC is a right angle (*stop and mark in the drawing*). What is the measurement of angle x in degrees? (*stop and mark in or circle what you are looking for in the drawing*).

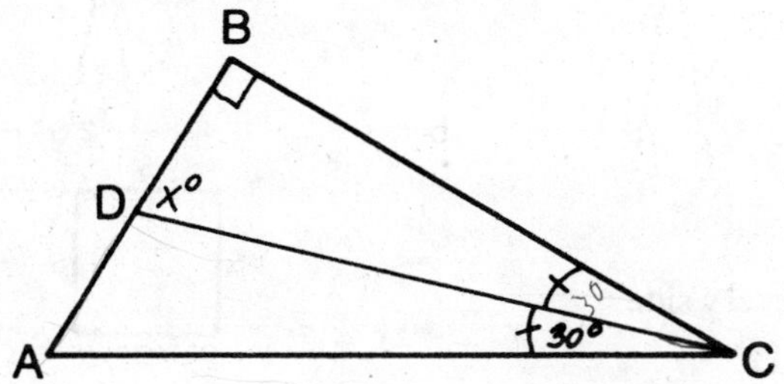

Now, with the drawing marked in, it is evident that, since angle ACD is 30°, angle BCD is also 30° because they are formed by an angle bisector (divides an angle into two equal parts). Since angle ABC is 90° (right angle) and BCD is 30°, angle x is 60° because there are 180° in a triangle.

$$180 - (90 + 30) = 60$$

The correct answer is (C). ALWAYS MARK IN DIAGRAMS AS YOU READ DESCRIPTIONS AND INFORMATION ABOUT THEM. THIS INCLUDES WHAT YOU ARE LOOKING FOR.

DRAW DIAGRAMS

Drawing diagrams to meet the conditions set by the word problem can often make the problem easier for you to work. Being able to "see" the facts is more helpful than just reading the words. *For example:*

1. If all sides of a square are doubled, the area of that square
    (A) is doubled
    (B) is tripled
    (C) is multiplied by 4
    (D) remains the same

One way to solve this problem is to draw a square and then double all its sides. Then compare the two areas:

Your first diagram:

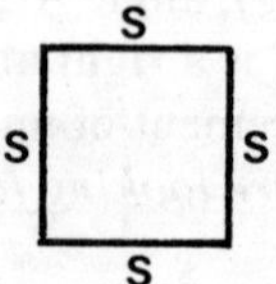

Doubling every side:

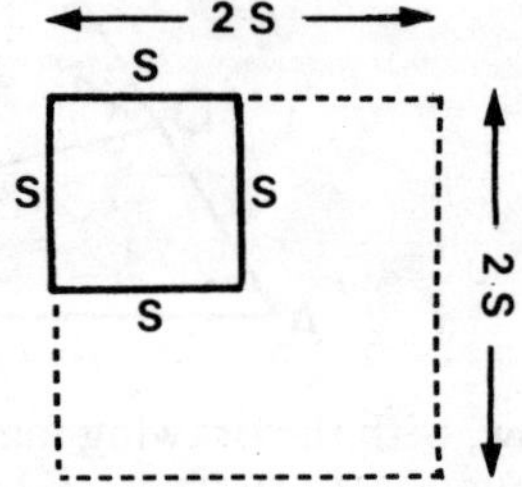

Notice that the total area of the new square will now be four times the original square. The correct answer is (C).

2. A hiking team begins at camp and hikes 5 miles north, then 8 miles west, then 6 miles south, then 9 miles east. In what direction must they now travel in order to return to camp?
   (A) north
   (B) northeast
   (C) northwest
   (D) west

For this question, your diagram would look something like this:

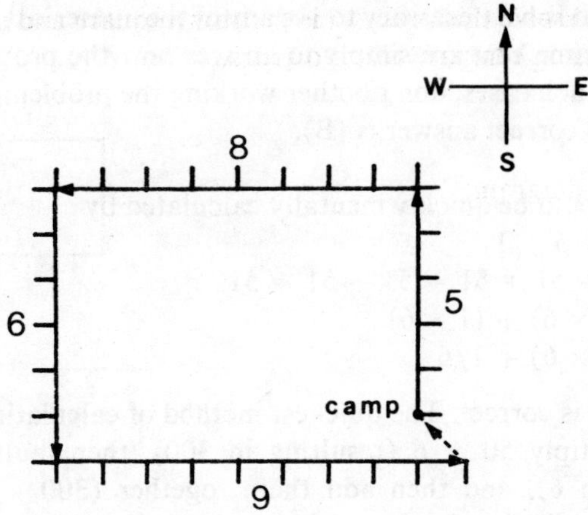

Thus, they must travel northwest (C) to return to camp. Note that in this case it is very important to draw your diagram very accurately.

PROCEDURE PROBLEMS

Some problems may not ask you to solve and find a correct numerical answer. Rather, you may be asked *how to work* the problem. *For example:*

1. To find the area of the following figure, a student would use which of the formulas below?

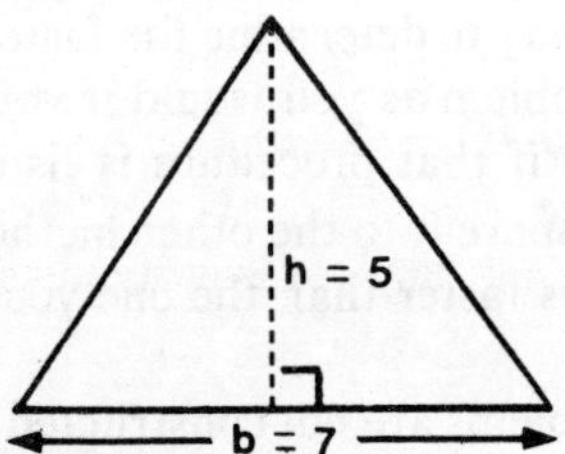

(A) area = base times height
(B) area = ½ times base times height
(C) area = one side squared
(D) area = ½ times base plus height

Notice that it is not necessary to use any of the numerical values given in the diagram. You are simply to answer how the problem is to be worked. In such cases, don't bother working the problem; it's a waste of time. The correct answer is (B).

2. 51 × 6 could be quickly mentally calculated by
    (A) 50 × 6 + 1
    (B) 51 + 51 + 51 + 51 + 51 + 51
    (C) (50 × 6) + (1 × 6)
    (D) (50 × 6) + 1/6

Answer (C) is correct. The quickest method of calculating 51 × 6 is to first multiply 50 × 6 (resulting in 300), then multiply 1 × 6 (resulting in 6), and then add them together (300 + 6 = 306). Answer (B) will give the correct answer as well (306), but it isn't the best way to *quickly* calculate the answer.

Sometimes, however, actually working the problem can be helpful. *For example:*

3. The fastest method to solve (7/48) × (6/7) would be to
    (A) invert the second fraction and then multiply
    (B) multiply each column across and then reduce to lowest terms
    (C) find the common denominator and then multiply across
    (D) divide 7 into the numerator and denominator, divide 6 into the numerator and denominator, and then multiply across

In this problem, the way to determine the fastest procedure may be to actually work the problem as you would if you were working toward an answer. Then see if that procedure is listed among the choices. You should then compare it to the other methods listed. Is one of the other *correct* methods faster than the one you used? If so, select the fastest.

These types of problems are not constructed to test your knowledge of *obscure* tricks in solving mathematical equations. Rather, they test your knowledge of common procedures used in standard mathematical equations. Thus, the fastest way to solve this problem would be to first divide 7 into the numerator and denominator:

$$\frac{^{1}7}{48} \times \frac{6}{7_{1}} =$$

Then divide 6 into the numerator and denominator:

$$\frac{^{1}7}{_{8}\cancel{48}} \times \frac{\cancel{6}^{1}}{7_{1}} =$$

Then multiply across:

$$\frac{^{1}7}{_{8}\cancel{48}} \times \frac{\cancel{6}^{1}}{7_{1}} = \frac{1}{8}$$

The correct answer is (D).

SEQUENCE PROBLEMS

Some problems may ask you to identify a sequence of either numbers or figures. If numbers are given, look for an obvious pattern (odd numbers then even numbers, increasing, decreasing, etc.). You may wish to first check for a common differnce between the numbers. *For example:*

1. Which of the following is the next number in the series 1, 3, 6, 10, 15, ___?
   (A) 20
   (B) 21
   (C) 25
   (D) 26

Notice that the pattern here is based on the difference between the numbers:

$$\begin{array}{ccccccccccc} & +2 & & +3 & & +4 & & +5 & & +6 & \\ 1, & & 3, & & 6, & & 10, & & 15, & & \text{---} \end{array}$$

Therefore, the answer is 21, (B).

If a series of figures is given, you may wish to work the problem by analyzing the pattern of each part of the figure. Sometimes this part-by-part analysis can be helpful. *For example:*

2. The sequence below follows a certain pattern. Answer the question that follows by finding the pattern.

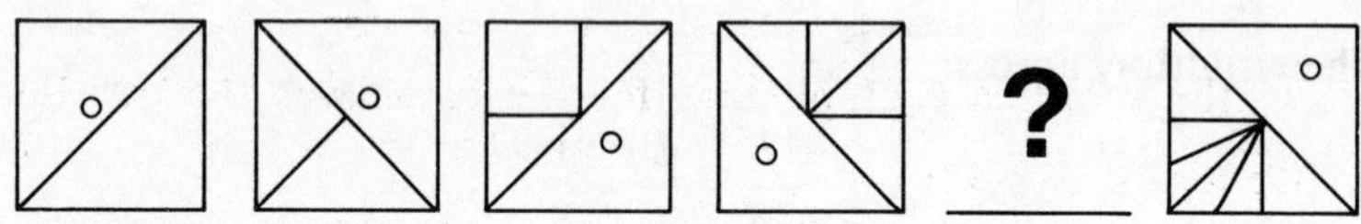

The missing design in the sequence is

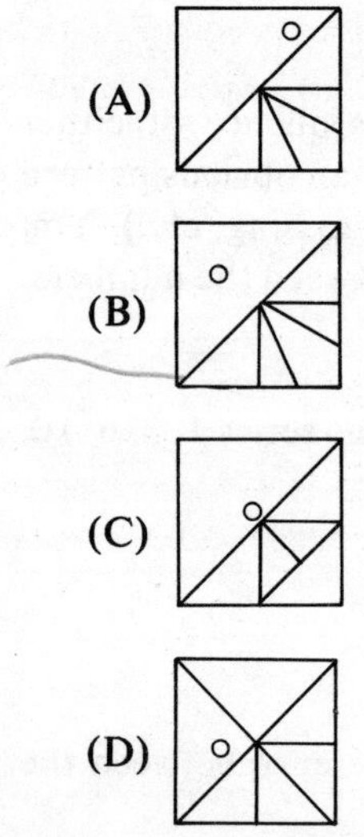

(A)

(B)

(C)

(D)

With each successive figure, one more line is added from the center. Since the missing figure is between 3 "center lines" and 5 "center lines," the missing figure will have 4 lines coming from the center. This eliminates choices (C) and (D). The only difference between choices (A) and (B) is the placement of the small circle. Notice that in the series the circle is slowly moving from the center toward the corner opposite the diagonal. Choice (B) continues this path of the circle. The answer is (B).

COORDINATE GRAPH PROBLEMS

You should be familiar with coordinate graphs. Know how to read points, find coordinates, calculate midpoints and lengths of line segments, identify equations of a line or area (inequalities), and find the slope of a line. *For example:*

1. Use the coordinate graph that follows to answer the question below.

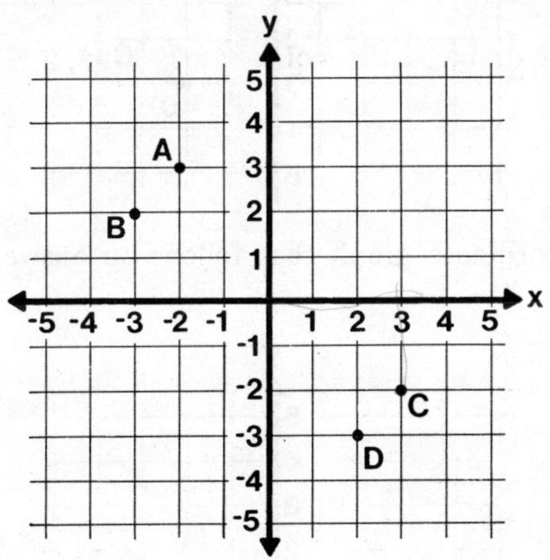

Which of the points has coordinates $(3, -2)$?
(A) A
(B) B
(C) C
(D) D

The answer is (C). Starting at the origin $(0, 0)$, the first coordinate (x) is across (right for positive, left for negative). The second coordinate is up for positive and down for negative. Therefore, the point with coordinates $(3, -2)$ is, starting from the origin, 3 to the right and down 2.

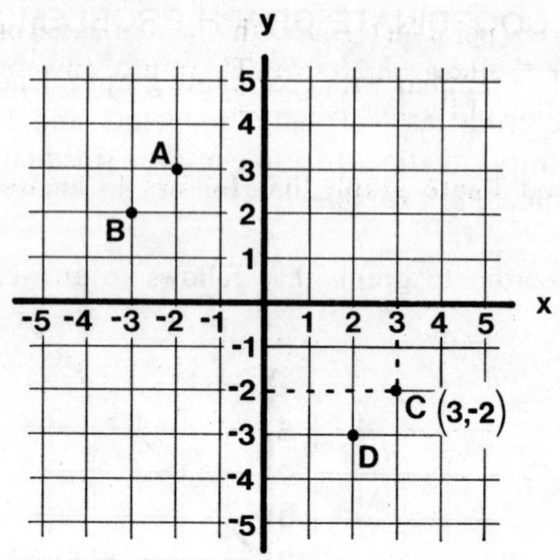

2. Use the coordinate graph that follows to answer the question below.

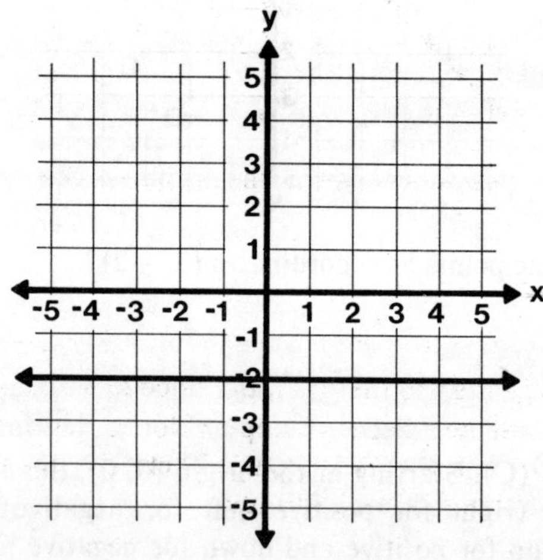

The graph above shows a representation of which of the following equations?
(A) $x = 2$
(B) $x = -2$
(C) $y = 2$
(D) $y = -2$

Notice that every point on the straight line indicated on the graph is 2 "steps" below the horizontal axis. Therefore, since y is -2 on this line, the equation of the line is $y = -2$.

3. Use the coordinate graph that follows to answer the question below.

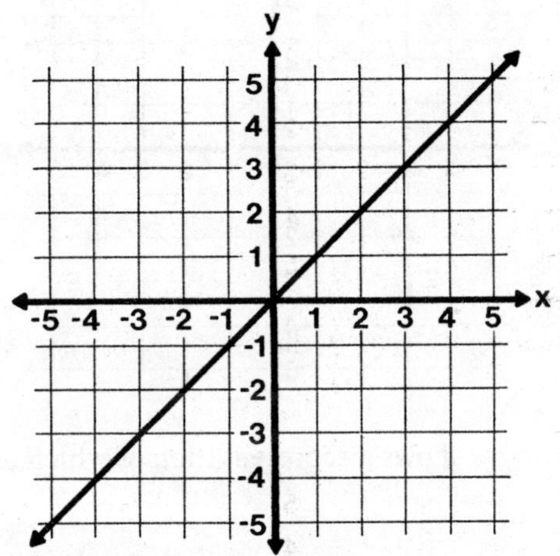

What is the slope of the line in the graph above?
(A) -1
(B) ½
(C) 1
(D) 2

Since the line goes up to the right, the slope must be positive. (Down to the right would be a negative slope.) Notice that for every 1 space to the right, the line goes 1 space up. Therefore, the slope is 1. You could have used the following formula:

$$\text{slope} = m = \frac{y_2 - y_1}{x_2 - x_1}$$

Selecting the points $(1, 1)$ and $(2, 2)$ for (x_1, y_1), (x_2, y_2) and plugging into the formula gives

$$m = \frac{2 - 1}{2 - 1} = \frac{1}{1} = 1$$

4. Use the coordinate graph that follows to answer the question below.

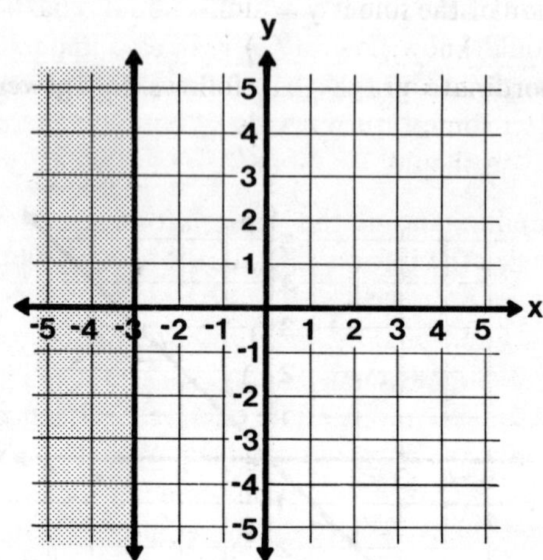

The graph above shows a representation of which of the following
(A) $x \geq 3$
(B) $x \leq 3$
(C) $x \geq -3$
(D) $x \leq -3$

Every point on the straight line indicated on the graph is 3 steps to the left of the vertical axis. Therefore, since x is always -3, on this line the equation would be $x = -3$. But since the area to the left is shaded, the inequality is $x \leq -3$. The answer is (D).

CHARTS, TABLES, AND GRAPHS

The TASP will ask some questions about charts, tables, and graphs. You should know how to (1) read and understand information given, (2) analyze and apply the information given, and (3) spot trends and predict some future trends. When you encounter a chart, table, or graph, you should:

1. Focus on understanding the important information given.
2. Not memorize the information, but refer to it when you need to.
3. Review any additional information given with a graph (headings, scale factors, legends, etc.).
4. Read the question and possible choices, noticing key words.
5. Look for obvious large changes, high points, low points, trends, etc. Obvious information often leads to an answer.
6. Skim the questions, which can sometimes be helpful.

CHARTS AND TABLES

Charts and tables are often used to give an organized picture of information, or data. Be sure that you understand *what is given.* Column headings and line items give the important information. These titles give the numbers meaning.

Questions 1 to 3 are based on the following chart.

BURGER SALES FOR THE WEEK OF AUGUST 8 TO AUGUST 14

Day	Hamburgers	Cheeseburgers
Sunday	120	92
Monday	85	80
Tuesday	77	70
Wednesday	74	71
Thursday	75	72
Friday	91	88
Saturday	111	112

1. On which day were the most burgers sold (hamburgers and cheeseburgers)?
   (A) Saturday
   (B) Monday
   (C) Thursday
   (D) Friday

The answer is (A). Working from the answers is probably the easiest method of answering this question.

   (A) Saturday $111 + 112 = 223$
   (B) Monday $85 + 80 = 165$
   (C) Thursday $75 + 72 = 147$
   (D) Friday $91 + 88 = 179$

Another method is to *approximate* the answers.

2. On how many days were more hamburgers sold than cheeseburgers?
   (A) 7
   (B) 6
   (C) 5
   (D) 4

The answer is (B). Hamburgers outsold cheeseburgers every day except Saturday.

3. If the pattern of sales continues,
    (A) the weekend days will have the fewest number of burger sales next week.
    (B) the cheeseburgers will outsell hamburgers next week.
    (C) generally, when hamburger sales go up, cheeseburger sales will go up.
    (D) hamburgers will be less expensive than cheeseburgers.

The answer is (C). You should notice this trend. Most days that hamburger sales go up, cheeseburger sales go up (with the exception of Saturday to Sunday).

4. As shown in the following chart, the *difference* in temperature between the point at which oxygen freezes and the point at which iron melts is

Temperature of Object in Degrees Centigrade	
absolute zero	−273
oxygen freezes	−218
oxygen liquefies	−183
water freezes	0
human body	37
water boils	100
wood fire	830
iron melts	1535
iron boils	3000

(A) 1317
(B) 1535
(C) 1718
(D) 1753

The answer is (D). The freezing temperature of oxygen is −218 degrees centigrade. Iron melts at 1535 degrees centigrade. To find the difference between the two, you must subtract.

$$1535 - (-218) = 1535 + 218 = 1753$$

A more complex chart might look like this:

Questions 5 and 6 are based on the following chart.

AVERAGE EXPENDITURES FOR MONTHLY HOUSING EXPENSES

Metropolitan Area	Mortgage Payment	Property Tax	Hazard Insurance	Utility Cost	Total Monthly Expenses
Large					
Chicago	$291	$ 64	$14	$60	$429
Houston	292	48	26	74	439
Los Angeles	403	99	15	50	567
New York	291	111	25	70	497
San Francisco	445	99	20	50	614
Washington	388	85	14	91	578
All U.S. metropolitan areas with populations of 1.5 million or more	$299	$ 70	$13	$60	$442
All of the United States	$273	$ 54	$13	$60	$400

5. Which city's total monthly expenses were closest to the total monthly expenses for areas with populations of 1.5 million or more?
   (A) Chicago
   (B) Houston
   (C) New York
   (D) Los Angeles

The answer is (B). First, you must determine the total monthly expenses for all U.S. cities with a population of 1.5 million or more. The last column of the next to last line shows that the number is $442 per month. The column at the left shows the *area,* and the last column shows the *total monthly expenses.* Second, you must determine which city's total monthly expenses are closest to the $442 monthly figure. The correct answer is Houston, which has a total monthly expense of $439.

6. You could conclude which of the following statements from information presented in the chart?
   - (A) Los Angeles residents have larger incomes than residents in New York.
   - (B) The median mortgage payment in Los Angeles is lower than that in Washington.
   - (C) Housing dollars would stretch further in smaller cities.
   - (D) Hazard insurance is higher as total monthly expenses increase.

The answer is (C). The information in choice (A) cannot be determined from the data in the table. (Don't choose as an answer information that is *not presented* in the chart or graph, even if the statement might be based on accepted fact.) You can quickly eliminate choice (B) because the mortgage payment table shows that the Los Angeles average is $403, while the Washington average is $388. You can see that choice (D) is false by looking at the Houston hazard insurance ($26), the highest in the chart, and Houston's total monthly expenses ($439), one of the lowest in the chart. Notice that the monthly expense column is *not* in rank order—lowest to highest. Choice (C), the correct answer, can be supported by data presented in the chart. Notice that all cities with populations of 1.5 million or more have a total monthly expense figure of $442. "All of the United States" (the United States considered as a whole) has a total monthly expense of $400. This means that many small cities reduced the $442 total monthly figure. So you can conclude that housing dollars would stretch further in smaller cities.

GRAPHS

Information may be displayed in many ways. The four basic types of graphs you should know are *pictographs, bar graphs, line graphs,* and *pie graphs* (or *pie charts*).

Pictographs

Pictographs use *pictures* to help you see information and make comparisons.

Questions 7 and 8 are based on the following pictograph.

During the summer months, Phil works by the beach selling surfboards. Phil decided to chart his sales. Each circle represents $1000 in sales.

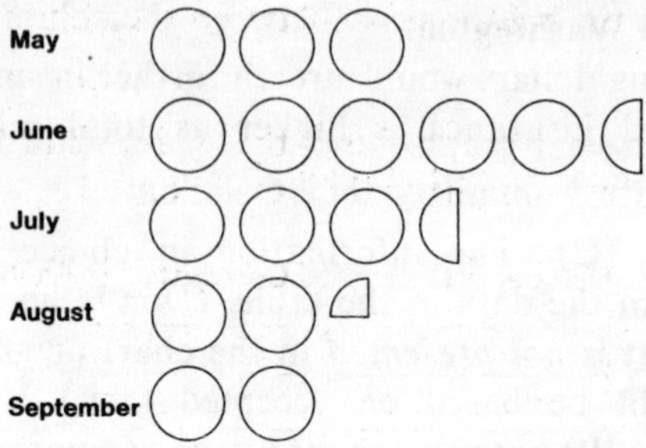

7. About how much money did Phil receive in sales in July?
   (A) $3000
   (B) $3500
   (C) $4000
   (D) $5000

The answer is (B). Since each circle stands for $1000, each half circle stands for $500. July has 3½ circles, which equals $3500.

8. About how much more money did Phil receive in his best month than he did in his worst month?
   (A) $1500
   (B) $2500
   (C) $3500
   (D) $4500

The answer is (C). In Phil's best month, June, he had sales of $5500. In his worst month, September, he had sales of $2000. Now, subtracting gives

$$\$5500 - \$2000 = \$3500$$

Bar Graphs

Bar graphs convert the information in a chart into separate bars or columns. Some graphs list numbers along one edge and places, dates, people, or things (individual categories) along another edge. Always try to determine the *relationship* between the columns in a graph or chart.

9. The following bar graph shows that Candidate 1 has how many more delegates committed than Candidate 2?

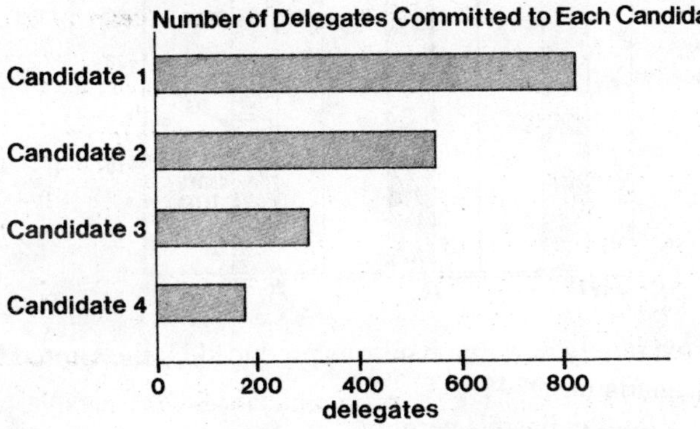

    (A) 150
    (B) 200
    (C) 250
    (D) 400

The answer is (C). Notice that the graph shows the "Number of Delegates Committed to Each Candidate," with the numbers given along the bottom of the graph in increases of 200. The names are listed along the left side. Candidate 1 has approximately 800 delegates (possibly a few more). The bar graph for Candidate 2 stops about three quarters of the way between 400 and 600. Now, consider that half way between 400 and 600 would be 500. So Candidate 2 is at about 550. 800 − 550 = 250

A slightly more difficult bar graph might look like this:

Questions 10 and 11 are based on the following bar graph.

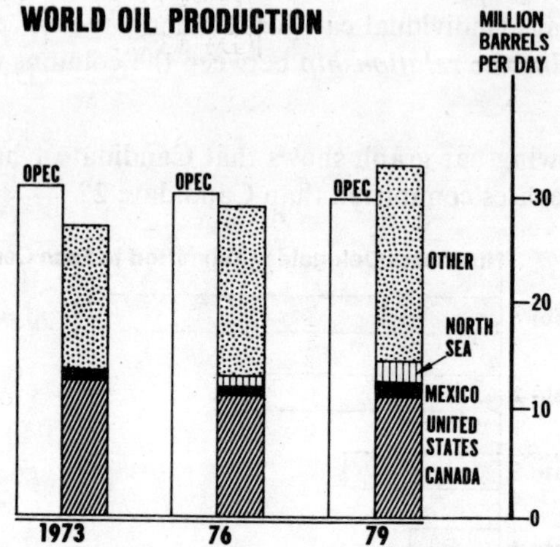

10. Approximately how much oil was produced by the United States and Canada in 1979?
    (A)   8 million barrels per day
    (B)   11 million barrels per day
    (C)   13 million barrels per day
    (D)   20 million barrels per day

The answer is (B). The bar graph shows the years in study on the horizontal line along the bottom of the graph (1973–1979). The vertical line at the right shows the number of barrels per day stated in millions. Note that the vertical line at the right is spaced in increments of 10 million barrels per day (0 to 10, 10 to 20, etc.). In 1979, the United States and Canada produced approximately 11 million barrels per day.

11. Since 1973, the rate of United States and Canadian oil production has
    (A) risen sharply.
    (B) outpaced OPEC production.
    (C) dropped dramatically
    (D) declined gradually

The answer is (D). You can see from the graph that the production of U.S. and Canadian oil has declined *slightly* over the 1973–1979 period.

Line Graphs

Line graphs convert data into points on a grid. These points are then connected to show a relationship among the items, dates, times, etc. Notice the slopes of the lines connecting the points. These lines will show increases and decreases. The sharper the slope *upwards,* the greater the *increase.* The sharper the slope *downwards,* the greater the *decrease.* Line graphs can show trends, or changes, in data over a period of time.

Questions 12 and 13 are based on the following line graph.

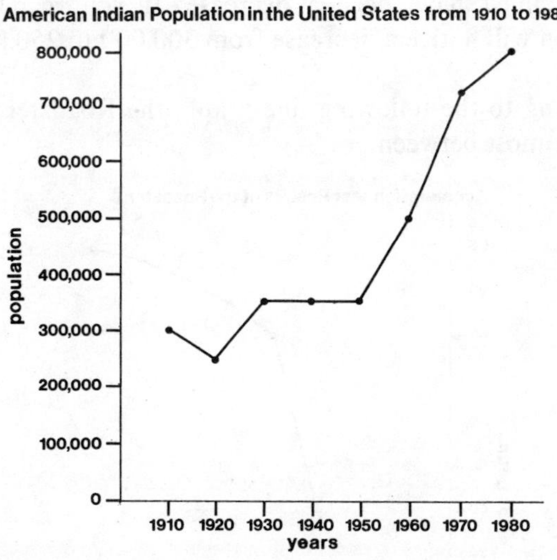

12. In which of the following years were there about 500,000 American Indians?
    (A) 1930
    (B) 1940
    (C) 1950
    (D) 1960

The answer is (D). The information along the left side of the graph shows the number of Indians in increases of 100,000. The bottom of the graph shows the years from 1910 to 1980. You will notice that in 1960 there were about 500,000 American Indians in the United States. Using the edge of a sheet of paper as a ruler will help you see that the dot in the 1960 column lines up with 500,000 on the left.

13. During which of the following time periods was there a decrease in the American Indian population?
    (A) 1910 to 1920
    (B) 1920 to 1930
    (C) 1930 to 1940
    (D) 1960 to 1970

The answer is (A). Since the slope of the line goes *down* from 1910 to 1920, there must have been a decrease. If you read the actual numbers, you will notice a decrease from 300,000 to 250,000.

14. According to the following line graph, the Roadster II accelerated the most between

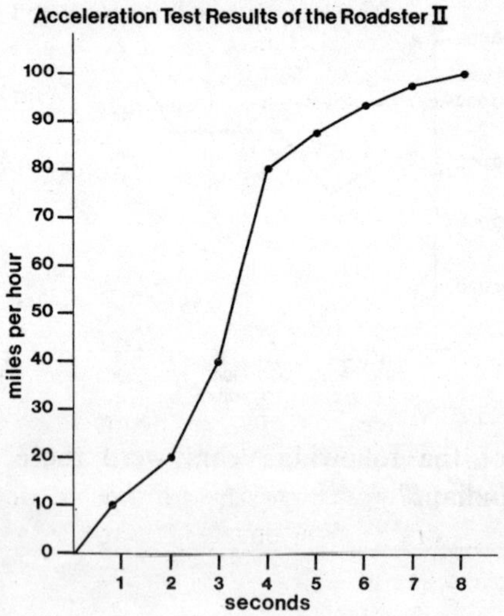

    (A) 1 and 2 seconds.
    (B) 2 and 3 seconds.
    (C) 3 and 4 seconds.
    (D) 4 and 5 seconds.

The answer is (C). The numbers on the left side of the graph show the speed in miles per hour (mph). The information at the bottom of the graph shows the number of seconds. The movement of the line can give important information and show trends. The *more the line slopes upward,* the *greater the acceleration.* The greatest slope upward is between 3 and 4 seconds. The Roadster II accelerates from about 40 to about 80 mph in that time.

The following graph is a little more complex.

Questions 15 and 16 refer to the following line graph.

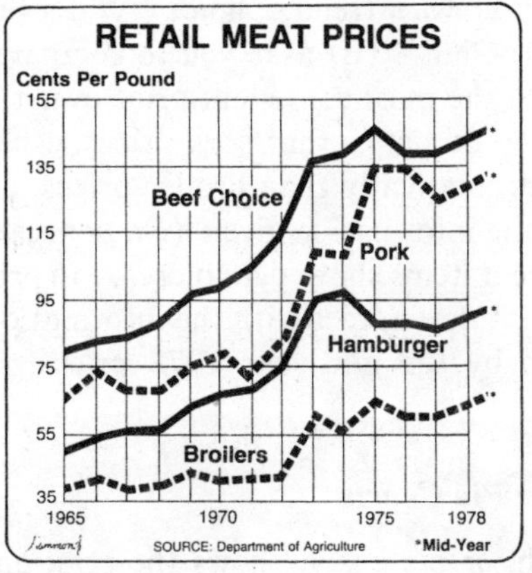

15. A pound of hamburger in 1975 cost approximately how much more than it did in 1970?
    (A) 20 cents
    (B) 25 cents
    (C) 30 cents
    (D) 35 cents

The answer is (A). Notice that the lower horizontal line indicates the time reference as given in years 1965 to 1978. Each line extending from it represents a one-year increment. The vertical line on the far left gives the price, or cents per pound (35¢ to $1.55 per pound). Each line extending from it represents a 20¢ increment (35¢ to 55¢; 55¢ to 75¢, etc.). In 1975 hamburger sold for slightly more than 85¢ per pound. The price increase from 1970 to 1975 was approximately 20¢ per pound.

16. Which of the following is an accurate statement based on the information provided in the chart?
    (A) The figures for mid-year 1978 indicate a downward trend in retail meat prices.
    (B) Pork prices increased more gradually than broiler prices.
    (C) More hamburger was sold than beef choice.
    (D) The figures for mid-year 1978 indicate a continued increase in retail meat prices.

The answer is (D). Mid-year 1978 is shown by the continuation of the lines representing meat prices beyond the 1978 line. Notice that all lines represent an *upward* trend. Choice (A) does not agree with the data in the chart. Choice (B) asks you to compare two items to see which one showed the most consistent price over the entire period of the study. You should notice that pork prices, especially since 1971, increased more dramatically than broiler prices. Choice (C) cannot be supported by the information given. (*Do not* read information into the chart.) *All* meat items showed an increase in price over the 1970s. The only statement that agrees with the information is (D). All meat prices, as shown by the mid-year 1978 prices, show a continued increase.

Circle Graphs, or Pie Charts

A circle graph, or pie chart, shows the relationship between the whole circle (100%) and the various slices that represent portions of that 100%. The larger the slice, the higher the percentage.

Questions 17 and 18 are based on the following circle graph.

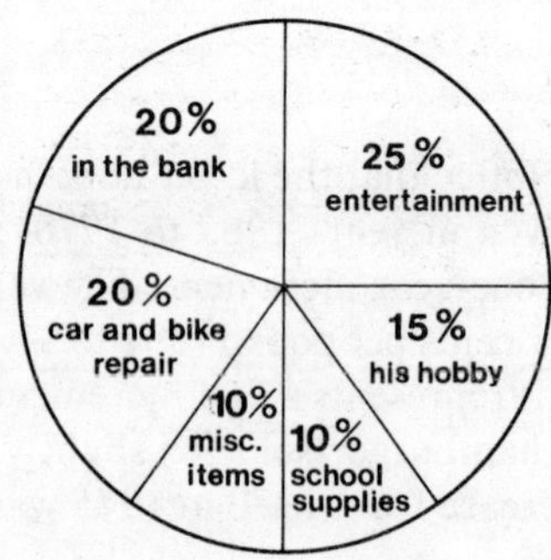

How John Spends His Monthly Paycheck

17. If John receives $100 on this month's paycheck, how much will
   he put in the bank?
   (A) $ 2
   (B) $20
   (C) $35
   (D) $60

The answer is (B). John puts 20% of his income in the bank. 20% of
$100 is $20. So he will put $20 in the bank.

18. What is the ratio of the amount of money John spends on his
   hobby to the amount he puts in the bank?
   (A) 1/6
   (B) 1/2
   (C) 5/8
   (D) 3/4

The answer is (D). To answer this question, you must use the
information in the graph to make a ratio.

$$\frac{\text{his hobby}}{\text{in the bank}} = \frac{15\%}{20\%} = \frac{15}{20} = \frac{3}{4}$$

Notice that the ratio 15%/20% reduces to 3/4.

*Questions 19 and 20 refer to the following circle graph of the budget
of the Pinewood School in 1988.*

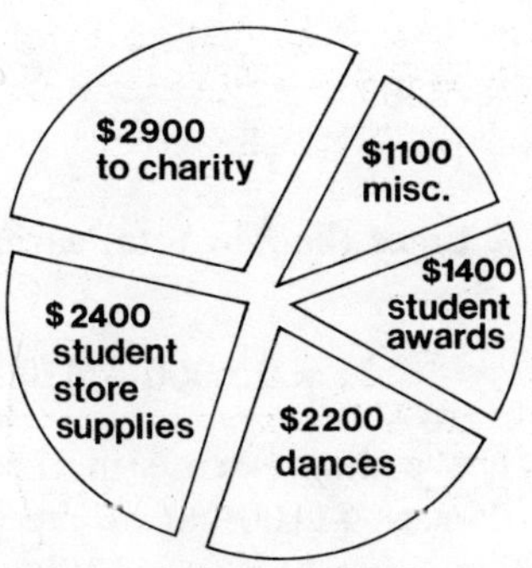

19. The amount of money given to charity in 1988 was approximately what percent of the total amount earned?
    (A) 15%
    (B) 30%
    (C) 40%
    (D) 60%

The answer is (B). By carefully reading the information in the graph, you will find that $2900 was given to charity. The information describing the graph explains that the total earnings were $10,000. Since $2900 is approximately $3000, the approximate *percentage* would be worked out as follows:

$$\frac{3000}{10,000} = \frac{30}{100} = 30\%$$

20. If the Pinewood School spends the same percentage on dances every year, how much will they spend in 1989 if their earnings are $15,000?
    (A) $1100
    (B) $2200
    (C) $2600
    (D) $3300

The answer is (D). To answer this question, you must find a percent and then apply this percent to a new total. In 1988 the Pinewood School spent $2200 on dances. This can be calculated to 22% by the following method:

$$\frac{2200}{10,000} = \frac{22}{100} = 22\%$$

Now, multiplying 22% times the *new* total earnings of $15,000 will give the right answer.

$$22\% = .22 \qquad .22 \times 15,000 = 3300 \text{ or } \$3300$$

You could use another common-sense method. If $2200 out of $10,000 is spent for dances, $1100 out of every $5000 is spent for dances. Since $15,000 is 3 × $5000, 3 × $1100 would be $3300.

21. According to the following pie charts, which field of study received the smallest number of earned masters degrees?

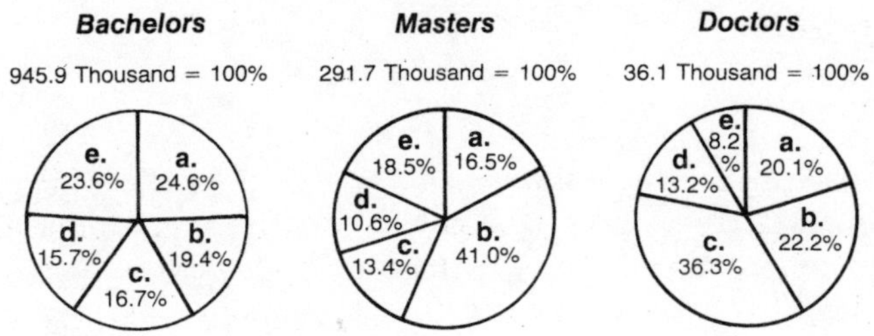

    a. social sciences
    b. education
    c. natural sciences
    d. humanities
    e. business, accounting, and others

(A) social sciences
(B) education
(C) natural sciences
(D) humanities

The answer is (D). Remember that a circle graph, or pie chart, shows the relationship between the whole circle (100%) and the slices or parts of that 100%. The larger the slice, the higher the percentage. A circle graph makes it easy to see the relationship among the parts that make up the total graph. Two or more circle graphs can be used in the same example to show many relationships. In this question, you must find the field of study that received the *least* number of masters degrees. You can see that the humanities, with 10.6% of the total amount, is the correct answer. Notice that with the data given, you could have calculated the *number* of masters degrees earned in the humanities, although to answer this question, you do not need to. 291.7 thousand equals 100% (see the information above the circle graph); therefore 10.6% of 291,700 would be approximately 30,920 earned degrees. This information could be calculated for each segment of the pie chart.

INTRODUCTION TO THE WRITING SECTION

The writing test has two parts, a writing sample and a 40- to 50-question multiple-choice section.

MULTIPLE-CHOICE SECTION

The multiple-choice section consists of 16 passages of prose, each usually about 250 words long, containing two or three paragraphs. The sentences or sentence fragments are numbered, and two or three multiple-choice questions follow each passage for a total of about 40 questions.

Ability Tested

The passages are representative of the range of prose you are likely to encounter in college. For example, there may be selections from textbooks (such as history, education, or sociology), selections in the style of a popular magazine or a letter to an editor, and selections in the style of student essays.

The passages and questions test how well you recognize effective organization, focus, and development; author's purpose and point of view; and correct standard written English (usage and mechanics).

Directions

Each of the passages is followed by questions based on the writing in the passage. Read each passage and answer each of the questions that follow. Each of the small raised numbers identifies the sentence or sentence fragment which follows it.

Analysis of Directions

Answer all the questions for one passage before moving on to the next one. If you don't know an answer, take an educated guess on your answer sheet.

Don't worry if some of the sentences or words used in the passage appear to be incomplete or incorrect. This will occur frequently, and questions will be based on the incorrect usage or organization.

Suggested Approach with Samples

At least one of the two or three questions on each passage will test your ability to *organize* a paragraph or paragraphs. For example, a passage might begin with the following excerpt from a sociology textbook.

[1]A fad is a short-lived mannerism or trait which is trivial and often irrational. [2]The Hula-Hoop, for example, was very popular in the 1950s. [3]In the 1960s, stuffing as many people as possible into a telephone booth was popular. [4]Fads occur in the world of the superficial. [5]Although they may be pervasive for a short while, they rapidly die out when their novelty wears thin or their utility as a device to enhance status disappears. [6]In the 1920s, swallowing as many goldfish as possible was a fad.

1. Which of these changes would make the sequence of ideas in this paragraph clearer?
    (A) Omit sentence 1.
    (B) Reverse the order of sentence 2 and sentence 3.
    (C) Reverse the order of sentence 4 and sentence 5.
    (D) Omit sentence 6.

The correct answer here is (D). The logical place for sentence 6 would be after sentence 1, as an example of the fad of the 1920s, to be followed by examples from the 1950s and 1960s. But sentence 6 is out of place after the earlier examples and the analysis of sentences 4 and 5. The paragraph would be clearer if it were left out.

Another kind of question using this paragraph might omit sentence 6 and leave a blank between sentence 1 and sentence 3, with a choice of one of four possible sentences to be inserted. For example,

[1]A fad is a short-lived mannerism or trait which is trivial and often irrational. [2] ____
[3]The Hula-Hoop, for example, was very popular in the 1950s. [4]In the 1960s, stuffing as many people as possible into a telephone booth was popular. [5]Fads occur in the world of the superficial. [6]Although they may be pervasive for a short while, they rapidly

die out when their novelty wears thin or their utility as a device to enhance status disappears.

One choice might be the sentence about goldfish (*In the 1920s, swallowing as many goldfish as possible was a fad.*), while the other three choices might cite fads of the 70s and 80s. The best choice would be the example from the 20s because the examples would then be in chronological order.

There will be other kinds of questions to test your ability to organize a paragraph. Some will expect you to recognize when a style or subject is appropriate or inappropriate in a work written for a specific kind of audience. For instance, a sentence using current student slang would not be likely to fit into a passage from a history text, but it might be suitable in a letter to a college newspaper. You may be asked to find a sentence in a paragraph which is *least* relevant or one that is repetitious.

Other questions will test your knowledge of standard English usage. Each passage will have common usage errors, such as faulty subject-verb agreement, errors of verb tense, misplaced modifiers, adjective and adverb confusions, or sentence fragments. There will also be some mechanical errors, especially with commas and apostrophes. The following letter to a student paper illustrates the kind of usage question you may be asked.

[1]The registration system requiring students to sign up for classes in alphabetical order <u>is unfair</u>. [2]My roommate who's name begins with "B" registered on the first day and got all the classes he wanted. [3]But because my name <u>begins with</u> "W," I couldn't register until the third day, and then all the classes I wanted to take were already filled. [4]This is the <u>most unfairest</u> system, unless your name happens to begin with an "A." [5]Something <u>should be done</u> to change it.

2. Which of the underlined phrases should be changed to correct a usage error?
    (A) Sentence 1: is unfair
    (B) Sentence 3: begins with
    (C) Sentence 4: most unfairest
    (D) Sentence 5: should be done

3. Which of these changes is needed?
   (A) Sentence 1: Change "up" to "upward."
   (B) Sentence 2: Change "who's" to "whose."
   (C) Sentence 3: Change "couldn't" to "couldnt."
   (D) Sentence 3: Change "were" to "was."

The correct answer to question 2 is (C). The superlative of the adjective is formed either by adding -*est* (*fairest*) or by using *most* and the original form of the adjective (*most fair*). But only one way or the other should be used, not both.

The correct response to question 3 is (B). The spelling *who's* is a contraction for *who is,* while the possessive form of *who* is *whose.*

SAMPLE PASSAGE 1

The following passage is followed by three sample questions. The test itself will contain 16 passages like this one and a total of approximately 40 questions, two or three on each passage. Read the passage carefully, and then answer the three multiple-choice questions.

Questions 4, 5, and 6 are based on the following excerpt from an education text.

[1]Nursery schools are becoming competitive prep schools for first grade. [2]Right or wrong, this is what many parents, teachers, and administrators now expect. [3]_______________________________
[4]There is pressure on teachers to have preschool children at a certain point in their reading ability when they enter first grade. [5]And there is pressure on parents to locate materials for home enrichment and to determine what theory to accept on the best way to teach reading.

[6]This frenzy on the part of many parents and teachers have created frustration and concern. [7]Why have they decided children must read before they reach a certain age? [8]Why should reading take precedence over everything else a child can learn in nursery school? [9]Parents hearing that five-year-olds in Scotland are successful readers. [10]When some American parents and teachers hear this news, they insist that our kindergartens must catch up immediately.

4. Which of these sentences would be most suitable to insert in the blank marked sentence 3?
   (A) Parents of high school seniors hoping to enter college also understand this pressure to achieve.
   (B) It is an attitude that has put unnecessary pressure on both teachers and parents.
   (C) The kids are expected to read like second graders of a few years ago.
   (D) The poor victims of this ambition, the innocent three- and four-year-old children, are too young to object.

5. Which of the following sentences is nonstandard?
   (A) Sentence 5
   (B) Sentence 7
   (C) Sentence 8
   (D) Sentence 9

6. Which of these changes is needed?
   (A) Sentence 6: Change "have" to "has."
   (B) Sentence 7: Change "have" to "has."
   (C) Sentence 8: Change the question mark to a period.
   (D) Sentence 10: Omit the comma after "news."

The correct answer to question 4 is (B). The sentence refers clearly to the sentence before it (*the attitude*) and connects with the following sentences by referring to pressure and to teachers (sentence 4) and parents (sentence 5). Choice (A) is not strictly relevant. The real subject of the passage is kindergarten, not high school, students. Choice (C) uses more informal language (*kids*) than the rest of the passage. Choice (D) is wordy and sentimental (*poor victims, innocent*) in a style quite unlike the rest of the passage.

Questions 5 and 6 are about usage. The nonstandard sentence (question 5) is sentence 9, choice (D). The verb is a participle, not a main verb, so the sentence is a fragment. The other error in the paragraph (question 6) is in sentence 6, choice (A). The subject of the sentence is the singular noun *frenzy*, so the agreeing verb must be the singular *has*.

SAMPLE PASSAGE 2

Questions 7, 8, and 9 are based on the following excerpt from a social studies text.

[1]The President of the United States is the most powerful official of any democratic state in the world. [2]The President has been characterized by some writers as the most powerful official in the history of the world. [3]______________, the powers and prerogatives demanded of American Presidents have undoubtedly caused many of them to wring their hands in frustration, stalemated in the courses of action they deemed best for the nation and its people.

[4]The authors of the United States Constitution were quite indefinite about what they considered to be the proper role of the President in the American government. [5]Article II of the Constitution, which creates the presidency, is both brief and sketchy when compared with the length and detail of Article I, which created and circumscribed the legislative branch of government. [6]Article I describes fully the roles of the Senate and the House of Representatives. [7]Because of the brevity of Article II, the great powers of the President of the United States grow less out of the Constitution than they do out of practice, precedent, and custom. [8]Once a President exercises power, that exercise has established a precedent which will serve as a source of power for future Presidents.

[9]Those who wrote the United States Constitution created a presidency which is not duplicated by any governmental system in the world. [10]The American presidency is unique in the assemblage of powers vested in a single leader, unique in the way the leader is chosen, and equal unique in the relationship between the leader and the legislative branch of government.

7. Which of these would most logically fit in the blank in sentence 3?
   (A) And so
   (B) Consequently
   (C) And yet
   (D) Therefore

8. Which of these sentences is *least* necessary?
   (A) Sentence 5
   (B) Sentence 6
   (C) Sentence 7
   (D) Sentence 8

9. Which of these changes is needed in sentence 10?
   (A) Omit the first use of the work "unique."
   (B) Omit the second use of the word "unique."
   (C) Omit the third use of the word "unique."
   (D) Change "equal" to "equally."

Answers

Question 7: The correct answer is (C). The paragraph begins by describing the power of the American President, but the third sentence describes the frustration of a stalemated officeholder. The conjunctions introducing this different idea should signal the change in the line of argument. Of the four choices, only *And yet* does so. Choices (A), (B), and (D) suggest continuation, not change.

Question 8: The correct answer is (B). The focus of the passage and of this paragraph is on the presidency and its powers. In this paragraph, four of the five sentences are about these subjects. But the sixth sentence is about the Constitution and the congress, and not about the President.

Question 9: The correct answer is (D). Though the sentence could easily be rewritten to eliminate the repetition of the word "unique," the author is deliberately stressing this word, and there is no grammatical error in its repetition. There is an error, however, in using the adjective *equal* to modify another adjective, *unique*. The correct word here is the adverb *equally*.

SAMPLE PASSAGE 3

Questions 10, 11, and 12 are based on the following excerpt from an education text.

[1]The question of teaching a foreign language in the elementary school continues to be mildly controversial. [2]Some proponents list two good reasons for the teaching of a foreign language. [3]Because of America's present role in the world, more American children need to acquire culture, preferably through the medium of a foreign language. [4]Also, young children learn to speak foreign languages more easily, and with more accurate accent, than do older children or grownups. [5]But the elementary school faces a number of problems with relation to the addition of foreign languages to the already crowded curriculum. [6]The question of time and how to fit language instruction into the daily program is uppermost. [7]Another question is who will teach it? [8]The regular classroom teacher or a specialist?

[9]At the present time television appears now to have temporarily solved today's problems of cost and the shortage of qualified teachers. [10]However, the usual problem yet prevails. [11]All too often, schools have started enthusiastically with foreign languages but have failed to carry on the work consistently for a sustained period of years. [12]Typically, a foreign language program will begin in a school with great fanfare, only to be found, upon another glance two years later, to have faded into a memory.

10. Which of these sentences, if inserted between sentences 6 and 7, would be most consistent with the style and intent of the passage?
    (A) What subject should be dropped to make room for language study?
    (B) You can't add a language without getting rid of something else.
    (C) Kids can't be expected to spend more time in school.
    (D) Language study had been common in European elementary schools.

11. Which of these changes is needed?
    (A) Sentence 3: Omit the comma after "world."
    (B) Sentence 6: Change the period to a question mark.
    (C) Sentence 7: Change the question mark to a period.
    (D) Sentence 8: Change the question mark to a period.

12. Which of these sentences should be changed to reduce its repetition?
    (A) Sentence 9
    (B) Sentence 10
    (C) Sentence 11
    (D) Sentence 12

Answers

Question 10: The correct answer is (A). The language, tense, and person of choice (A) are like those of the rest of the passage, and the direct question is parallel to sentence 8. Choice (B) introduces the second person (you), but the rest of the passage uses only the third person. Choice (C) uses the word *Kids,* while the language of the rest of the passage is more formal. Choice (D) requires a change in the verb tense, to the past perfect, while the rest of the passage uses the present tense.

Question 11: The correct answer is (C). Sentence 7 is a statement, not a question, and so the punctuation should be a period, not a question mark. The punctuation in the other choices is correct.

Question 12: The correct answer is (A). Sentence 9 is needlessly repetitive. The meaning of the phrase *At the present time* is repeated by the word *now* and again by the use of *today's.* The sentence can be revised leaving out both *now* and *today's.*

Special Time-Saving Techniques

As you read the passages, you may notice certain errors or inconsistencies in sentence structure, word usage, punctuation, etc. If an error is particularly obvious, you may wish to circle it on your test booklet and make a quick notation in the margin. Or you may find something confusing—for instance, several ideas out of order. Here too a quick notation in the margin (perhaps a question mark) will help you refer to this problem area later when answering the questions.

Try the sample passage which follows. If you can detect any errors as you're reading, mark them so they'll be easy to find when you get to the questions.

But remember, don't spend forever trying to edit the passage; just note the obvious errors.

SAMPLE PASSAGE

Questions 1 through 5 are based on the following excerpt from an anthropology text.

[1]People pondering the origin of language for the first time usually arrive at the conclusion that it developed gradually as a system of conventionalized grunts, hisses, and cries and must have been a very simple affair in the beginning. [2]But when we observe the language behavior of what we regard as primitive cultures, we find it strikingly complex and complicated. [3]Stefansson, the explorer, said that in order to get along reasonably well, an Eskimo must have at the tip of their tongue a vocabulary of more than 10,000 words, much larger than the active vocabulary of an average businessman whom speaks English. [4]Moreover, these Eskimo words are far more highly inflected than those of any of the well-known European languages, for a single noun can be spoken or written in several hundred different forms, each having a precise meaning different from that of any other. [5]The Eskimo language is, therefore, one of the most difficult in the world to learn, with the result that almost no traders or explorers have even tried to learn it. [6]Even more numerous than these nouns are the verbs.

[7]Consequently, there has grown up, in interactions between Eskimos and whites, a jargon similar to the pidgin English used in China. [8]With a vocabulary of from 300 to 600 uninflected words, most of them derived from English, Danish, Spanish, Hawaiian, and other languages. [9]It is this jargon which is usually referred to by travelers as "the Eskimo language."

As you read the passage, you might have made the following notations:

[1]People pondering the origin of language for the first time usually arrive at the conclusion that it developed gradually as a system of conventionalized grunts, hisses, and cries and must have been a very simple affair in the beginning. [2]But when we observe the language behavior of what we regard as primitive cultures, we find it strikingly complex and complicated. [3]Stefansson, the explorer, said that in order to get along reasonably well, an Eskimo must have at the tip of their tongue a vocabulary of more than 10,000 words, much larger than the active vocabulary of an average businessman whom speaks English. [4]Moreover, these Eskimo words are far more highly inflected than those of any of the well-known European languages, for a single noun can be spoken or written in several hundred different forms, each having a precise meaning different from that of any other. [5]The Eskimo language is, therefore, one of the most difficult in the world to learn, with the result that almost no traders or explorers have even tried to learn it. [6]Even more numerous than these nouns are the verbs.

[7]Consequently, there has grown up, in interactions between Eskimos and whites, a jargon similar to the pidgin English used in China. [8]With a vocabulary of from 300 to 600 uninflected words, most of them derived from English, Danish, Spanish, Hawaiian, and other languages. [9]It is this jargon which is usually referred to by travelers as "the Eskimo language."

• Questions

1. Which of these changes is needed?
   (A) Sentence 1: Change "developed" to "develops."
   (B) Sentence 3: Change "their tongue" to "his tongue."
   (C) Sentence 7: Change "has grown up" to "have grown up."
   (D) None of these changes is needed.

2. The order of which of these pairs of sentences ought to be reversed to make the sequence of ideas in the passage clearer?
   (A) Sentence 1 and sentence 2
   (B) Sentence 3 and sentence 4
   (C) Sentence 5 and sentence 6
   (D) Sentence 7 and sentence 8

3. Which of the following is a nonstandard sentence?
   (A) Sentence 3
   (B) Sentence 5
   (C) Sentence 7
   (D) Sentence 8

4. Which of the following is a redundancy which should be corrected?
   (A) Sentence 1: hisses and cries
   (B) Sentence 2: complex and complicated
   (C) Sentence 3: active vocabulary
   (D) Sentence 4: precise meaning

5. Which of these changes is needed?
   (A) Sentence 3: Change "whom" to "who."
   (B) Sentence 4: Change "Moreover" to "However."
   (C) Sentence 7: Change "has" to "have."
   (D) None of these changes is needed.

• *Answers*

1. (B) The subject of the phrase *an Eskimo must have at the tip of their tongue* is singular (*an Eskimo*). Therefore, the modifying adjective (*their*) must also be singular, <u>*his*</u> *tongue.*

2. (C) The order of sentence 5 and sentence 6 should be reversed. Sentence 4 refers to the many forms of nouns in the Eskimo language. Sentence 6 states that Eskimo verbs are even more numerous that the nouns mentioned in sentence 4. Sentence 5, between the nouns and the verbs, is a "summarizing" sentence about the entire language, which should logically follow both sentences 4 and 6. Therefore, sentence 5 should be the final sentence of that paragraph.

3. (D) Sentence 8 is a sentence fragment (not a complete sentence). It has no clear subject and verb. It can be corrected by simply replacing the previous period with a comma and adding the sentence fragment to the previous sentence: *Consequently, there has grown up, in interactions between Eskimos and whites, a jargon similar to the pidgin English used in China, with a vocabulary of from 300 to 600 uninflected words, most of them derived from English, Danish, Spanish, Hawaiian, and other languages.*

4. (B) The words *complex* and *complicated* are synonyms; they have almost exactly the same meanings. Therefore, using both these words is unnecessary.

5. (A) In sentence 3, the phrase *whom speaks English* requires the nominative form of the pronoun, *who,* since it is the subject of that phrase: *who speaks English* not *whom speaks English.*

ENGLISH REVIEW

The following pages review the major concepts, rules, and possible errors covered in the TASP multiple-choice writing section. This review also includes many helpful study techniques.

Before reading the review in full, skim through it and read the headings of each section. Then read first those sections that are most important to you, the sections that cover your personal "trouble spots." After you read a section, close the book and try to write a summary of what you've read to check your understanding.

PUNCTUATION

Instances of incorrect or omitted punctuation appear on the TASP in the multiple-choice writing section. The most important marks of punctuation tested are the comma(,) and semicolon(;). Typically, the TASP tests *obvious* and *basic* punctuation skills rather than subjective, stylistic uses of the comma or semicolon.

The Comma

Use a comma

- before words like *and, or, but, so, for,* and *yet* that join two or more complete sentences (each with a subject and verb and able to stand alone and make sense) into a compound sentence:

The horrifying aftermath of the fire was reported on all the news stations, and the arson squad worked diligently to uncover the cause of the tragedy.

Linguists expect to find primitive languages simple and uncomplicated, but they find instead that early language systems were strikingly elaborate and complex.

NOTE: To punctuate a compound sentence when the two or more clauses themselves contain commas, a semicolon is sometimes needed. See the review section on the semicolon for further explanation.

- to set off interrupting or introductory words or phrases:

Safe in the house, we watched the rain fall outside.

Regrettably, many of my friends will not attend the party.

Tom, after all, is one of twelve children.

Your home is in Lincoln, Nebraska, isn't it?

One must, of course, save a great deal of money before one goes into business for oneself.

- to separate a series of words or word groups:

The threat of runaway inflation, the heightened tension regarding foreign affairs, and the lack of quality education in many schools are issues that will be addressed in political campaigns for years to come.

- to set off nonessential clauses and phrases that are descriptive but not needed to get across the basic meaning of the sentence:

Truman, who tried to continue Roosevelt's conciliatory approach to the Soviet Union, adopted a much tougher policy toward the Russians by 1946.

The clause *who tried . . . Union* is not necessary. Truman's name is sufficient and the clause is merely descriptive not definitional. The clause is then nonessential and therefore set off by commas.

My wealthy Aunt Em, exceeding the trait of being economical, is so parsimonious she washes paper plates to be used again.

The phrase *exceeding the trait of being parsimonious* is set off by commas because it is extra information and descriptive, not essential and definitional.

Remember, clauses and phrases that *are* essential and definitional are *not* set off by commas.

Any teacher who ignores the varying and individual skill levels of his or her students is apt to devise lesson plans either too elementary or too advanced for effective sequential learning of new skills.

The clause *who ignores the varying . . . students* is essential; without it the reader might wonder *which* teachers. Because it defines precisely which teachers, it is not set off by commas.

Nothing was allowed to be published in Iron Curtain countries except material that had secured the approval of the Communist Party.

The clause *that had secured . . . Party* is essential here and is therefore not set off by commas. Without this clause the sentence meaning would be quite ambiguous. Again the reader would not know *which* material because the definitional clause is necessary here.

• to set off appositives (second nouns or noun equivalents that give additional information about a preceding noun):

Mr. Johnson, a teacher, ran for Chairman of the School Board.

Robert's wife, Marsha, played the harp.

When the second noun is needed to identify and to distinguish the first noun from others of its kind, the second noun is not set off with commas:

The word tenacious *was misspelled.*

My daughter Wendy loves to swim more than her sister does.

Since there are two daughters, *Wendy* is essential to distinguish which daughter loves to swim, and the word is therefore not set off by commas.

- after introductory clauses or phrases:

Although the thirteen-year-old boys grew restive under the new discipline policy, the girls seemed unperturbed by it.

When finishing an essay, do not end with an apology for not having said anything or with an indignant statement about the unfair allotment of time.

The following are some situations in which commas should *not* be used. Some of these sentence constructions may appear on the TASP.

Do NOT use a comma

- to separate a subject and its verb or a verb and its complement:

Requiring the study of grammar in our secondary English classes, is, somewhat controversial. (Incorrect)

The first comma unnecessarily separates *requiring* and *is* (subject and verb); the second separates *is* and *somewhat controversial* (verb and its complement).

- to separate a verb from its object:

Dolly Parton combines, a buxom blonde appearance, a homespun country-western sense of humor, and a dynamic vocal range. (Incorrect)

In this sentence the first comma separates *combines* (verb) from *appearance . . . sense . . . range* and splits the verb from the objects.

- to connect independent sentences without also using conjunctions such as *but, and, or, so, for,* and *yet:*

At the last school board meeting, an irate school administrator argued that principals should be given the right to suspend appropriate students if necessary to enforce board policies, that right was conceded. (Incorrect)

Both a comma and *and* are needed after *policies* to connect the two independent sentences correctly. A semicolon would also be correct here. See the review section dealing with semicolons for more information.

- to set off essential modifying information from the word modified:

A steadily increasing incidence of school vandalism is an appalling reality, characteristic of the inner-city neighborhoods, in many metropolitan areas. (Incorrect)

The two commas in this sentence are unnecessary and separate modifying phrases from the two words they modify.

NOTE: To avoid some of the punctuation errors involving either misuse of or omission of commas, try reading the sentence out loud (in a whisper) to yourself. Often your ear will catch an error your eye might overlook. Read over the examples in the section headed "Do *not* use a comma," and you will *hear*, in most cases, the correct punctuation.

The Semicolon

Use a semicolon

- to separate two complete sentences when they are not joined by words like *and, but, for, or, nor,* or *yet:*

The winter was exceptionally cold; once again fuel shortages plagued the northeastern cities.

Long-awaited relief from the six-month drought was in sight; the barometric pressure readings indicated a rainstorm was on its way.

A common error in punctuation is to connect sentences such as the two above with a comma only. One way of avoiding this error is to read the sentences out loud. A long pause between the two sentences indicates the need for a semicolon. Also, remember that two independent sentences may be punctuated as separate sentences with periods at the end of each or as two connected sentences punctuated with a semicolon (;) alone or with a comma and a conjunction (,and)(,but)(,or).

- before words like *however, therefore, moreover, then,* and *consequently* when they are used to link two complete sentences:

It was raining outside; however we felt quite warm and dry inside the house.

I feel happy about my new job; consequently I work quickly and efficiently.

My friend spends afternoon hours watching TV talk shows; then he watches situation comedies all evening.

- before words like *and, but, for, or, nor,* and *yet* that join two complete sentences of a compound sentence if either of the two sentences contains a comma:

Kim, my sister, could not take time off from work in August; but she took her vacation in September to travel to Canada, where she camped for two weeks.

The Colon

Use a colon

- to formally introduce a statement, a quotation, or a series of terms:

Introducing a statement—*The members of the community all hold the following belief: We should all love our neighbors.*

Introducing a quotation—*John F. Kennedy is remembered for these words: "Ask not what your country can do for you; ask what you can do for your country."*

Introducing a series—*The most familiar punctuation devices are these: the period, the comma, the semicolon, the colon, and the question mark.*

Playing the Punctuation Game: Some Extra Practice

In addition to the practice this book provides, you can strengthen your punctuation skill by doing the following. Have a friend recopy for you a long newspaper or magazine article or editorial, leaving out all the punctuation marks. Then your task becomes putting the punctuation marks back in. Use the original article to check your choices. In current magazine and newspaper articles, there may be a wide range of uses of some marks of punctuation, especially the comma. Your practice time is well spent, however, because you have practiced looking for the appropriate places for punctuation. Practicing this editing skill will help you on the TASP.

GRAMMAR, USAGE, AND SENTENCE STRUCTURE

Pronouns

- Use *I, he, she, we,* and *they* in place of the *subject* of a sentence. (The subject is the *doer.*):

  <u>Bill</u> wrote a sentence.
  <u>He</u> wrote a sentence.
  <u>I</u> wrote a sentence.

  <u>Susan</u> was late for work.
  <u>She</u> was late for work.

  <u>My family</u> always takes a summer vacation.
  <u>We</u> always take a summer vacation.

  <u>Jerry's family</u> always takes a summer vacation.
  <u>They</u> always take a summer vacation.

- Use *me, him, her, us,* and *them* in place of the *object* of a sentence. (The object is the *receiver.*):

  Bill greeted <u>Jerry</u>.
  Bill greeted <u>him</u>.
  Bill greeted <u>me</u>.

  The boss fired <u>Susan</u>.
  The boss fired <u>her</u>.

  Camille helped <u>Christopher and me</u> pack our suitcases.
  Camille helped <u>us</u> pack our suitcases.

  The lifeguard saved <u>three people</u> from drowning.
  The lifeguard saved <u>them</u> from drowning.

- Use *who* as a *subject* (a *doer*):

  <u>Who knocked</u> at the door?

  Do you know <u>who knocked</u> at the door?

  No doubt it was a neighbor <u>who</u>, a few minutes ago, <u>knocked</u> at the door.

- Use *whom* as an *object* (a *receiver*):

To whom were you speaking?

Your line was busy, and I wondered to whom you were speaking.

I'm the person whom you telephoned yesterday.

PRONOUN REVIEW CHART
PERSONAL PRONOUNS

	Nominative (subject)		Objective (object)		Possessive (ownership)	
	singular	*plural*	*singular*	*plural*	*singular*	*plural*
First Person	I	we	me	us	my mine	our ours
Second Person	you	you	you	you	your yours	your yours
Third Person	he she it	they	him her it	them	his her, hers its	their theirs

RELATIVE PRONOUNS

Nominative (subject)	Objective (object)	Possessive (ownership)
who (persons) which (things) that (things and persons)	whom	whose

Verb Tense

- Most verbs are regular. For these verbs add *-ed* to talk about the past and *will* or *shall* to talk about the future.

Past: *I walked yesterday.*
Present: *I walk today.*
Future: *I will walk tomorrow.*

One way to practice the basic forms of regular verbs is to recite the *past tense* and *past participle* when you are given only the *present tense*. Here are some examples:

PRESENT	PAST (-ED)
I talk today.	*I talked yesterday.*
I help you today.	*I helped you yesterday.*
I close shop early today.	*I closed shop early yesterday.*

PAST PARTICIPLE (-ED)

I have talked on many occasions.
I have helped you often.
I have closed shop early for a week.

• Some verbs are *irregular* and require special constructions to express the past and past participle. Here are some of the most troublesome irregular verbs:

PRESENT	PAST	PAST PARTICIPLE
begin	began	begun
burst	burst	burst
do	did	done
drown	drowned	drowned
go	went	gone
hang (to execute)	hanged	hanged
hang (to suspend)	hung	hung
lay (to put in place)	laid	laid
lie (to rest)	lay	lain
set (to place in position)	set	set
sit (to be seated)	sat	sat
shine (to provide light)	shone	shone
shine (to polish)	shined	shined
raise (to lift up)	raised	raised
rise (to get up)	rose	risen
swim	swam	swum
swing	swung	swung

Subject-Verb Agreement

- If a subject is plural, the verb must be plural; if a subject is singular, the verb must be singular. The following sentence is *incorrect:*

Here on the table is an apple and three pears.

Focus on the verb (*is*) and then locate the subject. In this sentence, the subject (*an apple and three pears*) *follows* the verb. Since the subject is plural, the verb must be plural, and the sentence should say:

Here on the table are an apple and three pears.

Here is another example that is *incorrect:*

The man, along with his friends and neighbors, support the home-town candidate.

The verb is *support.* Since the subject is singular (*man*), the verb must be singular—*supports* instead of *support.* Notice that in this case many words separate the subject from the verb; subject and verb will not always be close to one another.

Adjectives and Adverbs

- Adjectives describe nouns:

Holidays are happy occasions. (*Happy* describes *occasions.*)

His was a narrow escape. (*Narrow* describes *escape.*)

Jesse Owens was a successful athlete. (*Successful* describes *athlete.*)

- Adverbs describe verbs:

We all sang happily. (*Happily* describes *sang.*)

He narrowly missed an oncoming car. (*Narrowly* describes *missed.*)

Jesse Owens successfully completed the race. (*Successfully* describes *completed.*)

• Making comparisons—Adjectives normally add *-er* or *-est* to make comparisons.

Use *-er* to compare two items: *Cindy was the great**er** of the two athletes.*

Sometimes use *more* to compare two items: *Christopher was the **more** handsome of the twins.*

Use *-est* to compare more than two items: *Cindy was the great**est** athlete on the team.*

Sometimes use *most* to compare more than two items: *Christopher was the **most** handsome member of the family.*

Adverbs normally use *more* or *most* to make comparisons:

*Bob ran **more** quickly today than he did yesterday.*

*Bob runs **most** quickly in the early morning.*

NOTE: The first sentence compares only two items, today and yesterday, and so it requires *more*. The second sentence compares one time (early morning) with many other possible times, and so it requires *most*.

• Use an adjective after a verb that expresses being, feeling, tasting, or smelling.

*Harry seems **happy**.* (not *happily*)

*Bill feels **bad**.* (not *badly*)

*The candy tastes **sweet**.* (not *sweetly*)

*The flowers smell **sweet**.* (not *sweetly*)

Idiom

To native English speakers, certain expressions "sound right" because they are so commonly used. Such expressions are called "idiomatic" and are correct simply because they are so widely accepted. Here is a list of examples:

<table>
<tr><td>IDIOMATIC</td><td>UNIDIOMATIC</td></tr>
<tr><td>addicted to</td><td>addicted from</td></tr>
<tr><td>angry with</td><td>angry at</td></tr>
<tr><td>capable of</td><td>capable to</td></tr>
<tr><td>different from</td><td>different than</td></tr>
<tr><td>identical with</td><td>identical to</td></tr>
<tr><td>obedient to</td><td>obedient in</td></tr>
<tr><td>on the whole</td><td>on a whole</td></tr>
</table>

Remember that the standard of correctness is standard written English. Be alert to idiomatic expressions not acceptable in or characteristic of standard *written* English.

Double Negatives

- To use a double negative is incorrect in standard written English. When words like *hardly, scarcely,* and *barely,* considered "negative" words, are used along with other negative words such as *not, no, none, never,* and *nothing* in the same sentence to express the same negative meaning twice, a "double negative" occurs. For example:

The puppy <u>didn't</u> have <u>no one</u> to love.

The notion that there is not anyone to love is expressed twice—once by the *didn't (did + not)* and once by *no one.*

After a hard day's work, Susan <u>can't hardly</u> stay awake.

Susan's not being able to stay awake is expressed twice—once with the *can't (can + not)* and again with *hardly.* Here are some other examples of "double negatives":

You <u>don't</u> have <u>scarcely</u> anything to worry about.

The fans <u>can't hardly</u> wait for the concert to begin.

NOTE: Merely the occurrence of two negative words in the same sentence does not necessarily result in a "double negative" as in the following example:

I had <u>no</u> time available on weekends, so I decided I would <u>not</u> take the part-time job offer.

The *no* and the *not* in this sentence express two different negatives and are therefore not considered "double negatives."

Either/Or—Neither/Nor

• Use *either* or *neither* to compare two items (*either* is sometimes used to compare more than two items):

Uncle Joe will arrive <u>either</u> today or tomorrow morning.

<u>Neither</u> of these two shirts fits me very well.

• Use *either* with *or:*

Uncle Joe will arrive <u>either</u> today <u>or</u> tomorrow.

• Use *neither* with *nor:*

<u>Neither</u> the white shirt <u>nor</u> the blue shirt fits me very well.

Exact Word Choice

• Sometimes words that sound alike are confused with one another. Checking their dictionary meanings will help you avoid their misuse. Here are some commonly confused words:

1. adapt/adept		9. lay/lie	
2. affect/effect		10. persecute/prosecute	
3. capital/capitol		11. precede/proceed	
4. detain/retain		12. raise/rise	
5. elicit/illicit		13. set/sit	
6. foreword/forward		14. their/there/they're	
7. human/humane		15. weather/whether	
8. incite/insight			

Special Problems

Fewer/Less

- *Fewer* is used with *countable* items:

  There are <u>fewer people</u> in the room than I had expected.

- *Less* is used with *uncountable* items:

  There has been <u>less rain</u> this year than in years past.

Many/Much

- *Many* is used with *countable* items:

  There are <u>many people</u> at the meeting tonight.

- *Much* is used with *uncountable* items:

  Frank spends too <u>much time</u> worrying about the future.

Sentence Fragments

- A sentence fragment is an *incomplete* sentence that is written and punctuated as if it were a *complete* sentence. Here are some examples of sentence fragments:

  Fragment: *Although Fred must leave for work early each morning.*
  Problem: *Although* suggests another action that would make the sentence complete.
  Complete Sentence: *Although Fred must leave for work early each <u>morning, he never gets to bed before one</u> A.M.*

  Fragment: *Hard study, a baseball game with friends, or just some sleep.*
  Problem: There is no subject (doer) and no verb (action).
  Complete Sentence: *<u>Tim</u> [subject] <u>could not decide</u> [verb] whether to devote his afternoon to hard study, a baseball game with friends, or just some sleep.*

Fragment: *People who sing loudly and happily in the shower.*
Problem: *People who* signals the need for additional information, what the people who sing do.
Complete Sentence: *People who sing loudly and happily in the shower often start the day feeling optimistic.*

Wordiness

- Saying the same thing twice is one common type of wordiness. Here are some examples with the repetitions underscored:

At 8 A.M. in the morning it suddenly started to rain without warning.

In this modern world of today there are hundreds of millionaires with a great deal of money.

Several separate and distinct programs signaled a new era of economic progress.

Students found the lectures Professor Smith gave while he was speaking difficult to understand and comprehend.

Parallelism

- Items in a sentence are *parallel* when they have the same *form.* Here are three series of parallel items:

to join the army, to find a job, to enroll in college

joining the army, finding a job, enrolling in college

the army, a job, college

- The following sentence *mixes forms,* an example of *faulty parallelism:*

Faulty: *Once he turned eighteen, the young man's choices were joining the army, to find a job, or college.*

Correct: *Once he turned eighteen, the young man's choices were the army, a job, or college.*

- Sometimes faulty parallelism occurs in just two items instead of three:

Faulty: *The youngster needed to choose between <u>playing</u> outdoors with friends and <u>to study</u> for a test.*

Correct: *The youngster needed to choose between <u>playing</u> outdoors with friends and <u>studying</u> for a test.*

Misplaced Modifiers

- A misplaced modifier occurs when a *description* does not clearly refer to the *item described:*

Faulty: *<u>Galloping</u> across the finish line, <u>I</u> realized I had bet on the wrong horse.*

The sentence structure indicates that *I* am doing the *galloping*.

Correct: *As the winner galloped across the finish line, I realized I had bet on the wrong horse.*

Here are some other misplaced modifiers. Notice that in each case the *description* does not clearly refer to the *item described*.

A <u>piano</u> [item described] *is for sale by an <u>elderly woman</u> with <u>walnut legs</u>* [description].
(The item described is not clearly connected with its description.)

<u>To keep cool</u> [description] *during summer weather, my air conditioner ran constantly.*
(The item described—a person—is omitted altogether.)

Corrections:

<u>A piano with walnut legs</u> is for sale by an elderly woman.

<u>To keep cool</u> during summer weather, <u>I</u> run my air conditioner constantly.

Comparisons

- As/than—*As* and *than* are often used to structure comparisons, sometimes incorrectly and incompletely:

Correct combinations: *as . . . as . . . than*
                          as . . . as

Incorrect combinations: *as . . . than*

Correct Sentences:

She is as pretty as, if not prettier than, any other girl.

Linda is as pretty as any of her sisters.

Incorrect Sentences:

She is as pretty, if not prettier than, any other girl.

Linda is as pretty than any of her sisters.

WRITING SAMPLE

The writing sample portion of the TASP writing test consists of one assigned topic on which you are to write from 300 to 600 words.

Ability Tested

The writing sample tests your ability to read a topic carefully, organize your ideas before you write, and write with clarity and precision.

Basic Skills Necessary

This section requires a basic high school level writing background. Papers are scored on the writers ability to perform the following: development and organization of ideas with supporting evidence or specific examples; understanding of the essay's intended audience (for example, a speech urging members of the Board of Education to vote a certain way); comprehension of assigned task(s); skillful use of language; and correctness of mechanics, usage, and paragraphing.

Directions

For this section, you should spend approximately 60 minutes to plan and write your essay. You may use the bottom of your directions page to organize and plan before you begin writing. You should plan your time wisely, using enough time to understand the question, plan and outline, write, and finally reread your essay and revise if necessary.

You must write on the specified topic. An essay on another topic will not be acceptable.

Your essay must be written on the lined pages provided. No other paper may be used. Your writing should be neat and legible. Do not skip lines, do not write excessively large, and do not leave large margins.

Your essay will be judged for its

- being on topic

- clarity

- support and development

- organization

- use of correct standard written English

No reference materials (dictionary, thesaurus, etc.) may be used.

Analysis of Directions

You will have space below the topic for planning. Use this space to organize your thoughts. Double check to determine how much space (lined paper) you have in which to write your essay (normally three sides).

Pay careful attention to the criteria on which your essay will be scored:

- being on topic: Have you addressed the topic and the tasks required by the topic? Have you used language appropriate for the essay's intended audience?

- clarity: Is your main idea clearly expressed?

- support and development: Are your points well supported with specific examples and specific details?

- organization: Do you use correct paragraph form, with each paragraph consisting of one main idea?

- use of correct standard written English: Does the essay use correct grammar, usage, and sentence structure, as well as proper punctuation and spelling?

Some General Tips

- Read the topic twice—three times if necessary—before writing. Circle key words. This will help you focus on the assigned task(s).

- Plan before you begin writing your actual essay. This planning may consist of outlining, brainstorming, clustering, etc.

- Spend at least 5 minutes organizing your thoughts before you begin writing. A poorly written essay is often the result of inadequate planning.

- Don't let spelling slow down your writing. Keep the flow of your writing going; come back later to correct spelling errors.

- Leave time after you write the essay to reread and edit/correct your essay. Don't make extensive changes when you reread; correct spelling errors and other minor flaws.

SAMPLE TOPIC, TECHNIQUES, AND ESSAYS

Sample Topic

Some have said that Americans are becoming a nation of spectators rather than a nation of doers. Others have argued the opposite, that Americans have become more active participants rather than just passive observers. Write an essay to be read by a history teacher in which you take one side of the argument. Support your position using examples from your own experience, reading, and/or observations.

Outlining

One way of planning is outlining. A simple outline for this sample might go something like this:

Americans—Spectators, Not Doers

I. Sporting events
   A. Attendance figures highest ever
   B. More teams being watched

II. Television and films
   A. Homes with TVs
   B. TVs on more and more

III. Elections
   A. Only half of eligible voters vote
   B. More watch on TV than participate

OR

Americans—Doers, Not Spectators

I. Recreation—more popular than ever
   A. More sporting equipment sold than ever before
      1. Athletic shoes: its own industry
      2. Athletic outfits
   B. On weekends parks are filled
      1. Tennis courts hard to get
      2. Ballfields always used

II. Public involved in fundraisers
   A. For social concerns
      1. Aid to Africa
      2. Farm Aid
      3. Comic Relief
      4. Door-to-door for diseases
   B. For political candidates
      1. More PAC money raised than ever before

Clustering

Here's another quick way to organize your ideas:

Sample Essay

A sample essay from the first outline might go something like this:

It has been said that Americans are becoming a nation of spectators, rather than a nation of participants. From my observations, I can easily agree with this statement. In recent years, Americans have increasingly demonstrated their passive, nonparticipatory status. This is most apparent in the increase in popularity of spectator sports, the rise of the visual media, and unfortunately, the decline of electoral participation.

The popularity of spectator sports has risen dramatically. The number of sports teams has expanded and continues to grow. At one time, there were only 16 major league baseball teams; now there are 27. Once major league football teams played only in the East and Midwest; now they include the major cities in the South and West as well. Professional hockey once consisted of only six major league teams; now there are almost two dozen. Total attendance has likewise grown. It is impossible to get tickets to some football games, as they are sold out months, sometimes years, in advance. If you don't have season tickets, you may not be able to get in the stadium. Sell-outs, once uncommon, are an everyday event. Each year, total attendance for individual sports breaks the previous year's records.

The rise of the visual media is also indicative of a more passive society. Nearly every home has at least one, if not more, television sets. Recent studies have found that watching television, a passive entertainment (unlike reading or card playing), consumes hours of the average American's day. Once there were only about a half-dozen television stations; now there are dozens, including cable films, 24-hour sporting events, and many more yet to come. Americans' appetite for television appears to be insatiable.

Unfortunately, the increasingly passive nature of the American citizen is also reflected in the American electoral process. Fewer voters than ever take the time to fulfill their responsibility to vote. In the last presidential election, nearly half of the eligible voters stayed home instead of going to the polls. It was estimated that more Americans <u>watched</u> the election on television than voted. Sad to say, but the growing passivity of the American character may have grave consequences for the future of our democracy.

American passivity is exemplified by the recent growth of spectator sports and television and the decline of participatory electoral democracy. Hopefully, however, this trend is only a temporary one.

The "Why" Essay

One good way to approach a question which asks you to explain, analyze, or evaluate is to use a "why" essay format. A "why" essay is built around a thesis sentence. The thesis sentence begins with your opinion, followed by the word *because* and then a list of the most important reasons that the opinion is valid, reasonable, or well founded. For example,

I am against the "Back to Basics" movement because it inhibits creativity, fails to recognize the importance of the arts, and restricts the curriculum.

The thesis statement comes at the end of the introductory paragraph followed by paragraphs that explain each of your reasons. Finally, the paper ends with a summary of the reasons and a restatement of the thesis sentence.

The "why" essay format could look like this in outline form:

"WHY" ESSAY FORMAT

Paragraph	*Content*
1	Introduction—Thesis Sentence
2	Reason 1
3	Reason 2
4	Reason 3
5	Conclusion

The introduction invites the reader to read on. Your reasons (three are often sufficient) that follow should give examples or evidence to support each reason. Your concluding paragraph summarizes your reasons and restates the thesis statement.

Examples

In most essay questions, regardless of "type" (*compare,* or *describe,* or *explain*), you will need to use *examples* to support your thoughts. Thinking in terms of examples will also be helpful in planning your writing.

PRACTICE ESSAY TOPICS

Following are topics you may use for practice. Allow about 60 minutes to plan and write each essay. Give yourself about a half-page to organize your notes and three sides on lined 8½″ by 11″ paper to write the actual essay. Then, upon completion of each essay, evaluate, or have a friend evaluate, your writing using the checklist provided.

Topic 1

Some people argue that it is difficult, if not impossible, to earn a good living nowadays without at least a high school diploma. In fact, these people argue that an undergraduate college degree may often also be a necessity for a good job. Others, however, argue that college degrees are meaningless, that a high school diploma or college degree is usually irrelevant to the demands of the real world of work. These poeple maintain that on-the-job training, not a college degree, is often the best preparation for a particular job. Choose one side of this debate and write an essay supporting your position, using examples from your experience, reading, and/or observations.

Topic 2

Some have argued that imagination is not as important as perspiration, that hard work is far more significant to the success of any endeavor than even the most creative and imaginative ideas. Others argue that without the creative spark, all the hard work in the world would be meaningless. Write an essay to be read by an English teacher in which you take one side of the argument. Support your position using examples from your own experience, reading, and/or observations.

Topic 3

Some educators have argued that an all-male or all-female environment is beneficial to learning. Others have maintained that a single-sex environment is actually detrimental to learning. Write an essay to be read by a school board considering a policy making all school classes either single sex or coeducational. Take one side of the argument. Support your position using examples from your own experience, reading, and/or observations.

Topic 4

Some have argued that technology is a blessing, that it makes our lives easier and more enjoyable. Others have argued that the results of technology are actually troublesome, making our lives more stressful and less healthful. Write an essay to be read by a social studies teacher in which you take one side of the argument. Support your position using examples from your own experience, reading, and/or observations.

Essay Checklist

Use the following checklist to evaluate your finished essay:

A well-written essay will

☐ be on topic: Does your essay address the assignment? Does it complete all the tasks set by the topic?

☐ be written clearly: Is your essay consistent in its tone and its arguments? Is it carefully focused on the assignment?

☐ be well developed: Does your essay use lots of specific examples and details to support its points?

☐ use language correctly and skillfully: Is your essay written in standard written English, with only minor flaws, if any, in grammar, sentence structure, and punctuation?

☐ be well organized: Is each paragraph one main idea? Are there smooth transitions between paragraphs? Is the entire essay unified?

☐ be legible: Is your handwriting neat enough to be read and understood?

Part III: Practice-Review-Analyze-Practice

Two Full-Length Practice Tests

This section contains two full-length practice simulation TASPs. The practice tests are followed by complete answers, explanations, and analysis techniques. The format, levels of difficulty, question structure, and number of questions are similar to those on the actual TASP. The actual TASP is copyrighted and may not be duplicated, and these questions are not taken directly from the actual tests.

When taking these exams, try to simulate the test conditions by following the time allotment for the complete test carefully.

PRACTICE TEST 1

Section I: Reading—40 Questions
Section II: Mathematics—40 Questions
Section III: Writing—Multiple-Choice—40 Questions
                Essay—1 300 to 600 word essay

The total time allowed for the test is four hours (with one additional hour allowed if necessary). You may work on any section of the test during this time period.

READING

Several questions follow each of the passages in this section. Using only the stated or implied information given in the passage, answer the questions by choosing the best answer from among the four choices given.

Questions 1 through 5 are based on the following passage.

THE ULTIMATE TEACHING MACHINE

1   A new aid to rapid—almost magical—learning has made its appearance. Indications are that if it catches on all the electronic gadgets will be so much junk. The new device is known as BUILT-IN ORDERLY ORGANIZED KNOWLEDGE. The makers generally call it by its initials, BOOK.

2   Many advantages are claimed over the old-style learning and teaching aids on which most people are brought up nowadays. It has no wires, no electronic circuits to break down. No connection is needed to an electricity power point. It is made entirely without mechanical parts to go wrong or need replacement. Anyone can use BOOK, even children, and it fits comfortably into the hands. It can be conveniently used sitting in an armchair by the fire.

3   How does this revolutionary, unbelievably easy invention work? Basically BOOK consists only of a large number of paper sheets. These may run to hundreds where BOOK covers a lengthy program of information. Each sheet bears a number in sequence, so that the sheets cannot be used in the wrong order. To make it even easier for the user to keep the sheets in the proper order, they are held firmly in place by a special locking device called a "binding."

4   Each sheet of paper presents the user with an information sequence in the form of symbols, which he absorbs optically for automatic registration on the brain. When one sheet has been assimilated, a flick of the finger turns it over and further information is found on the other side. By using both sides of each sheet in this way, a great economy is effected, thus reducing both size and cost of BOOK. No buttons need to be pressed to move

from one sheet to another, to open or close BOOK, or to start it working.

5   BOOK may be taken up at any time and used by merely opening it. Instantly it is ready for use. Nothing has to be connected up or switched on. The user may turn it at will to any sheet, going backwards or forwards as he pleases. A sheet is provided near the beginning as a location finder for any required information sequence.

6   A small accessory, available at trifling extra cost, is the BOOKmark. This enables the user to pick up his program where he left off on the previous learning session. BOOKmark is versatile and may be used in any book.

7   The initial cost varies with the size and subject matter. Already a vast range of BOOK is available, covering every conceivable subject and adjusted to different levels of aptitude. One BOOK, small enough to be held in the hands, may contain an entire learning schedule. Once purchased, BOOK requires no further cost; no batteries or wires are needed, since the motive power, thanks to the ingenious device patented by the makers, is supplied by the brain of the user.

8   BOOK may be stored on a handy shelf, and for ease of reference, the program schedule is normally indicated on the back of the binding.

9   Altogether the Built-in Orderly Organized Knowledge seems to have great advantages with no drawbacks. We predict a big future for it.

1. Which of these phrases best defines the term *motive power* as it is used in paragraph 7?
   (A) strong motivation to read
   (B) power by which BOOK operates
   (C) BOOK's built-in electric generator
   (D) patented device for giving power to the brain

2. The main idea of the passage is best expressed by which of the following?
   (A) When conceived of as a machine, a book is an unbeatable, incredibly easy device to aid learning.
   (B) A book, no matter how dramatically it is described, is highly overrated as a learning tool.
   (C) BOOK is a technical wonder, a kind of computer program, far advanced over ordinary books.
   (D) Because so much modern new teaching technology is now available, books have outlived their usefulness.

3. Which of the following is the best description of the author's tone in discussing BOOK?
   (A) The author's tone conveys an affectionate attitude toward readers.
   (B) By employing language used to describe machines, the author adopts a dehumanizing attitude toward readers.
   (C) The author's tone is informal, especially when describing how BOOK works.
   (D) The author adopts the enthusiastic attitude of a public-relations promoter.

4. The author of this passage would most likely agree with which of these statements?
   (A) Machines powered by electricity tend to perform better than machines powered by hand.
   (B) The human body can be described as a remarkably efficient and resourceful machine.
   (C) Even after BOOK becomes popular, electronic teaching devices will continue to play an important educational role.
   (D) One disadvantage of BOOK is that it is too difficult for most young children to understand.

5. Which of the following groups of topics bests shows the content organization of the passage?
   (A)   I. BOOK's history and inventor
          II. BOOK's pros and cons
          III. BOOK's many uses
   (B)   I. Advantage of BOOK over other teaching aids
          II. The way BOOK works
          III. Other features of BOOK
   (C)   I. Types of teaching machines
          II. Teacher's role in introducing BOOK to students
          III. Parent's role in introducing BOOK to children
   (D)   I. User's attitudes about BOOK
          II. The many uses and types of BOOKmark
          III. BOOK of the future

Questions 6 through 10 are based on the following passage.

THE GRANT PRESIDENCY

1   The presidency of Ulysses S. Grant is generally considered to be one of the lowest points in American history. Unprecedented scandals shocked the nation as it had never been shocked before, and the President's own relatives were implicated in several of the scandals. Although Grant possessed considerable physical courage and unquestioned personal integrity, he was woefully unprepared to be president of the United States. He was not a politician; in fact, he loathed politics. Grant had voted only once in a presidential campaign—for Buchanan. The general, who in his earlier life had tasted real poverty, was overawed by the adulation of the wealthy, and so he accepted such lavish gifts from them as a house in Philadelphia, the use of private railroad cars, and cash. He assumed that these gifts were his due; it never occurred to him that he was being used.

2   As president, Grant was everything the Civil War conqueror of Robert E. Lee was not—weak, vacillating, and indecisive. Seldom has a president depended so much on his Cabinet or been so ill served. A poor judge of men, Grant appointed a Cabinet that was unparalleled for ineptness as well as corruption. Of a total of twenty-five appointments, only six men really proved to be competent: E. R. Hoar, Attorney General; J. D. Cox, Secretary of the Interior; J. A. J. Creswell and M. Jewell, Postmasters General; B. H. Bristow, Secretary of the Treasury; and H. Fish, Secretary of State. As a further example of his ineptness, Grant eventually fired all of these men except Fish. As Allan Nevins demonstrates so clearly in his book *Hamilton Fish: Inner History of the Grant Administration,* Fish was the bulwark of the Grant Administration; again and again he saved it from major blunders in both foreign and domestic affairs.

3   The greatest failure of the Grant administration was the widespread corruption it brought to national politics. Practically every government agency was tainted with a major scandal during his eight years as president. Grant was a stubborn man who prided himself on his loyalty to friends and relatives; he could not believe that his associates would betray him and the public trust. Thus, whenever charges of corruption were made against

his associates, Grant felt that the attacks must be part of the usual slander of political opponents. When J. F. Casey, his brother-in-law, was charged with using his post as Collector of Customs at New Orleans to defraud the government, and there was clear evidence of his guilt, Grant, nevertheless, reappointed him for four more years. In another instance, Treasury Secretary William Richardson was discovered stealing a good portion of delinquent tax collections. Grant refused to take any action against Richardson until a congressional committee had prepared a censure vote against him. Grant finally accepted Richardson's resignation and then appointed him to a federal judgeship. Worst of all was the case of Orville Babcock, Grant's close friend and private secretary. When Babcock was caught redhanded as one of the key figures in the Whiskey Ring (a conspiracy to defraud the government of excise taxes), Grant supported him with the full prestige of the presidency. He ordered federal agencies to suppress the evidence and asked to testify personally in Babcock's behalf. Fortunately, wise minds prevailed and Grant had to content himself with writing a letter in support of Babcock. Eventually Babcock was acquitted despite ample evidence of his guilt; a conviction might have made it appear that the President had collaborated with his corrupt friend. After the trial Grant fired all government officials who had cooperated with the prosecution and appointed Babcock Inspector of Lighthouses.

4   Historians generally agree that the Grant presidency was a tragedy both for him and for the nation. This country cannot afford eight years of bungling and corruption, and certainly not during a critical time such as the Reconstruction period. Another disastrous consequence of the Grant years was the shattered prestige of the presidential office. The congressional Radicals dominated the government from 1866 until the inauguration of Rutherford B. Hayes in 1877.

6. Which of these phrases best defines the word *ineptness* as it is used twice in the second paragraph?
   (A) emotional emptiness
   (B) hunger for power
   (C) lack of aptitude
   (D) decisive judgment

7. The main idea of the passage is best expressed by which of the following?
   (A) The Grant presidency, a severe set-back to the nation's recovery after the Civil War, was marked by incompetent leadership and widespread government corruption.
   (B) The American public, who admired Grant as a Civil War hero, would have been able to respect him as president if his Cabinet had not been corrupt and incompetent.
   (C) Grant was weak, vacillating, and indecisive both as a general during the CIvil War and as president of the United States.
   (D) The worst consequence of Grant's poor leadership was that the American public became mistrustful of the authority associated with the presidential office.

8. Which individual is used to illustrate the author's claim that *the President's own relatives were implicated in* government scandals?
   (A) Orville Babcock
   (B) Hamilton Fish
   (C) J. F. Casey
   (D) William Richardson

9. Which of these statements from the passage is an opinion held by the author rather than a fact?
   (A) Grant had voted only once in a presidential campaign—for Buchanan.
   (B) Eventually Babcock was acquitted despite ample evidence of his guilt.
   (C) Grant refused to take any action against Richardson until a congressional committee had prepared a censure against him.
   (D) He assumed that these gifts were his due; it never occurred to him that he was being used.

10. Which of these statements best summarizes the information in the passage?

(A) Grant's loyalty to his friends in government was short-lived. Although he would, for a time, support his political associates against slanderous accusations of corruption, he eventually would fire them, just as he fired five of his most competent Cabinet members. His poor judgement led him to accept Richardson's resignation and to fire the government officials who assisted in the prosecution of Babcock.

(B) Perhaps no president was worse equipped for political office than was Grant. During his disastrous presidency, Grant depended on a notoriously unqualified and dishonest Cabinet and was foolishly loyal to a number of corrupt govenment associates who scandalized the nation with their behavior. His presidency struck a dreadful blow to the nation during the Reconstruction period.

(C) Grant, the Civil War general, was a strong, decisive leader who struggled to direct and guide the American people through the Reconstruction period. Although poor counsel from a misguided and greedy Cabinet hindered Grant in his work of uniting the North and South, he managed to win modest public support for his domestic policies. Today, historians praise this courageous post-war president for holding on to his personal integrity even while associating with a self-serving Cabinet.

(D) Scandals involving members of Grant's administration made it difficult for Hamilton Fish, Secretary of State, to guard the president against making errors in domestic and foreign affairs. In the Whiskey Ring case, Fish advised Grant to limit his suppoort to a letter written in Babcock's behalf. Despite the wise, protective counsel of Fish, Grant was forced to accept that by the time his presidency ended the prestige of his office had been destroyed.

Questions 11 through 15 are based on the following passage.

COURSE OUTLINE FOR RELIGION 201
Professor Dale Renick

1   Religion is an experience which is found among all classes of people. Primitive man had his peculiar religious beliefs and practices, and the same is true of people in all stages of civilization. The expression of religion varies with the needs, customs, and education of the people involved, and for this reason, it is difficult to state precisely what religion is and to differentiate it from other forms of experience. There is no uniformity of religious beliefs, and the same is true of the various types of religious activity. For the purposes of this course, we will use the following definition: "Religion is an intense loyalty and devotion to whatever it is one regards as most worthful in human life."

2   The objectives for Religion 201 are to trace the rise and development of religious consciousness, to survey the main religions of the world, and to examine the Christian belief in God.

3   The required textbooks for the course are *Charting the Religious Sensibility* by Mildred Carruthers and *The Christian Faith* by William Stoner. Please make sure that you purchase the fourth edition of the Stoner text. He has made many revisions and added entire new sections since the publication of the third edition. For example, his discussion of the Reformation period has been entirely revamped, and for the first time includes a chronology of Martin Luther's life.

4   I will lecture on your reading on Mondays and Wednesdays. Because this class is intended to help you clarify your views on matters of faith and religion, Fridays are reserved for discussions in which I will challenge you to express your opinions and to ask questions of me and your classmates.

5   As an incentive to you to keep up with the reading, I will be giving unannounced quizzes throughout the term. There will be about eight in all. To ensure that you come informed to Friday discussions, I will require that you turn in a weekly reaction paper based on your understanding of the reading. The paper, one page typed and double spaced, should give your response to one of the many discussion questions I will hand out each week.

6   Quizzes and reaction papers make up only a small part of your grade. The bulk of your grade will be based on two ten-page papers you will write for me. Each paper must be argumentative in form. Essentially, this means you should begin by introducing your paper's central claim or thesis, then go on to support it with a strong reasoned argument and defend it against plausible objections.

7   This course will be of great value to students who are willing to examine what is "most worthful" in their lives. According to our definition of religion, even students who do not believe in God may be surprised to discover that they, indeed, are quite religious.

11. Which of these words or phrases best defines the word *revamped* as it is used in paragraph 3?
   (A) divided into sections
   (B) lengthened
   (C) condensed
   (D) made over

12. Why does the writer use the phrase *they, indeed, are quite religious* in the last paragraph?
   (A) to highlight a broader concept of what it means to be religious
   (B) to emphasize that deep down most people believe in God
   (C) to evoke a sense of how a soul can be transformed through self-examination
   (D) to differentiate between atheism and God-centered religion

13. Which of the following would most likely be an incorrect tactic in writing an argumentative paper as defined by Professor Renick?
   (A) citing a quotation from an authority in the field of psychology
   (B) defending the paper's thesis against invalid objections
   (C) exploring a topic of personal interest and importance
   (D) taking a stand that is controversial

14. Which of these statements from the passage is an opinion held by
    the author rather than a fact?
    (A) This course will be of great value to students who are willing
        to examine what is "most worthful" in their lives.
    (B) The objectives for Religion 201 are to trace the rise and
        development of religious consciousness, to survey the main
        religions of the world, and to examine the Christian belief in
        God.
    (C) For example, his discussion of the Reformation period has
        been entirely revamped, and for the first time includes a
        chronology of Martin Luther's life.
    (D) Quizzes and reaction papers make up only a small part of
        your grade. The bulk of your grade will be based on two
        ten-page papers you will write for me.

15. According to the passage, religion is a form of experience
    (A) similar to the experience of beauty.
    (B) less highly devloped among primitive people, especially
        those who believe in many gods.
    (C) common to people at all levels of civilization.
    (D) which reveals itself in uniform types of religious activity.

Questions 16 through 20 are based on the following passage.

AESOP

1   Three early Greek prose writers of importance are Lysias, Demosthenes, and Aesop. Lysias, a noted Athenian orator and professional speech writer, was born about 445 B.C. and died about 380 B.C.. He is known for his ability to identify with clients, for whom he served as a legal advocate, and to typify their station, lifestyle, and idiosyncrasies with application of suitable examples and logic. Demosthenes (384–322 B.C.) holds a place among the great speakers of history. He was eulogized by an ancient critic as follows: "Our orator, owing to the fact that in his vehemence— and in his speed, power, and intensity—he can as it were consume by fire and carry away all before him, may be compared to a thunderbolt or a flash of lightning." Aesop, our subject in what follows, is today perhaps the best known of the three Greeks.

2   The semilegendary writer and/or collector of 350 fables, Aesop (620?–560? B.C.) was a slave from Phrygia, or Lydia, who served Iadmon on the island of Samos before being freed. After extensive travels, he is thought to have been thrown from a cliff at Delphi after envious Delphians, angered by his ironic tales, hid a golden bowl in his luggage and accused him of theft. The city is said to have suffered a plague and was forced to pay blood-money to Iadmon's grandson to atone for its savagery. However, this story, like most episodes attached to Aesop's name, contains the elements of legend.

3   An ancient biographer of Aesop pictures him as a Greek Uncle Remus—a jolly teller of tales and dispenser of homespun wisdom who confounds the learned men of his day with common sense. The bits of orally transmitted folklore, proverbs, and yarns attributed to Aesop were probably written down around 300 B.C. by Demetrius Phalereus. The collection known as "Aesop's Fables" is the product of Phaedrus (ca. 15–50 A.D.), a Roman slave of the Christian era who compiled books of pointed, satiric verse which got him into dificulty with the Emperor Tiberius.

4   Four overlapping manuscripts of Aesop's contain a series of animal fables as well as stories of men and gods, particularly the mythic narratives about Hermes the Trickster. For the purpose of educating young readers, each story ends with an explicit moral,

such as "To change place is not to change your nature," "The greedy who demand more lose all," and "There is always someone worse off than you." The stories were used as classroom exercises in composition and declamation and as illustrations by many orators, including Abraham Lincoln. Whatever the truth of Aesop's life, it is obvious that he was respected and loved, as indicated by the statue in his honor in Athens.

16. Which of these words best defines the word *confounds* as it is used in paragraph 3?
    (A) convinces
    (B) amazes
    (C) bores
    (D) amuses

17. The main idea of the passage is best expressed by which of the following?
    (A) Because his fables had satiric messages, Aesop, a slave to Iadmon, was accused of theft by his master's grandson and then thrown off a cliff at Delphi.
    (B) It is probable that Aesop did not write any of the fables attributed to him, but rather was a collector of fables he had heard while he was a slave.
    (C) It is probable that Aesop originally wrote the fables without moral endings and that a later compiler added them so they could be used for instruction.
    (D) Legends surround Aesop's life, but it is certain that, in his time and for centuries to come, he was greatly admired for his moral-bearing fables.

18. The moral "Danger often comes from where we least expect" probably could be used at the end of a story about
    (A) a cat named Lyle who, just as he pounces on a mouse, gets his tail snapped in a mousetrap.
    (B) a king who will turn over his kingdom to the first honest person he meets.
    (C) a leopard named Leonard who one day discovers that his spots have turned into tiger stripes.
    (D) a goddess named Mirea who starts a rainstorm by flying through a cloud and causes thunder by yelling into it.

19. Which city, according to legend, suffered a plague?
    (A) Phrygia
    (B) Lydia
    (C) Delphi
    (D) Samos

20. Which of the following groups of topics best shows the content
    organization of the passage beginning with paragraph 2?
    (A)   I. The known facts about Aesop
          II. The use of Aesop's fables
         III. Famous orators, including Lincoln
    (B)   I. Truth and legend about Aesop
          II. The compiling of Aesop's fables
         III. About the fables and their use
    (C)   I. The danger of satire
          II. Animal fables versus the mythic tales
         III. Present-day Aesops
    (D)   I. The storytelling slaves of Samos
          II. Samos's most renowned storyteller
         III. A statue honoring Aesop

Questions 21 through 25 are based on the following passage.

WINDOW TINTS PUT VALUE, LAW IN THE SHADE

1   **Question:** I have been noticing recently that a lot of cars have tinted windows. I like the way they look, but I am wondering about how well they hold up. Some of the window films look terrible, as if they had formed bubbles or cracks. What are the advantages and disadvantages of window films?

2   **Answer:** Window tinting is growing in popularity, but it is something that consumers must exercise great caution in purchasing. You hit a bull's-eye when you raised concern about the longevity of the product. In addition. there are other important considerations in the quality and legality of window films.

3   Manufacturers of window films make the claim that they cut glare and reduce solar heating by at least 35% and as much as 65%. With less heat shining into the car, the load on the air conditioning during summer is reduced; supposedly that will save gas. Another key advantage to window tinting is that it filters out damaging ultraviolet light, which can crack plastic dashboards and rot upholstery fabrics. Plastic and cloth interiors are attacked by ultraviolet light and atmospheric pollutants, but it is the ultraviolet light that does the most damage.

4   The problem is that in many states, including California, it is illegal to tint either the windshield or the front side windows of cars. In fact, the California Highway Patrol recently issued a letter to window tint installers, warning them that such applications are illegal. The letter asserted that tinted windows "dangerously reduce a driver's ability to see after dark" and that they increase the possibility of accidents by eliminating eye contact between drivers. Martin Processing, a major manufacturer of window tinting films, launched an attack on the letter, calling it "misleading and ill-informed." It cited a scientific study that reported tinted windows improve drivers' response times under glaring sunlight conditions.

5   Motorists should be reluctant to violate state laws forbidding the use of the tints on front side windows and windshields, because many police agencies will issue tickets. In fact, a General Motors public relations representative told me recently that he

was pulled over by the police while driving a promotional Pontiac that had illegally tinted windows used for a GM ad.

6   In addition, federal laws forbid the selling of cars with extremely dark tinting, commonly known as limousine tints, which permits as little as 5% of light to pass through, on any window. But federal agencies have not enforced these regulations in the resale market.

7   Aside from the safety issue, window tint films have major disadvantages over the long haul. Although they may look good when new, they tend to age quickly. Even the highest quality window films, which are available only through professional installation shops, will last only several years. Then, they begin to form cracks and fade to a sick purple color. These higher-quality films cost anywhere from $125 to $300 to install. The cheaper films sold in auto parts stores for home application don't hold up as well, partly because the adhesives are designed to be easier to apply and thus are not as strong. They will purple much sooner, especially in sunny areas.

21. Which of these phrases best defines the word *applications* as it is used in paragraph 4?
    (A) written requests for permission to tint windows
    (B) written invitations to consumers to buy tints
    (C) the adding of tints to windows
    (D) advertisements for window tinting

22. The author's main purpose is to
    (A) alert readers to how disadvantages of window tinting outweigh advantages.
    (B) encourage readers to resist unfair laws forbidding the use of window tints.
    (C) promote the use of rear-window tinting as a way to reduce solar heating on the back-end upholstery.
    (D) offer a neutral presentation of the advantages and disadvantages of window films.

23. In paragraph 3, the author states, "supposedly that will save gas." The use of the word *supposedly* implies that the author
    (A) has no doubts about the claim made by manufacturers.
    (B) is about to predict the logical benefit of the manufacturer's claim.
    (C) is not convinced that there will be significant gas savings.
    (D) is guessing about the value of a reduced air-conditioning load.

24. How is the scientific study cited by the major manufactuer of tinting films used to demonstrate that the letter from the California Highway Patrol is *misleading and ill-informed?*
    (A) The study shows that the letter neglects to consider how tints promote safer driving in glaring sunlight conditions.
    (B) The study shows that tints actually improve a driver's ability to see more clearly after dark because they eliminate oncoming headlight glare.
    (C) The study shows that the elimination of eye contact between drivers has no bearing on driving safety.
    (D) The study demonstrates that the response times of drivers after dark are equal to those of drivers under glaring sunlight conditions.

25. Which of the following groups of topics best shows the content organization of the passage's Answer section?
    (A) I. A few advantages of tinting
         II. The legal and saftey problems of tinting
         III. The major disadvantages of aging tints
    (B) I. The benefits of solar heating
         II. Damages due to atmospheric pollutants
         III. The benefits of using professional installers
    (C) I. State and federal tinting laws
         II. Civil disobedience to laws against tinting
         III. Federal enforcement of laws restricting tinting
    (D) I. Manufacturers' guarantees on tinting
         II. Improving tinting products for use at home
         III. The development of heat-proof car interiors

Questions 26 through 30 are based on the following passage.

EXCERPT FROM *ADAM BEDE* BY GEORGE ELIOT

1   The schoolmaster, Bartle Massey, lived in a small house in the village. When Adam reached the house that evening, he could see, through the curtainless window, that there were eight or nine heads bending over the desks, lighted by thin candles.

2   When he entered, a reading lesson was going forward, and Bartle Massey merely nodded, leaving him to take his place where he pleased. He had not come for the sake of a lesson tonight, and his mind was too full of personal matters for him to amuse himself with a book till school was over; so he sat down in a corner, and looked on with an absent mind. It was a sort of scene which Adam had beheld almost weekly for years; he knew by heart ever flourish in the framed specimen of Bartle Massey's handwriting which hung over the schoolmaster's head, by way of keeping a lofty ideal before the minds of his pupils; he knew the backs of all the books on the shelf running along the white-washed wall above the pegs for the slates; and from the place where he sat, he could make nothing of the old map of England that hung against the opposite wall, for age had turned it a fine yellow brown. Adam felt a momentary stirring of the old fellow-feeling, as though he looked at the rough men painfully holding pen or pencil, with their cramped hands, or humbly labouring through their reading lesson.

3   The reading class now seated in front of the schoolmaster's desk consisted of three most backward pupils. Adam would have known it, only by seeing Bartle Massey's face as he looked over his spectacles. The face wore its mildest expression; the bushy eyebrows had taken their angle of compassionate kindness, and the mouth was relaxed so as to be ready to speak a helpful word or syllable in a moment. This gentle expression was the more interesting because the schoolmaster's brow has that peculiar tension which always impresses one as a sign of a keen, impatient, temperament.

4   "Nay, Bill, nay," Bartle was saying in a kind tone, as he nodded to Adam, "begin that again, and then perhaps it'll come to you what d, r, y, spells. It's the same lesson you read last week, you know."

5   "Bill" was a sturdy fellow, aged four-and-twenty, an excellent sawyer, but he found a reading lesson in words of one syllable a harder matter to deal with than the hardest stone he ever had to saw. The letters, he complained, were "so alike, there no tellin' one from another."

6   Bill had a firm determination that he would learn to read, founded chiefly on two reasons: first, that Tom Hazelow, his cousin, could read anything whether it was print or writing, and Tom had sent him a letter from twenty miles off, saying how he was prospering in the world, and had got an overlooker's place; secondly, that Sam Phillips, who sawed with him, had learned to read when he was turned twenty; and what could be done by a little fellow like Sam Phillips, Bill considered, could be done by himself, seeing that he could pound Sam into wet clay if circumstances required it. So here he was, pointing his big finger towards three words at once, and turning his head on one side that he might keep better hold with his eye of the one word which was to be discriminated out of the group.

26. Which of the following best defines the word *sawyer* as it is used in paragraph 5?
    (A) speaker
    (B) farmer
    (C) carpenter
    (D) stone cutter

27. The passage is presented primarily from the viewpoint of which of the following?
    (A) Adam
    (B) Bartle Massey
    (C) Bill
    (D) Sam Phillips

28. Which of the following words best descibes Bartle Massey as he is presented in this passage?
    (A) stern
    (B) impatient
    (C) sympathethic
    (D) sentimental

29. From the passage, we can infer that Bill's motives for learning to
    read are
    (A) to raise his wages and be able to read the Bible.
    (B) to prove himself superior to his cousin and help his court-
         ship.
    (C) to improve his position at work and to show he is the equal of
         a fellow worker.
    (D) to be able to send and receive letters from his family and to
         impress his coworkers.

30. The details of the passage suggest that the scene at Bartle
    Massey's is familiar to Adam because
    (A) he was once a student himself.
    (B) he is also a teacher.
    (C) he is related to Bartle Massey.
    (D) he is a school inspector or supervisor.

Questions 31 through 35 are based on the following passage.

DISEASES OF THE DIGESTIVE SYSTEM

1   Diseases of the digestive system are often transmitted by water and food; the mouth is the portal of entry. Some food- and water-borne diseases caused by bacteria include typhoid fever, salmonellosis, bacillary dysentery, cholera, brucellosis, and staphylococcal food poisoning.

2   **Typhoid Fever** is a common disease in areas with poor sanitation; epidemics often occur in times of war and floods. It is caused by the bacterium *Salmonella typhosa,* which may survive for weeks in water. Symptoms of the disease are inflammation and ulcers in the intestine, diarrhea, fever, enlargement of the spleen, rose spots on the trunk, and toxemia (presence of toxin in the blood). The organisms also enter the lymph and bloodstream. Diagnosis depends on identification of *S. typhosa* cells in the blood or feces of the patient. Recovery from an attack confers immunity. The disease may be controlled by modern sanitation methods and vaccination.

3   **Salmonellosis** is an acute gastroenteritis (inflammation of stomach and intestinal membranes) accompanied by diarrhea, stomach cramps, and vomiting; it may be caused by several species of *Salmonella* and is sometimes called salmonella food poisoning. The bacteria produce an endotoxin that is absorbed through the intestine. Symptoms begin about 12 hours or longer after ingestion of the organisms; recovery occurs in about three days. Control methods are similar to those for typhoid fever.

4   **Bacillary dysentery** is transmitted much as typhoid fever. *Shigella dysenteriae* lives in the intestine and produces both an exotoxin (a neurotoxin) and an endotoxin. Symptoms vary from patient to patient but include mild to severe abdominal pains and diarrhea; feces contain blood and mucus. Natural immunity following recovery is short-lived; no vaccines are available. Control is primarily by sanitary measures.

5   **Cholera** is mostly confined to southeastern Asia; it is now rare in the Western Hemisphere. It is characterized by vomiting, abdominal pain, and a severe diarrhea that rapidly dehydrates the body and causes intense thirst. *Vibrio comma* living in the intestines releases an endotoxin and enzymes that cause the

breaking away of small patches of intestinal lining. The untreated patient usually dies in a coma in less than three days. Man is the only natural host of *V. comma*. Control is largely by sanitation, boiling of drinking water, and thorough cooking of food. Vaccination produces immunity for about six months.

6   **Brucellosis** is a disease of humans and cattle. It is spread by milk and dairy products, by direct contact with diseased animals, and by droplet infection. In man there is a typical undulating fever accompanied by chills, sweating, headaches, and muscular aches. The organisms enter the lymph and blood and are carried to other parts of the body, where they grow intracellularly. Recovery usually confers immunity. In cattle, the disease causes abortion of fetuses and results in economic losses. Control measures include pasteurization of dairy products and destruction of diseased cattle. Vaccination of humans is usually not practiced, but calves are vaccinated.

7   **Staphylococcal food poisoning** may result from eating unrefrigerated custards, creamed foods, sandwich spreads, or processed meats. *Staphylococcus aureus* usually is introduced into food by food handlers. It grows rapidly in unrefrigerated foods, especially in summer. Within a few hours the cells produce a heat-stable exotoxin that can survive 30 minutes of boiling. When ingested it produces nausea, vomiting, cramps, diarrhea, and extreme discomfort. Symptoms usually begin three to four hours after eating contaminated food, and recovery usually occurs within 24 hours. Control depends on sanitary practices by food handlers and refrigeration.

31. Which of the following best defines the word *ingested* as it is used in the last paragraph?
    (A) boiled in water
    (B) injected into the skin
    (C) causing indigestion
    (D) swallowed

32. From the discussion of cholera in paragraph 5, it can be inferred
    that
    (A) a treatment for cholera exists.
    (B) dehydration of the body is the cause of severe diarrhea.
    (C) the United States has a cholera vaccine that produces
        lifelong immunity.
    (D) to purge water of cholera bacteria it must be boiled for at
        least 30 minutes.

33. According to the passage, one way to control salmonella food
    poisoning is through
    (A) modern sanitation methods.
    (B) the early identification of endotoxins.
    (C) natural immunity following recovery.
    (D) the quarantining of disease carriers.

34. Which of these best expresses the author's purpose?
    (A) to explain how most water-borne diseases are transmitted in
        a manner similar to typhoid fever
    (B) to describe how recovery from disease attacks guarantees
        future immunity
    (C) to identify the causes, symptoms, and control methods of
        selected diseases transmitted by food and water
    (D) to demonstrate the social impact of epidemic diseases
        caused by bacteria

35. The author would most likely agree with which of the following
    statements?
    (A) Some individuals are born with natural immunity to all
        bacterial diseases.
    (B) Other food poisoning diseases not selected for discussion in
        the passage may be controlled by taking careful sanitary
        measures.
    (C) Vaccination of humans against the onset of brucellosis is
        ineffective.
    (D) Because control methods for typhoid fever and salmonello-
        sis are similar, both diseases have nearly equivalent recov-
        ery periods.

Questions 36 through 40 are based on the following passage.

JULIUS CAESAR

1   One of the world's renowned military and political strategists, Gaius Julius Caesar was born to an old, illustrious family which claimed to be able to trace its ancestry back to Iulus, Aeneas' son. By luck, Caesar possessed the right combination of talents and opportunities to skyrocket him to the greatest position of power in the known world.

2   According to his earliest biographer, Suetonius, Caesar was an imposing, energetic figure with a magnetic personality and a remarkably alert mind. He capitalized on his stature and good looks by fastidious grooming and striking dress. He was careful to hide indications of weakness, such as premature baldness, migraine headaches, and epileptic seizures, and chose the surest path to power, leaving himself open to the designation of genius and/or opportunist, labels which succeeding generations have debated.

3   Caesar cultivated membership in the *populares,* or people's party, partly as a result of his kinship with its leader, Marius. Early in his career, Caesar was appointed a *flamen,* or priest, of Jupiter. He strengthened his political position by marrying Cornelia, daughter of Cinna (the consul, not the poet), but he was unprepared for the aggressive political moves on the part of Sulla, a powerful consul who defeated Marius' supporters, confiscated Caesar's property and ordered him to divorce Cornelia.

4   Caesar refused to give up his wife and sought refuge in Asia Minor in 81 B.C., but returned to Rome upon the death of Sulla. There he climbed the traditional ladder to political success, impressing his seniors with his oratorical prowess, which he gained from study under Apollonius Molon at Rhodes. Caesar made steady political progress—from *quaestor* in 68 B.C. to *aedile* two years later. In 63 B.C. he was elected *pontifex maximus* (chief priest), and the following year, he became a *praetor,* or judge.

5   After a successful term as *propraetor,* or provincial governor, of Spain, Caesar's widespread popularity increased when he returned to Rome and joined a coalition with Pompey and Crassus—a triumvirate which made the most of Crassus' money,

Pompey's military experience, and Caesar's popularity. From one success to another, his influence spiraled. He served as *consul* in 59 B.C., governed the northern provinces of Italy, and fought a series of Gallic wars from 58 to 51 B.C., during which time he chronicled the exploits of his skillfully organized military operation, thereby securing his place as the people's favorite.

36. Which of these phrases best defines the word *triumvirate* as it is used in the last paragraph?
    (A) a financial investment
    (B) a triumphant success
    (C) an organization led by Pompey and Crassus
    (D) a united group of three leaders

37. What reason is given for Caesar's being able to secure membership in the people's party?
    (A) He was related to Marius.
    (B) He studied oratory under Apollonius Molon.
    (C) He used his influence as a priest of Jupiter.
    (D) He hid all signs of personal weakness.

38. The author's main purpose is to
    (A) convince the reader that Caesar was a genius.
    (B) trace Caesar's rise as a popular and powerful leader.
    (C) explain why Caesar fled to Asia Minor.
    (D) describe Caesar's military strategies and battle techniques.

39. According to information in the passage, Sulla
    (A) was a supporter of Marius.
    (B) wanted to marry Caesar's wife.
    (C) interrupted Caesar's political progress.
    (D) died in 82 B.C.

40. Which of the following groups of topics best shows the content organization of the passage?

(A)   I. Caesar's family background, personality, and physical traits
      II. His early rise within the people's party
      III. His flight to Asia Minor and return
      IV. His growth in power and popularity

(B)   I. Caesar's marriage to Cornelia
      II. His study under Apollonius Molon
      III. His successful term as *propraetor*

(C)   I. Description of Caesar's illustrious family
      II. Debate over whether Caesar was an opportunist or a genius
      III. An alliance formed with Sulla
      IV. Caesar's account of the Gallic wars

(D)   I. Caesar's attempt to reform Rome
      II. His concealment of physical weaknesses
      III. The death of Sulla
      IV. His continued political progress

MATHEMATICS

DIRECTIONS

Solve each problem in this section by using the information given and your own mathematical calculations. Then select the one correct answer of the four choices given.

Following are some mathematical symbols and formulas for reference during your exam.

Common Math Symbols

Symbol References:

$=$ is equal to	$\geq$ is greater than or equal to
$\neq$ is not equal to	$\leq$ is less than or equal to
$>$ is greater than	$\parallel$ is parallel to
$<$ is less than	$\perp$ is perpendicular to

Math Formulas

Triangle	Perimeter $= s_1 + s_2 + s_3$ Area $= \frac{1}{2}bh$
Square	Perimeter $= 4s$ Area $= s \cdot s$, or s^2
Rectangle	Perimeter $= 2(b + h)$, or $2b + 2h$ Area $= bh$, or lw
Parallelogram	Perimeter $= 2(l + w)$, or $2l + 2w$ Area $= bh$
Trapezoid	Perimeter $= b_1 + b_2 + s_1 + s_2$ Area $= \frac{1}{2}h(b_1 + b_2)$, or $h\left(\dfrac{b_1 + b_2}{2}\right)$
Circle	Circumference $= 2\pi r$, or πd Area $= \pi r^2$

Pythagorean theorem (for right triangles) $a^2 + b^2 = c^2$

The sum of the squares of the legs of a right triangle equals the square of the hypotenuse.

Cube	Volume $= s \cdot s \cdot s = s^3$ Surface area $= s \cdot s \cdot 6$
Rectangular Prism	Volume $= l \cdot w \cdot h$ Surface area $= 2(lw) + 2(lh) + 2(wh)$

1. 24% of what is 72?
   - (A) 150
   - (B) 200
   - (C) 250
   - (D) 300

2. Simplify the following expression.

   $5^2 - 2(3 + 7)$

   - (A)   5
   - (B)   24
   - (C)   33
   - (D) 900

3. Of the following, which is the smallest?
   - (A) $2/9$
   - (B) $3/10$
   - (C) $6/11$
   - (D) $5/12$

4. Give the closest approximation for

   $$\frac{.55 \times 4.02}{1.08}$$

   - (A) 24
   - (B) 20
   - (C)   2
   - (D)   0.5

5. Do the following operations.

   $1\frac{1}{4} - 3\frac{1}{2} + \frac{1}{6}$

   - (A) $-4\frac{7}{12}$
   - (B) $-2\frac{5}{12}$
   - (C) $-2\frac{1}{12}$
   - (D) $2\frac{11}{12}$

6. $\dfrac{48 \times 10^7}{16 \times 10^2} =$

    (A) 3×10^5
    (B) 3×10^9
    (C) 32×10^5
    (D) 32×10^9

7. An arithmetic teacher is putting together her final examination. Of the 50 problems, 46% are on fractions, 20% are on decimals, 18% are on percent, and 16% are on basic computation. How many total problems are on fractions and percent?
    (A) 18 problems
    (B) 32 problems
    (C) 46 problems
    (D) 64 problems

8. The inventory of a new-car dealership is composed of hardtops and convertibles. If there are 15 hardtops for every 2 convertibles, how many hardtops are there out of a total of 136 cars?
    (A) 16
    (B) 32
    (C) 120
    (D) 134

9. A customer at a restaurant purchases food totaling $8.80. If the customer leaves a tip of 20% and pays with a $20 bill, how much change will that customer receive?
    (A) $ 1.76
    (B) $ 9.44
    (C) $10.56
    (D) $11.20

10. Answer the following question by using the information given in the graph below.

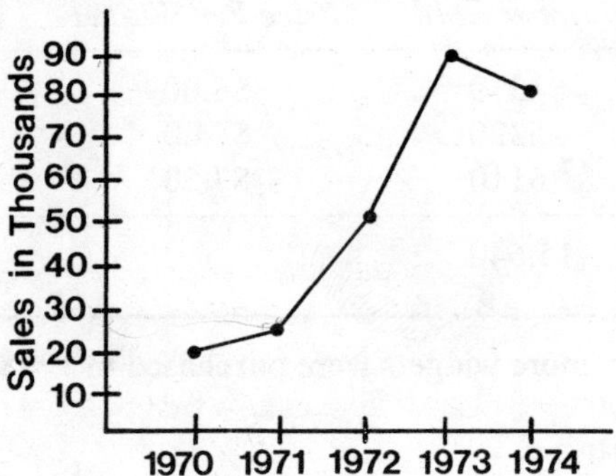

Between what years was there the greatest increase?
(A) 1970 and 1971
(B) 1971 and 1972
(C) 1972 and 1973
(D) 1973 and 1974

11. Use this pie chart to answer the following question.

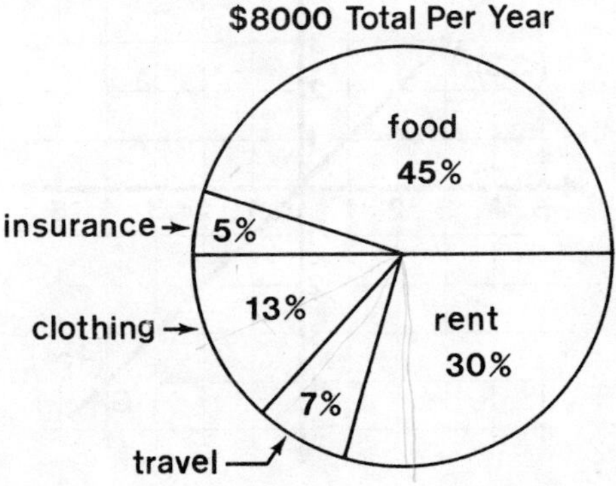

How much more money was spent on clothing than on insurance?
(A) $ 160
(B) $ 400
(C) $ 640
(D) $1440

12. Use this table to answer the following question.

Year	Number Sold	Price Per Widget	Total Dollars
1977	4210	$6.00	$25,260.00
1978	5320	$7.00	$37,240.00
1979	6110	$7.50	$45,825.00
Totals	15,640		$108,325.00

How many more widgets were purchased in 1978 than in 1977?
(A)   790
(B)   1110
(C)   1900
(D) 11,980

13. Use the coordinate graph that follows to answer the question below.

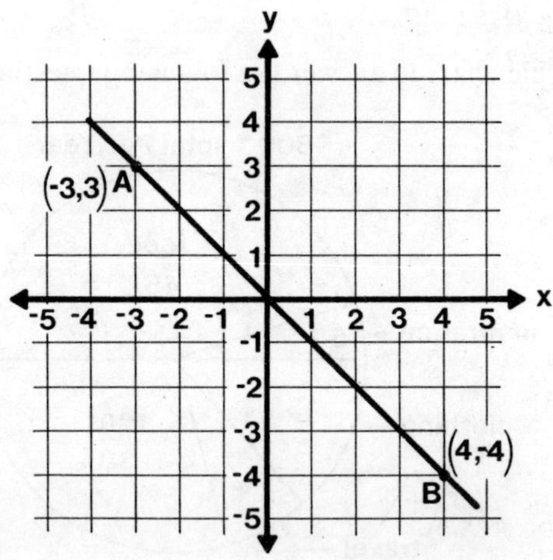

Which of the following points lie on line AB?
(A) $(-3, -3)$
(B) $(2, 2)$
(C) $(-3, 1)$
(D) $(2, -2)$

14. Use the coordinate graph that follows to answer the question below.

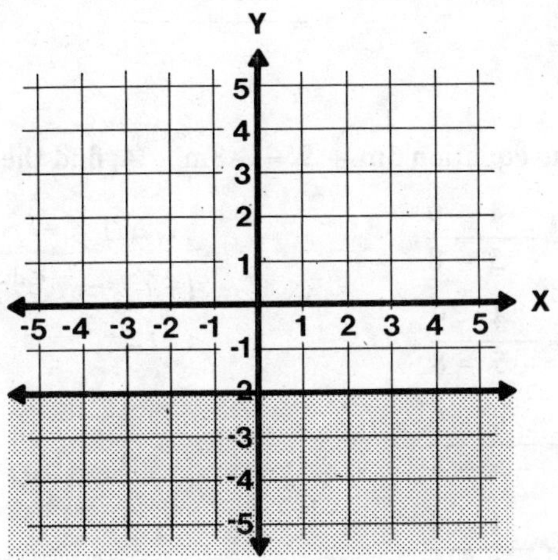

The graph above shows a representation of which of the following inequalities?
(A) $x \geq 2$
(B) $x \geq -2$
(C) $y \leq 2$
(D) $y \leq -2$

15. Given the equation $5x + 9 = -16$, the value of $\frac{1}{5}x - 2$ is
     (A) -5
     (B) -3
     (C) -1
     (D) 1

16. What is the value of x?
     $5x + 6y = 9$
     $3x - 2y = 11$

     (A) 21
     (B) $10\frac{1}{2}$
     (C) 10
     (D) 3

17. In the linear equation $y = 3x - 9$, what is the slope of the line?
(A) -9
(B) -3
(C) $\frac{1}{3}$
(D) 3

18. Given the equation $5m + 9 = -8m - 4$, find the value of m.

(A) $m = \dfrac{-4 - 9}{5 - 8}$

(B) $m = \dfrac{4 - 9}{-5 - 8}$

(C) $m = \dfrac{4 + 9}{-5 + 8}$

(D) $m = \dfrac{-4 - 9}{5 + 8}$

19. Three years ago, Tina was half as old as she is now. Which of the following equations could be used to find Tina's age today, T?
(A) $2(T + 3) = T$
(B) $T - 3 = \frac{1}{2}T$
(C) $\frac{1}{2}(T - 3) = T$
(D) $T - 3 = 2T$

20. What is the value of c in the equation $3c = 12c - 8$?
(A) $-\frac{8}{15}$
(B) $\frac{8}{15}$
(C) $\frac{8}{9}$
(D) $\frac{9}{8}$

21. The sum of the 4 angles of a quadrilateral is 360 degrees. Two angles have the same measure. The largest angle is 60 degrees greater than the smallest angle. If each of the two middle angles is twice the size of the smallest angle, which of the following equations correctly represents the relationship among the angles?
(A) $n + 2n + 2n + (n + 60) = 360$
(B) $n + n + 2(n + 60) = 360$
(C) $2n + n + 2(n - 60) = 360$
(D) $n + 2n + 2n + (n - 60) = 360$

22. Sara has \$16.20 with which to buy stamps. If she needs 22¢ stamps and 50¢ stamps, what is the greatest number of 22¢ stamps she could buy without receiving any change?
(A) 10
(B) 35
(C) 60
(D) 75

23. Given the quadratic equation $x^2 + 3x + 1 = 0$, solve for the value of x.
(A) $\dfrac{3 \pm \sqrt{5}}{2}$

(B) $\dfrac{-3 \pm \sqrt{5}}{2}$

(C) $\dfrac{-3 \pm \sqrt{13}}{2}$

(D) $\dfrac{-3 \pm \sqrt{5}}{4}$

24. Put the following into its simplest form.

$(6x^3y^2 - 3x^3y - 5x^2y^3 + xy) - (-7x^3y^2 + 2x^3y + 3x^2y^3 + 4xy)$

(A) $-x^3y^2 - x^3y - 8x^2y^3 + 5xy$
(B) $13x^3y^2 - x^3y - 8x^2y + 5xy$
(C) $13x^3y^2 - 5x^3y - 8x^2y^3 - 3xy$
(D) $13x^3y^2 - 5x^3y - 2x^2y^3 - 3xy$

25. The product of $(5z^2 + 8)$ and $(6z^2 + 9)$ is
    (A) $30z^4 + 93z^2 + 72$
    (B) $30z^4 + 48z^2 + 72$
    (C) $30z^4 + 30z^2 - 72$
    (D) $30z^4 + 72$

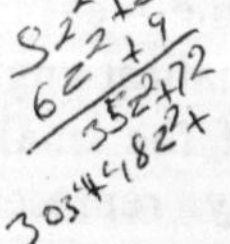

26. A real estate broker receives a monthly salary of $800 plus a commission of 2% on each property sold. To have a total income of $40,000 for the year, how much must the broker sell?
    (A) $ 800,000
    (B) $1,520,000
    (C) $1,960,000
    (D) $2,000,000

27. Put into simplest form.

$$\frac{15}{45x + 25} =$$

    (A) $\dfrac{1}{3}$

    (B) $\dfrac{1}{3x + 5}$

    (C) $\dfrac{3}{9x + 5}$

    (D) $\dfrac{1}{x + 5}$

28. Use this graph to answer the questions below.

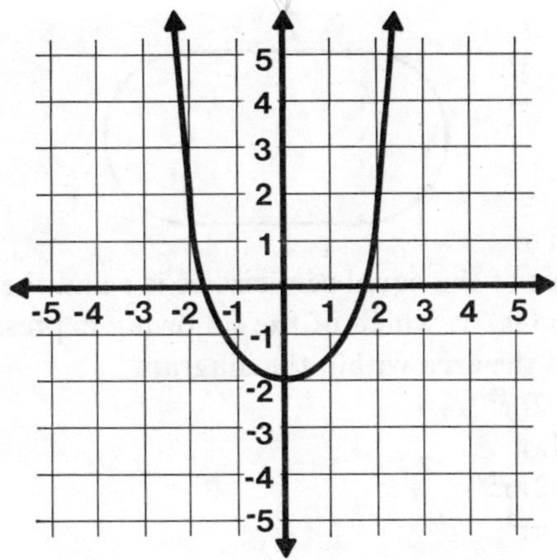

The equation represented by the graph above is
(A) $y = x^2 + 2$
(B) $y = -x^2 + 2$
(C) $y = x^2 - 2$
(D) $y = -x^2 - 2$

29. Given the equation $(x + 7)(x - 6) = 0$, find the greatest root.
(A)   7
(B)   6
(C)   −6
(D)   −7

30. Which of the following equations dealing with a constant cost, c, shows that price, p, varies in inverse proportion to number, n?
(A) $c = p - n$
(B) $c = pn$
(C) $c = p^2/n^2$
(D) $c = n - p$

31. Use this diagram to answer the question below.

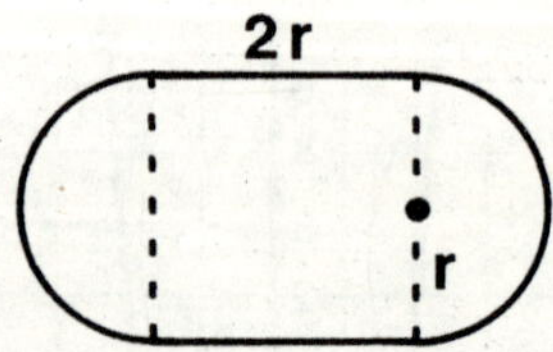

If the radius of the equal semicircles is r and the length of each straight line is 2r, which of the following expressions should be used to find the area within the diagram?
(A) $2r^2 + 2\pi r^2$
(B) $r^2 + 4\pi r^2$
(C) $4r^2 + 2\pi r^2$
(D) $4r^2 + \pi r^2$

32. Given that the radius of a circular area is 9 yards, which of the following is the closest approximation of the circumference of that circular area?
(A) 18 yards
(B) 54 yards
(C) 182 yards
(D) 300 yards

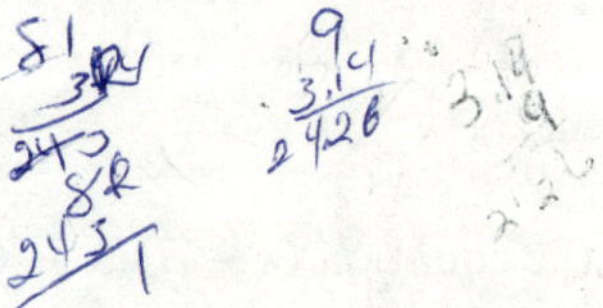

33. A book bindery calculates the number of books, B, it could bind in a 40-hour week by using the equation $B = 20w^2 - 6w$, where w is the number of workers working in the bindery at the time. If 5 workers worked for the first two weeks and 7 workers worked for the next two weeks, how many books could be bound in the 4 weeks?
(A)   1408
(B)   2816
(C)   2960
(D) 39,456

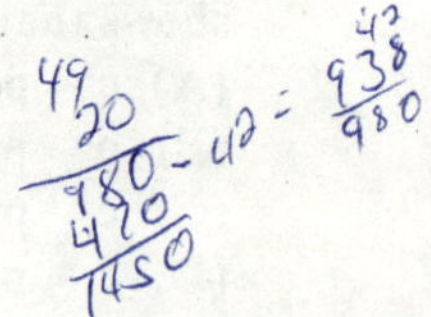

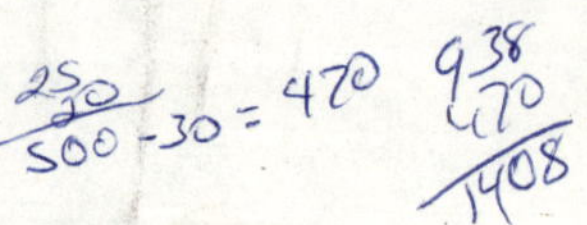

34. Use the diagram below to answer the question that follows.

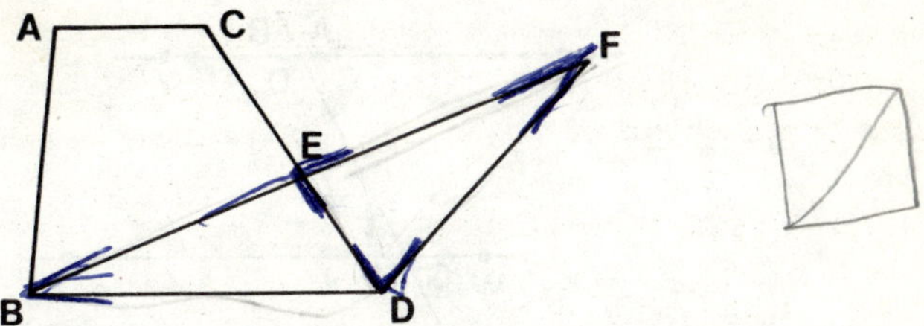

If ∠EBD = ∠EFD and ∠FDE = ∠FED, which of the following must be true?
(A) $\overline{CE} = \overline{ED}$
(B) $\overline{AC} = \frac{1}{2}\overline{BF}$
(C) $\overline{EF} = \overline{DB}$
(D) $\overline{ED} = \frac{1}{2}\overline{BE}$

35. Use this diagram to answer the following question.

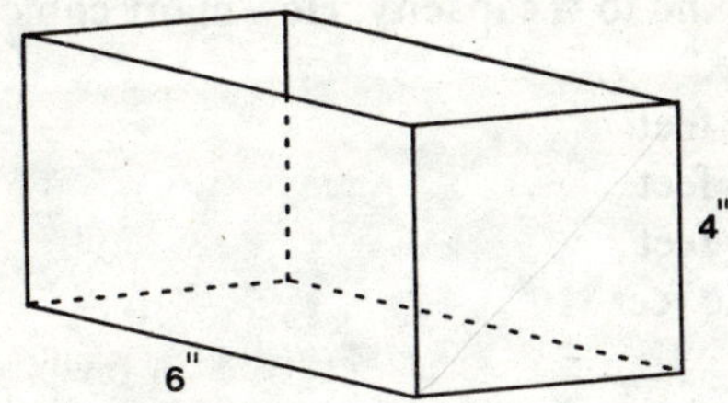

The side of the box is in the shape of a square. What is the length of the diagonal of that side of the box?
(A) $2\sqrt{2}$
(B) 4
(C) $4\sqrt{2}$
(D) 6

36. Use this diagram to answer the question below.

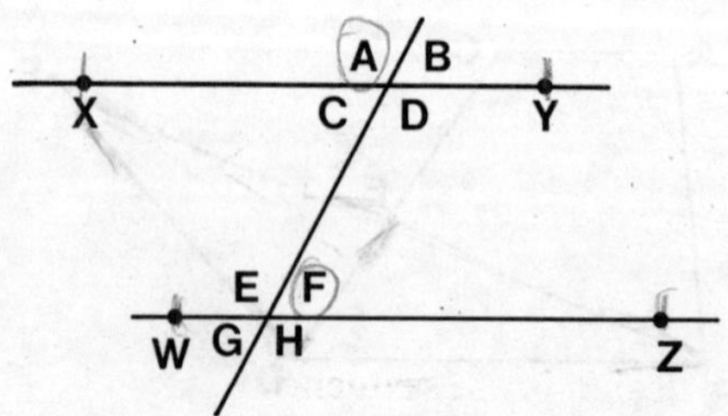

Given that line XY is parallel to line WZ, which of the following must be true about the relationships of angles A and F?
(A) $\angle A = \angle F$
(B) $\angle A = \angle F + 90°$
(C) $\angle A = 180° - \angle F$
(D) $\angle A = \angle F - 90°$

37. A sandbox that measures 5 feet wide by 6 feet long by 2 feet deep is filled with sand to ¾ capacity. How many cubic feet of sand are in the sandbox?
(A) 30 cubic feet
(B) 45 cubic feet
(C) 60 cubic feet
(D) 120 cubic feet

38. The sequence below follows a certain pattern. Answer the question that follows by finding the pattern.

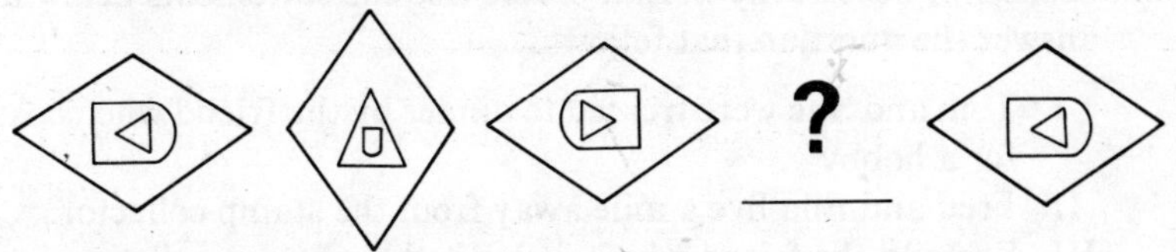

The missing design in the sequence is

(A) 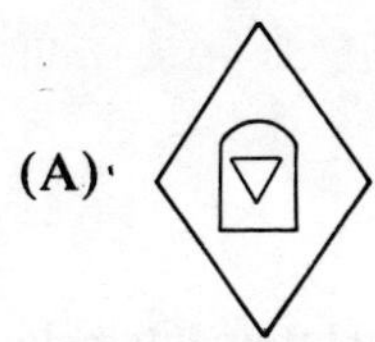

(B) 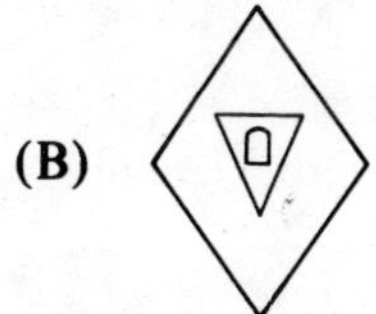

(C) 

(D) 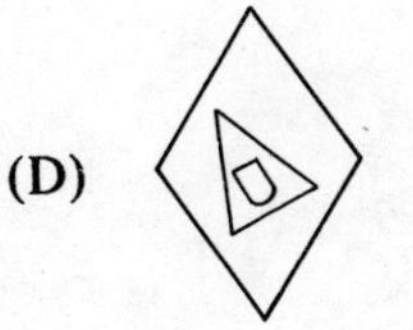

39. Four friends—Tom, Sue, Fred, and Ella—each have his or her own hobby. One collects stamps, one fishes, one knits, and one cooks, not necessarily in that order. Use the statements below to answer the question that follows.

   I. Tom and Sue were treated to dinner by the friend who cooks for a hobby.
   II. Fred and Ella live a mile away from the stamp collector.
   III. Sue and the friend who knits visited the stamp collector.

Who is the stamp collector?
(A) Tom
(B) Sue
(C) Fred
(D) Ella

40. Answer the following question by using the statements below.

   1. Games are played by children.
   2. All children have brown eyes.
   3. No toys are purchased by children.
   4. Arnold is one of the children.
   5. Toys are not games.

Of the following statements, which must be true?
(A) Toys and games are purchased.
(B) Arnold has brown eyes.
(C) Arnold purchases toys.
(D) Children play with toys.

WRITING—MULTIPLE CHOICE

DIRECTIONS

Each of the passages is followed by questions based on the writing in the passage. Read each passage and answer each of the questions that follow. Each of the small raised numbers identifies the sentence or sentence fragment which follows it.

Questions 1 and 2 are based on the following newspaper editorial.

[1]We have all heard about the importance of a balanced diet and seen posters illustrating the four basic food groups and advising us to eat something from each group every day. [2]Medical research has shown that the lack of a balanced diet can cause any number of physical problems, from fatigue to headaches to cancer. [3]But, if we take a wider view, we realize that it is not the lack of a balanced diet that causes problems. [4]A bad diet is the symptom of more deeper rooted social, cultural, and economic problems.

[5]When people don't eat right, it is chiefly because they cannot afford to do so. [6]Inundated with ads for fast food, many people find convenience more attractive than good health and seek the comfort of candy bars. [7]Poverty is the major cause of all the diet-related diseases. [8]Putting posters of the four food groups in our classrooms will not begin to solve the real social problems, which are too large to reduce to pictures on the wall.

1. Which of these changes is needed in the passage?
    (A) Sentence 1: Change "seen" to "see."
    (B) Sentence 3: Change "if" to "while."
    (C) Sentence 4: Change "deeper" to "deeply."
    (D) Sentence 6: Change "with" to "over."

2. Which of the following sentences draws attention away from the main idea of the second paragraph?
    (A) Sentence 5
    (B) Sentence 6
    (C) Sentence 7
    (D) Sentence 8

Questions 3, 4, and 5 are based on the following student essay.

[1]The "fight or flight" response is supposed to be a quality of only lower animals. [2]Humans are rational beings, supposedly, and do not mindlessly attack or run and hide when threatened. [3]Or do they? [4]Fourteen years ago, the families in my neighborhood behaved like animals when they brutalized an immigrant family trying to to join the community. [5]Facing the "unknown" (in the form of a family with Eastern European customs and clothes), they responded with fear and aggression (taunts and broken windows in the dead of night).

[6]I was raised in a small Midwestern town full of middle-American values. [7]Mom, the flag, and apple pie were the ideals that my parents and their friends worshipped. [8]When the Luzinskis moved to town, full of hope that they could share the American Dream of opportunity and prosperity, they were met by smiling, courteous, citizens—until the sun set. [9]After only two weeks of bruised hopes and shattered window panes, the Luzinskis quietly left. [10]I remember the nightly neighborhood meetings where angry neighbors claimed that the Luzinskis "didn't fit in" and organized groups to hide in the darkness, shouting insults at this new family and hurling rocks through their windows.

3. Which of the these changes is needed in the first paragraph?
   (A) Sentence 1: Change "is" to "are."
   (B) Sentence 2: Change "supposedly" to "supposed."
   (C) Sentence 4: Change "like" to "as."
   (D) Sentence 5: Change "Facing" to "Faced with."

4. Which of these changes would make the sequence of ideas in the second paragraph clearer?
   (A) Omit sentence 6.
   (B) Reverse the order of sentences 6 and 7.
   (C) Omit sentence 8.
   (D) Reverse the order of sentences 9 and 10.

5. Which of the following is the most convincing criticism of the
   relationship of sentences 1 and 2 to the rest of the passage?
   (A) Sentences 1 and 2 suggest that the passage will be about the
       "fight or flight" response, but the passage deals only with
       "fight."
   (B) Sentences 1 and 2 suggest that the passage will be about the
       "fight or flight" response, but the passage deals only with
       "flight."
   (C) By presenting both "fight" and "flight" as subhuman
       responses, the passage appears to criticize both the aggres-
       sors ("fight") and their victims ("flight").
   (D) Sentences 1 and 2 have no logical connection with the rest of
       the first or second paragraphs.

*Questions 6, 7, and 8 are based on the following excerpt from a
history text.*

[1]Water has always been precious in the American West. [2]The
scarcity of water in this brown and empty landscape have
confined human occupation since the earliest Indian and Spanish settlements. [3]Early-nineteenth-century mapmakers described most of the region as the "Great American Desert."
[4]Later settlers dammed the rivers and pierced the underground
reservoirs, but the most they created were scattered oases of
farms and towns across the high plains and dry uplands.
[5]Twentieth-century engineering has helped subdue the desert.
[6]But the desert endures and now threatens to cut short western
economic progress.

[7]Water use has already passed renewable natural supply in
some western states, and the demand for water is accelerating.
[8]Irrigated farms, growing cities, and new industries are all
competing for available water supplies. [9]Entire states and
regions are skirmishing over limited river flows, with economic
precepts at stake. [10]The West is dry and sometimes parched from
the 100th meridian, which runs through the heart of the Great
Plains, westward nearly to the Pacific Ocean.

6. Which of the these changes is needed in the first paragraph?
   (A) Sentence 1: Change "has always been" to "have always been."
   (B) Sentence 2: Change "have" to "has."
   (C) Sentence 4: Change "were" to "was."
   (D) Sentence 6: Change "threatens" to "threaten."

7. Which of the following sentences of the second paragraph is *least* relevant to the main idea?
   (A) Sentence 7
   (B) Sentence 8
   (C) Sentence 9
   (D) Sentence 10

8. Which of the underlined words in the second paragraph should be replaced by more precise or appropriate words?
   (A) is accelerating
   (B) all competing
   (C) are skirmishing
   (D) economic precepts

Questions 9 and 10 are based on the following student paper.

[1]Why do I prefer living in the city to living in the country? [2]I guess it's because I'm afraid I'd be bored if I had to depend on myself for entertainment. [3]What would I do in the country? [4]Milk cows? [5]Listen to wheat growing? [6]No, it's just too scary to think of.

[7]This just goes to show it's not the country I'm afraid of but myself. [8]Ten minutes without a television or a Walkman going and I'm a nervous wreck. [9]All that eerie silence, that peace and quiet, really spooks me. [10]To be face to face with myself with no distractions is more than I can face.

9. Which of the following sentences, if added between sentences 5 and 6, would be most consistent with the style and intent of the passage?
    (A) What if I wanted pizza late at night?
    (B) You have trouble finding an open pizza place late at night in the country.
    (C) Many rural areas have all the advantages of the urban locales.
    (D) We have difficulty in adjusting to a new environment.

10. Which of the following changes is needed in the second paragraph?
    (A) Sentence 7: Remove the apostrophe from "it's."
    (B) Sentence 7: Place a comma after "of."
    (C) Sentence 9: Remove the comma after "silence."
    (D) Sentence 10: Place a comma after "distractions."

Questions 11, 12, and 13 are based on the following excerpt from a history text.

[1]Working behind closed doors during the hot summer of 1787, a group of distinguished representatives from twelve of the American states debated, contended espoused, and compromised until they had produced a proposed new Constitution of the United States of America. [2]When the doors were thrown open and the results of their handiwork revealed to the world, a mixed response followed. [3]___________ the new document was instantly hailed by some scholars in Europe, it ___________ was viewed with suspicion and misgiving by many in the states who were expected to play a role in its adoption as the basic law of the land.

[4]The agrarian and debtor classes had not wanted it in the first place and were disinclined to be pleased. [5]They were satisfied with the simpler and weaker Articles of Confederation. [6]They had had no representatives at the convention, and some viewed the entire affair as a conspiracy promoted by the richer members of the community. [7]Much of their suspicion was based on the

fact that the new Constitution included no Bill of Rights with assurances of individual liberty—such as were common in the state constitutions. [8]They drew little comfort from assurances by Hamilton and others that a Bill of Rights would be unnecessary and that Article I did impose restraints on powers of the states and on the proposed new national government. [9]They wholly approved of Articles IV and V.

11. Which of the following words or phrases would most logically fit in order into the blanks in the third sentence?
    (A) Because—also
    (B) Although—nonetheless
    (C) Despite the fact that—furthermore
    (D) Of course—additionally

12. Which of the following sentences does *not* contribute to the main idea of the second paragraph?
    (A) Sentence 6
    (B) Sentence 7
    (C) Sentence 8
    (D) Sentence 9

13. Which of the following changes is needed in the first paragraph?
    (A) Sentence 1: Omit the comma after "1787."
    (B) Sentence 1: Insert a comma after "contended."
    (C) Sentence 2: Insert a comma after "mixed."
    (D) Sentence 3: Omit the comma after "Europe."

Questions 14 and 15 are based on the following excerpt from an economics textbook.

[1]In today's world there is almost universal agreement among economists that the benefits to be obtained from international trade outweigh any disadvantages or difficulties that might affect particular countries or particular commodities. [2]Even in such a large, rich, and powerful country as the United States, its people would suffer hardships and privations if international trade channels were to be seriously curtailed or blocked. [3]For

example, the United States depends heavily upon imports for essential items such as coffee, tea, sugar, bananas, and cocoa and for indispensable industrial raw materials such as cobalt, zinc, copper, lead, manganese, rubber, and diamonds. [4]These materials are indispensable, and we could not do without them.

[5]More important, however, is the possibility that the application of the principles of specialization and the division of labor on a world-wide scale will lead to higher and better living standards and will permit those who trade to use and enjoy a much greater variety of goods than otherwise possible. [6]When the trading area is widened and total demand increased, thus permitting each industry to expand to a point where it obtains maximum output.

14. Which of these sentences is unnecessarily repetitive?
     (A) Sentence 2
     (B) Sentence 3
     (C) Sentence 4
     (D) Sentence 5

15. Which of the following is a nonstandard sentence?
     (A) Sentence 1
     (B) Sentence 4
     (C) Sentence 5
     (D) Sentence 6

Questions 16, 17, and 18 are based on the following excerpt from an education text.

[1]Throughout the history of mankind, predictions of future events have found receptive audiences. [2]In the fifteenth century, Leonardo da Vinci wrote about tanks and helicopters. [3]In the nineteenth century, Jules Verne described trips to the moon. [4]During the thirteenth century, the English scientist Roger Bacon discussed the development of such things as optical instruments and motorboats. [5]Man has always been interested in where he is going. [6]Since humanity's continued existence is dependent upon its making intelligent decisions about the future, such fascination has taken on a very practical dimension.

7
____

⁸The subject is likely to hold the interest of students. ⁹At the same time, it will provide them with an understanding of some of the challenges they will face in five or ten or fifteen years. ¹⁰They may learn about issues as varied as ecology and social problems or family life and world politics.

¹¹It is vital that social studies teachers immerse themselves in the new field of futuristics—the study of future prospects and possibilities affecting the human condition. ¹²Futuristics, as an academic area, is already being taught at many major universities for the purpose of encouraging students to achieve an awareness that they can contribute to the development of a much better national and global society than they ever dreamed of. ¹³The perspective of futurism is very important for todays students, since they know they can do nothing about the past.

16. Which of the these changes would make the sequence of ideas in the first paragraph clearer?
    (A) Omit sentence 1.
    (B) Place sentence 4 before sentence 2.
    (C) Reverse the order of sentences 3 and 4.
    (D) Place sentence 6 before sentence 5.

17. Which of the following sentences, if inserted in the blank in sentence 7, would best introduce the main idea of the second paragraph?
    (A) The importance of the future cannot be overestimated.
    (B) The newly developed field of futuristics incorporated into social studies curriculum is a practical way to introduce these concepts.
    (C) Up until now, the study of the future has been disorganized and haphazard.
    (D) Studying the future will help us to make sensible decisions.

18. Which of the following changes is needed?
    (A) Sentence 11: Change "affecting" to "effecting."
    (B) Sentence 12: Omit the comma after "area."
    (C) Sentence 12" Change "dreamed of" to "dreamed about."
    (D) Sentence 13: Change "todays" to "today's."

Questions 19 and 20 are based on the following excerpt from an anthropology text.

[1]The hunting of animals can take many forms. [2]Lures may be used to attract the game traps may be concealed for animals to fall into. [3]Hunters may track and surround a quarry, with a group of hunters encircling or cornering the animal to be killed. [4]Hunters may take fish using spears or bow and arrow. [5]Or they may poison the water to stun the prey. [6]Gathering fruits and berries or digging for roots can be done with a few simple tools.

[7]A nonhunting culture may depend upon agriculture for food. [8]The basic implement of agriculture is the plow, but seed can be planted by using a simple stick. [9]The hoe, the sickle, and the scythe are all important tools in an agricultural society.

19. Which of these changes would strengthen the focus on the main idea of the first paragraph?
    (A) Omit sentence 1.
    (B) Reverse the order of sentences 3 and 4.
    (C) Omit sentence 5.
    (D) Omit sentence 6.

20. Which of these sentences is nonstandard?
    (A) Sentence 1
    (B) Sentence 2
    (C) Sentence 8
    (D) Sentence 9

Questions 21, 22, and 23 are based on the following excerpt from a communications text.

[1]More than two thousand years ago, Aristotle described how to make a good speech. [2]First, he said, the speechmaker must know the subject fully and must be aware of the facts that support both sides of the issue. [3]Second, the speechmaker must know the audience well and say things that will appeal to the audience's beliefs and interests. [4]Third, the speechmaker must have an absolute command of style and grammar; vague and incorrect sentences simply will not do. [5]__________________________

⁶A poor writer is usually someone who gives information that is either incomplete or too one sided; who offends, bores, or confuses the audience; who produces sentences that cannot be called standard English by any stretch of the imagination. ⁷The question is whether such writers can become better. ⁸If we turn to Aristotle, we learn his answer is no. ⁹He tells us that although some with talent can be trained to becoming an excellent communicator, those who are not born with such talent must simply be content with their lot. ¹⁰He would agree that good writers are born not made. ¹¹Someone who is not born a good writer will never become a good writer.

21. The first paragraph would best be ended and the second paragraph best prepared for by inserting which of the following in the blank labeled sentence 5?
    (A) Fourth, the speechmaker must speak clearly and concisely.
    (B) Fourth, the speechmaker must make sure that everyone in the audience can hear his words clearly.
    (C) Aristotle's advice is still useful, not only for speakers, but for writers as well.
    (D) The speaker who can follow all of of Aristotle's suggestions is bound to succeed.

22. Which of these sentences should be omitted to avoid unnecessary repetition?
    (A) Sentence 1
    (B) Sentence 4
    (C) Sentence 6
    (D) Sentence 11

23. Which change is needed?
    (A) Sentence 6: Change "usually" to "usual."
    (B) Sentence 6: Change "too" to "to."
    (C) Sentence 9: Change "becoming" to "become."
    (D) Sentence 9: Change "simply" to "simple."

Questions 24, 25, and 26 are based on the following letter to a college newspaper.

[1]The proposed <u>raising</u> in the student activity fee is ridiculous. [2]We are paying too much already. [3]And what do we get for our money? [4]The Student Activities Center is a rat-hole—filthy, noisy, and ill-equipped. [5]The rock concerts have attracted no audiences and have been given by no-name groups with no talent. [6]And the lecture series has been as bad as the concert series.

[7]The money we pay in student fees has been wasted on new clothes for the pom-pom girls and silly decorations for Greek Week. [8]Its time to lower or eliminate the student fees, not to raise them. [9]Why pour good money after bad?

24. Which of the following sentences, added between sentences 5 and 6, would be most consistent with the style and intent of the passage?
    (A) There have been several that were highly praised by discriminating audiences.
    (B) It is rumored that the only groups that are hired are relatives of the student body officers who control the cash.
    (C) In these concerts, the focus on sophisticated, minimalist music has alienated large segments of the audience.
    (D) The art exhibits, according to comprehensive gallery attendance figures, are immensely gratifying.

25. Which of these should replace the underlined word in sentence 1?
    (A) rising
    (B) hike
    (C) elevation
    (D) advancement

26. Which of the following changes is needed?
    (A) Sentence 7: Change "has been" to "have been."
    (B) Sentence 8: Change "Its" to "It's."
    (C) Sentence 8: Omit the comma after "fees."
    (D) Sentence 9: Change the question mark to a period.

Questions 27 and 28 are based on the following newspaper editorial.

[1]In landmark decisions of 1964 and 1967, the Supreme Court established that public officials or public figures bringing libel actions must prove that a damaging falsehood was published with "actual malice"—that is, with knowledge that the statements were false, or with reckless disregard of whether they were true or not. [2]_____________, a movie star or a senator falsely accused of drinking too much would be able to bring a libel action against a paper publishing the story only if the paper knew the story was fake or did not bother to confirm it. [3]_____________, these requirements would not apply to an obscure private citizen.

[4]Writing for the new majority in the ruling, it is not enough to examine all the circumstances of publication that would indicate whether there was malicious intent or not. [5]It is proper and constitutional now for "state-of-mind evidence" to be introduced. [6]The court is thus ordering a CBS television producer to answer questions about the thought processes that went into the preparation and airing of a segment of *60 Minutes.*

[7]That six justices of the Supreme Court fail to see this as a breach of the First Amendment is frightening. [8]The novelist George Orwell may have been mistaken only in the timing of his vision of a Big Brother government practicing mind control.

27. Which of these words or phrases would most logically fit in order into the blanks in sentences 2 and 3?
    (A) However—Therefore
    (B) Furthermore—Yet
    (C) In any case—Consequently
    (D) For example—On the other hand

28. Which of the following sentences uses nonstandard placement of a modifier?
    (A) Sentence 1
    (B) Sentence 4
    (C) Sentence 6
    (D) Sentence 8

Questions 29, 30, and 31 are based on the following magazine article.

[1]Sometimes the U.S. government goes out of its way to prove it can be an absolute nuisance. [2]Take the case of Southern Clay, Inc., which has a factory in Paris, Tennessee, putting out a clay product for cat-boxes best known as "Kitty Litter." [3]It's a simple enough process, but the federal Mine Safety and Health Administration insists that since clay comes from the ground—an excavation half a mile from the Kitty Litter plant—the company actually is engaged in mining. [4]Therefore, says the MSHA, Southern Clay <u>was</u> subject to all the rules that govern, say, coal miners working in shafts several hundred feet down.

[5]At its lowest point, Southern Clay's excavation is four feet deep. [6]Nevertheless, the company has been told to devise an escape system and firefighting procedure in case there is a fire in its "mine." [7]Southern Clay also must now give its 250 factory workers special training in how to escape a mine disaster. [8] ___

---

[9]One thing that has always impressed us about cats, in addition to their tidiness, is that they seem to watch the human world with a sense of wise and detached superiority, as though they wondered what the hustle and bustle is all about. [10]If they grin from time to time, as some people insist, it's no wonder. [11]It is probably the folly and foolishness of the government that they are grinning and smiling about.

29. Which of the following should replace the underlined word in sentence 4?

   (A) is

   (B) are

   (C) were

   (D) will have been

30. Which of the following sentences should be inserted in the blank lines labeled sentence 8 to best fit the pattern of development in the second paragraph?
   (A) Will they, we wonder, have to wear miners' lamps, though they work in the sunshine?
   (B) The number of deaths in mine disasters this century has declined steadily.
   (C) Safety in the workplace is the responsibility of both the state and federal governments.
   (D) The costs of these safety measures will probably affect the profitability of the company in this fiscal year and may result in a decline in the price of the company's common stock.

31. Which of these sentences should be changed to avoid its repetition?
   (A) Sentence 7
   (B) Sentence 9
   (C) Sentence 10
   (D) Sentence 11

Questions 32 and 33 are based on the following newspaper article.

[1]No matter what we think of Warren Beatty or his film *Reds,* we cheer his victory for artistic purity in preventing ABC from editing his movie for television. [2]An arbitrator ruled that Mr. Beatty's contractual right of "final cut" authority, which forbids editing he doesn't approve, prevented Paramount Pictures from granting that authority to ABC. [3]The scheduled showing of the film on ABC next week has been canceled.

[4]Most theatrical films (movies made for theaters) ultimately appear on network television, usually preceded by the brief message "Edited for Television." [5]The popular perception, argues Mr. Beatty, is that this editing removes obscenity. [6]Often, it does. [7]Yet, some editing is done purely in the interests of commercial and local programming. [8]Advertisements traditionally hover near hourly and half-hourly intervals. [9]And local affiliate stations zealously protect their 11:00 p.m. timeslots because it is commercially lucrative.

[10]Mr. Beatty's case illustrates why studios contracting with directors for films rarely grant the coveted right of final cut. [11]Televised theatrical movies receive wide exposure and are lucrative; Paramount has a $6.5 million contract with ABC for *Reds*. [12]True artistic control in filmmaking will come only when all directors receive final-cut guarantees, a right the Directors Guild of America hopes to obtain in future talks with movie producers. [13]Mr. Beatty's victory is a step in the direction of protection for film.

32. Which of these sentences, if placed between sentences 2 and 3, would best develop the main idea of the first paragraph?
    (A) Beatty is well known for his performances in a number of films, including *Splendor in the Grass* and *Shampoo*.
    (B) ABC is attempting to boost the ratings of its Wednesday night schedule by showing major Hollywood films with a wide audience appeal.
    (C) Beatty not only directed the film, but also appeared in its starring role.
    (D) The network planned to cut ten minutes from the film and air the shortened version.

33. Which of these changes is needed in the passage?
    (A) Sentence 7: Change "purely" to "pure."
    (B) Sentence 8: Change "Advertisements" to "Advertisement."
    (C) Sentence 9: Change "timeslots" to "timeslot."
    (D) Sentence 11: Change "Televised" to "Televising."

Questions 34, 35, and 36 are based on the following excerpt from a history text.

[1]Although the two nations were allies in World War I and again in World War II, the ideological discord between dictatorship and representative democracy, between socialism and capitalism, was seemingly heightened by the development of a new and awesome weapon. [2]Distrust has been the dominant characteristic of U.S.-Soviet relations ever since. [3]So much so that one hears common talk of a bipolarized world. [4]The United States is

the only nation on earth that has ever unleashed nuclear power as a destructive instrument of war. [5]After the holocaust of Hiroshima, where American nuclear war power was first tested, a mere seven years were to pass before both the United States and Russia were to have atomic bombs and the ability to deliver them as a destructive agent against each other.

[6]For a few anxious days in October 1962, it seemed as if the worst fears were on the brink of fulfillment. [7]United States aerial reconnaissance revealed that Russia was in the process of establishing a missile base in Cuba, which could have served as a launching pad for nuclear bombs aimed with deadly accuracy. [8]The nation's heart skipped a beat as President Kennedy readied the U.S. nuclear offensive and warned Russian Premier Khruschev that any attack on the United States would be answered by an attack, not on Cuba, but on the Soviet heartland. [9]A naval blockade was thrown up around Cuba which diverted Russian ships carrying additional weapons to that base. [10] ____________

____

[11]The Russian leader blinked, and the world could breathe more easily.

34. Which of these changes would make the sequence of ideas in the the first paragraph clearer?
    (A) Begin the paragraph with sentences 4 and 5.
    (B) Begin the paragraph with sentence 3.
    (C) Reverse the order of sentences 1 and 2.
    (D) Reverse the order of sentences 4 and 5.

35. Which sentence has no main verb?
    (A) Sentence 2
    (B) Sentence 3
    (C) Sentence 6
    (D) Sentence 9

36. Which of the following sentences, inserted in the blank labeled sentence 10, would be most consistent with the style and intent of the passage?
    (A) It was an eyeball-to-eyeball confrontation, a game of nuclear chicken.
    (B) The world wondered if the Yanks would dare to stand up to the Ruskies.
    (C) The leaders of the two most powerful nations on earth confronted one another eye to eye.
    (D) This suspenseful confrontation inspired trepidation throughout the entire civilized world.

Questions 37 and 38 are based on the following natural history article.

[1]Fossils are the remains or indications of ancient life on earth. [2]They tell us what plants and animals have existed in the past, what climatic and geologic environments they lived in, and what the age of a fossil-bearing rock is. [3]Fossils vary in size from microscopic, one-celled organisms to complete bodies of Ice-age mammals and entire skeletons of dinosaurs. [4]Age is not a criterion, ______________ skeletons of early man are regarded as fossils. [5]______________ footprints are as much fossils as are skeletons or bodies. [6]Ancient geologic features that are not of organic origin are not fossils, though often so called.

[7]Fossils usually consist of the hard parts of organisms. [8]Bones, teeth, scales, shells, and pollen are among the durable parts of animals and plants that are most apt to be preserved as fossils, while the softer parts decay. [9]Petrifaction is often produced by solutions that deposit silica. [10]Petrified fossils are more heavier and usually more durable than others.

37. Which words or phrases would most logically fit in order into the blanks in sentences 4 and 5?
    (A) because—However
    (B) although—On the other hand
    (C) and so—In addition
    (D) despite the fact that—Therefore

38. Which of the these changes is needed in the passage?
    (A) Sentence 7: Change "consist" to "consists."
    (B) Sentence 8: Change "that" to "these."
    (C) Sentence 10: Change "more heavier" to "more heavy."
    (D) Sentence 10: Change "more durable" to "durabler."

Questions 39 and 40 are based on the following college student paper.

[1]Two weeks before my twenty-first birthday, I was still engrossed in research about eighteenth-century educators and was delighted to discover that even then people were concerned about the growth of young minds. [2]In particular, I admired Descartes and was planning to write my final paper about the applications of his philosophy to modern educational problems. [3]However, as I was about to set pen to paper, a phone call from a friend and the offer of a well-paid job leaving me confused about what to do.

[4]Taking a job would leave me no time to write. [5]I was raising a family at the time, and housekeeping and working together would certainly occupy all my time. [6]I discussed the choice with both my husband and my parents, and they advised me to set aside the essay. [7]"You can write some other time," they explained; "Jobs are scarce," they explained; "Nobody really cares about the eighteenth century anyway," they explained. [8]Weak willed and easily persuaded, I agreed.

39. Which of the following changes would make the passage as a whole clearer?
    (A) Before sentence 1, add: I now regret that I did not finish college ten years ago.
    (B) Before sentence 2, add: I was taking a class in the philosophy of education.
    (C) After sentence 3, add: I could not make up my mind.
    (D) After sentence 8, add: I now believe I made a mistake.

40. Which of these sentences uses an incorrect verb form?
    (A) Sentence 2
    (B) Sentence 3
    (C) Sentence 6
    (D) Sentence 8

WRITING SAMPLE

DIRECTIONS

For this section, you should spend approximately 60 minutes to plan and write your essay. You may use the bottom of your directions page to organize and plan before you begin writing. You should plan your time wisely, using enough time to understand the question, plan and outline, write, and finally reread your essay and revise if necessary.

You must write on the specified topic. An essay on another topic will not be acceptable.

Your essay must be written on the lined pages provided. (For this simulation test, use three sides of an 8½″ by 11″ page.) No other paper may be used. Your writing should be neat and legible. Do not skip lines, do not write excessively large, and do not leave large margins.

Your essay will be judged for its

- being on topic

- clarity

- support and development

- organization

- use of correct standard written English

No reference materials (dictionary, thesaurus, etc.) may be used.

Topic

Most people would agree that the automobile has had a major impact on American society. However, there is much disagreement as to whether that impact has been positive or negative. Some people maintain that the invention of the automobile has brought about mostly positive results; others argue vehemently that its overall effect, in fact, has been decidedly negative. Write an essay to be read by a social studies instructor in which you take one side of the argument. Support your position using examples from your own experience, reading, and/or observations.

Essay Checklist

Use the following checklist to evaluate your finished essay:

A well-written essay will

☐ be on topic: Does your essay address the assignment? Does it complete all the tasks set by the topic?

☐ be written clearly: Is your essay consistent in its tone and its arguments? Is it carefully focused on the assignment?

☐ be well developed: Does your essay use lots of specific examples and details to support its points?

☐ use language correctly and skillfully: Is your essay written in standard written English, with only minor flaws, if any, in grammar, sentence structure, and punctuation?

☐ be well organized: Is each paragraph one main idea? Are there smooth transitions between paragraphs? Is the entire essay unified?

☐ be legible: Is your handwriting neat enough to be read and understood?

ANSWER KEY FOR PRACTICE TEST 1

Reading		Mathematics		Writing Multiple Choice	
1. B	21. C	1. D	21. A	1. C	21. C
2. A	22. A	2. A	22. C	2. B	22. D
3. D	23. C	3. A	23. B	3. D	23. C
4. B	24. A	4. C	24. D	4. D	24. B
5. B	25. A	5. C	25. A	5. C	25. B
6. C	26. D	6. A	26. B	6. B	26. B
7. A	27. A	7. B	27. C	7. D	27. D
8. C	28. C	8. C	28. C	8. D	28. B
9. D	29. C	9. B	29. B	9. A	29. A
10. B	30. A	10. C	30. B	10. B	30. A
11. D	31. D	11. C	31. D	11. B	31. D
12. A	32. A	12. B	32. B	12. D	32. D
13. B	33. A	13. D	33. B	13. B	33. C
14. A	34. C	14. D	34. C	14. C	34. A
15. C	35. B	15. B	35. C	15. D	35. B
16. B	36. D	16. D	36. C	16. B	36. C
17. D	37. A	17. D	37. B	17. B	37. C
18. A	38. B	18. D	38. B	18. D	38. C
19. C	39. C	19. B	39. A	19. D	39. A
20. A	40. A	20. C	40. B	20. B	40. B

ANALYZING YOUR TEST RESULTS

The following charts should be used to carefully analyze your results and spot your strengths and weaknesses. The complete process of analyzing each subject area and each individual question should be completed for this Practice Test. These results should be reexamined for trends in types of error (repeated errors) or poor results in specific subject areas. THIS REEXAMINATION AND ANALYSIS IS OF TREMENDOUS IMPORTANCE FOR EFFECTIVE TEST PREPARATION.

PRACTICE TEST 1: SUBJECT AREA ANALYSIS SHEET

	Possible	Completed	Right	Wrong
Reading	40			
Mathematics	40			
Writing—Multiple Choice	40			
TOTAL	120			

ANALYSIS—TALLY SHEET FOR QUESTIONS MISSED

One of the most important parts of test preparation is analyzing why you missed a question so that you can reduce the number of future mistakes. Now that you have taken Practice Test 1 and corrected your answers, carefully tally your mistakes by marking them in the proper column.

REASON FOR MISTAKE

	Total Missed	Simple Mistake	Misread Problem	Lack of Knowledge
Reading				
Mathematics				
Writing—Multiple Choice				
TOTAL				

Reviewing the above data should help you determine WHY you are missing certain questions. Now that you have pinpointed the type of error, when you take Practice Test 2, focus on avoiding your most common type.

ANSWERS AND COMPLETE EXPLANATIONS
FOR PRACTICE TEST 1

READING

1. (B) Choice (B) is correct since *motive power* in the context of paragraph 7 refers to the power from the brain, not requiring electrical wires or batteries, which makes BOOK operate. Because BOOK is being described as if it were a machine, Choice (A) is incorrect, as it defines motive power in psychological terms. Choice (D) reverses the direction of the power by saying that it is given to, rather than comes from, the brain.

2. (A) Choices (C) and (D) confuse the fact that the selection portrays the ordinary book as if it were a technical marvel unparalleled in its ability to teach. Choice (A) acknowledges how the selection exalts the ordinary book as the ultimate teaching machine.

3. (D) Contrary to choice (C), the writer's tone in describing how BOOK works (paragraph 3) is one of technical formality. The best support for Choice (D) is found in the flamboyant language of public-relations writing used to describe BOOK. BOOK is an aid to *almost magical* learning, is *revolutionary, unbelievably easy,* and has a *big future*.

4. (B) An ordinary book can be described as the ultimate teaching machine. One would expect that, in the same fashion, the writer would agree that the human body can be described as a remarkably efficient and resourceful machine. Thus, (B) is correct. Choice (D) is contradicted by the statement in paragraph 2 that *Anyone can use BOOK, even children.*

5. (B) Topic I in choice (A) refers to a person not spoken of in the selection. Topics II and III in choice (C) concern roles not discussed in the selection. Topic II in choice (D) is too narrow for use as an organizer of information in the selection. The best group of topics is presented by choice (B).

6. (C) The context of paragraph 2 makes clear that both Grant and his Cabinet were deficient in the skills needed for serving in their political posts. The selection provides ample examples of Grant's poor judgement and performance as president. The writer indicates the Cabinet's lack of aptitude in noting that only six out of its twenty-five members *proved to be competent*. Choice (D) is contradicted by the fact that Grant as president was *indecisive*.

7. **(A)** Choice (A) best covers the main idea about the nature and consequences of Grant's misguided presidency and of his associates' dishonest dealings. Choice (B) is mistaken in asserting that the selection deals with the sympathies of the American public. Choice (D) overstates the author's concern over the *shattered prestige of the presidential office;* the writer does not claim that the public's mistrust of authority is the worst consequence of Grant's poor leadership, only one of the major ones.

8. **(C)** J. F. Casey was Grant's brother-in-law. Choice (B) incorrectly cites Hamilton Fish, who was not a relative of Grant's or implicated in any scandal.

9. **(D)** Choices (A), (B), and (C) all state facts which can be verified by objective historical evidence. Choice (D) states an opinion about Grant's thinking process during his presidency. Although the author's opinion is probably quite justified, one cannot verify that Grant at *no time* ever thought that he might be being used.

10. **(B)** Choice (B) is the most accurate and inclusive summary. Choice (A) seems to suggest that Grant's friends in trouble were not corrupt. It also distorts the nature of Grant's loyalty to his friends. His loyalty, in fact, was constant and enduring. Choice (C) inaccurately portrays Grant, the president, as the same great leader he was as a general. Choice(D) overstates what is known about the role of Hamilton Fish.

11. **(D)** From the context of paragraph 3, it is clear that *revamping* has to do with the making of revisions and adding of sections. Choices (B) and (C) speak of changes dealing only with length; choice (D) suggests changes due both to revision and addition, making it the superior answer.

12. **(A)** Most people's concept of what it means to be religious is to believe in a personal God. However, the syllabus defines religion as devotion to what is *most worthful*—whatever that may be. So, according to this broader concept, even a person who does not believe in a transcendent higher power may still be very religious. Choices (B) and (D) deal with being religious in the limited sense of involving a belief in a supernatural God.

13. (B) Choice (D) suggests a tactic that would seem to be appropriate for an argumentative paper. The tactic stated in choice (C) would surely be encouraged, since the course is intended to help students clarify their *views on matters of faith and religion*. Choice (B) is the incorrect tactic. The better tactic would be to defend the paper's thesis against valid or, as the syllabus puts it, *plausible* objections.

14. (A) Any claim, such as the one made in choice (A), about the value of a course to students can be contested and is therefore an opinion. Choices (B), (C), and (D) state factual information, not really open to question.

15. (C) In support of choice (C), the selection points out that the religious experience and its expression are found *among all classes of people* and in *all stages of civilization*. The first paragraph of the syllabus speaks only of the commonality of religious experience, not of different levels of its development.

16. (B) The first sentence of paragraph 3 sets up a contrast between Aesop, a man of common sense, and the learned men of his day. His ironic stories, which according to paragraph 2 angered the Delphians, would also most likely have a strong emotional effect on the learned men. Choice (B) best defines *confounds*.

17. (D) Choice (D) correctly identifies the main idea: Aesop earned historic importance and respect although legends obscure the truth about his life. Choice (A), though not stating the main idea, would tend to support it, were it not that Iadmon's grandson did not accuse Aesop of theft. Choice (B) is not supported by evidence in the selection.

18. (A) Choice (A) is correct. The cat, Lyle, would not likely expect the danger he meets. None of the stories in choices (B), (C), and (D) have an obvious link to the moral about unexpected danger. The story of choice (B) might have a moral dealing with honesty. The story of choice (C) might have a moral dealing with sudden, unexpected changes. The story of choice (D) might more naturally be thought of as a myth to explain rain and thunder.

19. (C) Phrygia and Lydia are the same place. Aesop was originally from there, and served as a slave on the island of Samos. Once freed, he meets the people of Delphi, which is described as the city *said to have suffered a plague.*

20. (A) Choice (A) outlines the most accurate division of information in the selection. Choices (B), (C), and (D) identify topics not dealt with significantly, or at all, in the selection. Choice (B) can be eliminated because little mention is made of how Aesop's fables were compiled; choice (C) can be eliminated because no mention is made of an opposition between animal fables and mythic tales; and choice (D) can be eliminated because no mention is made of any storytelling slave of Samos other than Aesop.

21. (C) Choices (A) and (B) depend upon the more commonly thought-of meaning of *application* as a formal written request. However, when paragraph 4 uses the word *application,* it becomes clear that it should be understood in its secondary meaning as *something added* or *applied on.*

22. (A) Rather than being neutral as is asserted by choice (D), the author warns readers to purchase a window tint with *great caution.* Disadvantages of window tinting are shown to be greater than advantages. Choice (A) is correct. Choice (B) is contradicted by the author's statement that drivers *should be reluctant to violate* tinting laws.

23. (C) Paragraph 3 presents the claims of manufacturers, not necessarily those of the writer. That which is supposed about gas savings remains an open question for the writer until it is verified as an actual fact.

24. (A) Choices (B), (C), and (D) include factors that are not included in the account of the study cited. Only choice (A) relates the study to the California Highway Patrol letter. It shows that the letter is ill-informed and misleading for being ignorant of or, perhaps, intentionally dismissing the safety benefits of window tints.

25. (A) Choice (A) correctly indicates the three major divisions used in presenting information. Choices (B), (C), and (D) identify topics not dealt with significantly, or at all, in the passage. Consider

that little mention is given to the damages due to atmospheric pollutants or to federal enforcement of tinting laws. Also no mention is given to the benefits of solar heating or civil disobedience to tinting laws.

26. (D) A sawyer is one who saws (compare lawyer or clothier). The full sentence reveals that Bill is a stone sawyer by referring to reading as much harder than the *hardest stone he ever had to saw.*

27. (A) The passage describes Bartle Massey in the third paragraph, and refers only briefly to Sam Phillips in the sixth. The fifth and sixth paragraphs give the reader Bill's thoughts, but the viewpoint that is chiefly used is Adam's. Almost all of the first three paragraphs present the scene as Adam sees it.

28. (C) Though some of the physical details of Bartle Massey's face suggest he is capable of impatience, both the descriptive words (*mildest, compassionate, helpful*) and his gentle reply in the fourth paragraph make *sympathetic* the best choice.

29. (C) We are told that Bill's cousin who has learned to read has prospered and obtained an overlooker's place at work. We are also told that Bill does not like to be behind Sam Phillips in knowing how to read, especially since he regards himself as physically superior to Sam.

30. (A) We are told that Adam has witnessed a scene like this one almost weekly for years. We are also told he had *not come for the sake of a lesson tonight,* so we can infer that Adam was once a student in this school.

31. (D) The second to the last sentence in the passage makes clear that to *ingest* the poisonous exotoxin is essentially to *eat* it. The best available choice is (D). If choice (A) were correct, it would mean that boiling the exotoxin causes the symptoms. The fact is that exotoxins stand up well to boiling.

32. (A) To speak of *The untreated patient,* as paragraph 5 does, implies that some form of treatment for cholera exists. Choice (C) is contradicted by the fact that a vaccination is effective for about six months. The claim made in choice (B) should be reversed to say that diarrhea causes the dehydration.

33. (A) The control methods for salmonella and typhoid fever are similar. Therefore, choice (A) is correct because *modern sanitation methods* is one of the two controls identified for typhoid fever in paragraph 2. Choice (C) identifies a fortunate result of recovery from typhoid fever, not a control method.

34. (C) The passage catalogs a number of diseases of the digestive system. The author's aim is to discuss each disease—its causes, symptoms, and methods of control. Choice (A) makes typhoid fever more central to the author's discussion than is the case. Also, since social impact is not dealt with by the author, choice (D) does not state the purpose. Choice (B) is contradicted by the fact that natural immunity after recovery from bacillary dysentery is *short-lived*.

35. (B) All the diseases discussed in the selection require some kind of sanitary practice for their control. It seems likely that the author would agree that, as suggested by choice (B), other food poisoning diseases could be controlled by taking sanitary measures. Choice (D) makes a claim not substantiated by the passage, that how a disease is controlled is related to how long a victim needs for recovery. Choice (C) makes too strong a claim; the paragraph on brucellosis states only that vaccination of humans is not common. The effectiveness of such a vaccine is not indicated.

36. (D) The sentence using *triumvirate* speaks of a *coalition,* or a joining together, of three individuals: Caesar, Pompey, and Crassus. Choice (A) misinterprets the reference to Crassus' money. Although the triumvirate described in this selection makes the most of Crassus' money, a triumvirate is not by definition a financial investment. Choice (C) is incorrect because it leaves Caesar out of the organization.

37. (A) Choice (A) correctly restates the idea in paragraph 3 that Caesar became a member of the people's party *partly as a result of his kinship with its leader, Marius.* Choices (B) and (C) refer to facts of Caesar's life after securing membership in the people's party.

38. (B) Choice (A) is incorrect because the author leaves it an open question as to whether Caesar was a genius or an opportunist or both. Choice (C) refers to only one of the key events discussed about

Caesar's life. Choice (D) refers to a topic not dealt with in the passage. Choice (B) bests states the author's purpose because the passage serves to chart Caesar's growth in power and prestige.

39. (C) Choice (A) is incorrect because the selection reveals that Sulla defeated Marius' supporters. Choice (D) incorrectly suggests that Sulla died the year before Caesar fled to Asia Minor. Choice (B) misinterprets Sulla's wishes: he demanded only that Caesar divorce his wife. Choice (C) is the best answer because Caesar was not able to continue his political progress until after Sulla died.

40. (A) Each group of topics in choices (B), (C), and (D) contains at least one topic that is too narrow to use for organizing information or that is not discussed in the passage. In choice (B), Caesar's study under Apollonius Molon is too narrow a topic. In choice (D), the death of Sulla is also too narrow a topic. In choice (C), no alliance formed between Sulla and Caesar is discussed in the passage. Choice (A) is the best answer.

MATHEMATICS

1. **(D)** Since the answer choices are not close together in value, one technique for answering this question is to quickly estimate: 24% is almost 25%, or one quarter. So the problem can now be restated as "One quarter of what is 72?" Working from the answer choices shows that one quarter of 300 (choice D) is 75, which is closest to 72.

   Mathematically, "24% of what is 72?" can be changed to a proportion:

   $$\frac{24}{100} = \frac{72}{x}$$

   Then, cross multiplying gives

   $$24x = 7200$$

   Dividing by 24 gives $\qquad x = 300$

2. **(A)** If powers, multiplication, addition, parentheses, etc., are all contained in one problem, the order of operations is as follows: (1) parentheses, then (2) powers and square roots, then (3) multiplication and division, whichever comes first left to right, then (4) addition and subtraction, whichever comes first left to right. Therefore,

$$\begin{aligned} 5^2 - 2(3 + 7) &= 5^2 - 2\,(10) \\ &= 25 - 2(10) \\ &= 25 - 20 \\ &= 5 \end{aligned}$$

3. **(A)** You should be able to immediately realize that three of the choices are less than one half, while choice (C), 6 out of 11, is greater than one half. So choice (C) can be quickly eliminated. Of the three choices left, (A) and (B) are each considerably less than one half. Therefore, choice (D), which is slightly less than one half, can also be eliminated. Left with two fractions, simply cross multiply up; the smaller product will be above the smaller fraction. Choice (A), ⅖, is the smallest amount.

$$\frac{^{27}3}{10} \diagdown\!\!\!\!\diagup \frac{2^{20}}{9}$$

4. (C) To approximate the expression

$$\frac{.55 \times 4.02}{1.08}$$

first round off the numbers as follows:

$$\frac{.50 \times 4}{1}$$

Since .5 or $\frac{1}{2} \times 4 = 2$, you are left with $\frac{2}{1}$, which equals 2.

5. (C) You could have answered this problem by first getting a least common denominator of 12, changing each of the fractions to twelfths as follows:

$$1\frac{1}{4} = 1\frac{3}{12} \qquad -3\frac{1}{2} = -3\frac{6}{12} \qquad \frac{1}{6} = \frac{2}{12}$$

Then adding the two positive mixed numbers

$$1\frac{3}{12} + \frac{2}{12} = 1\frac{5}{12}$$

And then adding in the negative mixed number (subtract and keep the sign of the larger)

$$1\frac{5}{12} - 3\frac{6}{12} = -2\frac{1}{12}$$

6. (A) To quickly divide numbers in scientific notation, simply divide the first numbers and then subtract the powers of ten to get the second number. So

$$\frac{48 \times 10^7}{16 \times 10^2} = 3 \times 10^5$$

7. (B) Fraction problems (46%) and percent problems (18%) total 64% of all the problems, or 64% of 50:

$$.64 \times 50 = 32$$

8. (C) If there are 15 hardtops for every 2 convertibles, out of every 17 cars, 15 are hardtops. So ¹⁵⁄₁₇ of the total are hardtops:

$$\frac{15}{17} \times 136 = \frac{15}{\underset{1}{\cancel{17}}} \times \frac{\cancel{136}^{\,8}}{1} = 120$$

Notice that choices (A) and (B) are far too small.

9. (B) First compute twenty percent of $8.80 to determine the amount of the tip:

$$.20 \times \$8.80 = \$1.76$$

Add $1.76 to the food bill:

$$\$8.80 + \$1.76 = \$10.56$$

Now subtract from $20.00 to determine the amount of change:

$$\$20.00 - \$10.56 = \$9.44$$

10. (C) The greatest increase is indicated by the *steepest* rise in the graph lines, between 1972 and 1973. You could also have used the numerical grid along the left side of the chart to see the rise from 50,000 to 90,000 during those years.

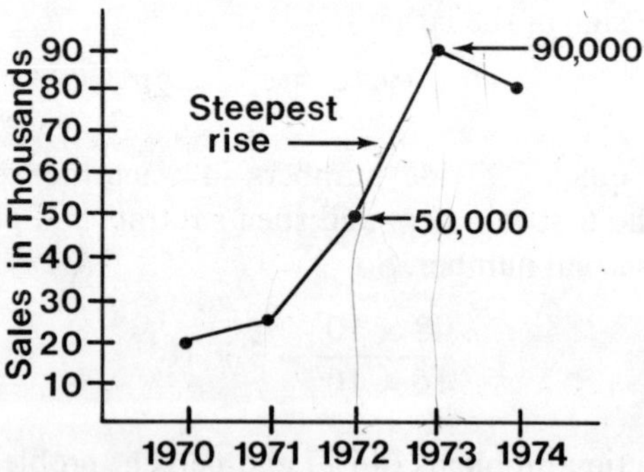

11. (C) The phrase "how much more" indicates subtraction. Clothing was 13% of the total. Insurance was 5% of the total. So 13% − 5%, or 8%, more of the total of $8000 was spent on clothing than on insurance:

$$.08 \times \$8000 = \$640$$

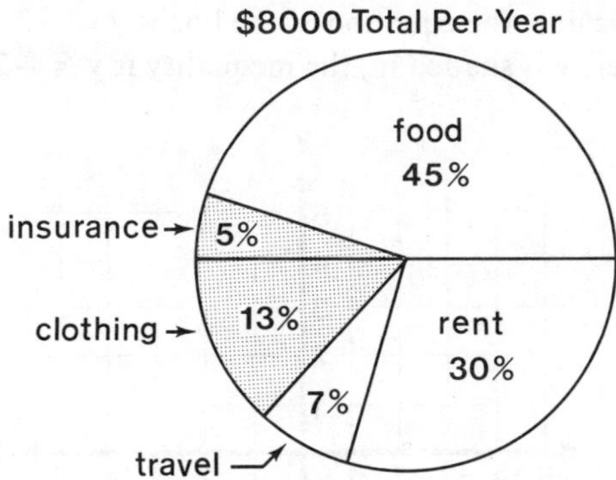

12. (B) The phrase "how many more" indicates subtraction. In 1978, 5320 widgets were sold; in 1977, 4210 widgets were sold. Therefore,

$$5320 - 4210 = 1110$$

13. (D) The line of the graph passes through points $(2, -2)$. So that point must lie on the line. (Notice that the coordinates for A $(-3, 3)$ are opposites, as are those for B $(4, -4)$

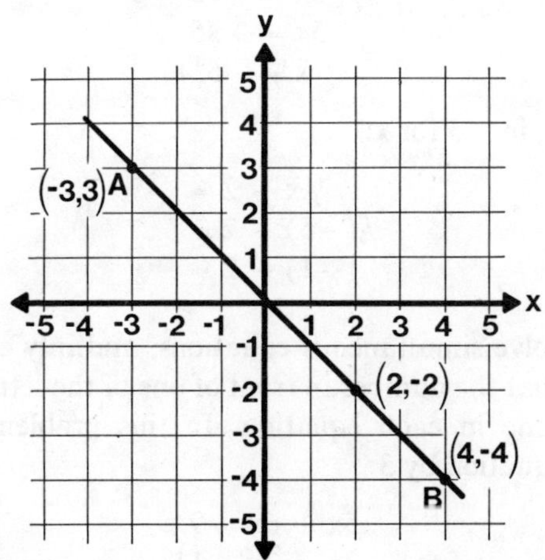

14. (D) Every point on the straight line indicated on the graph is 2 "steps" below the horizontal axis. Therefore, since y is always

-2 on this line, the equation of the line is $y = -2$. And since the section below is shaded in, the inequality is $y \leq -2$.

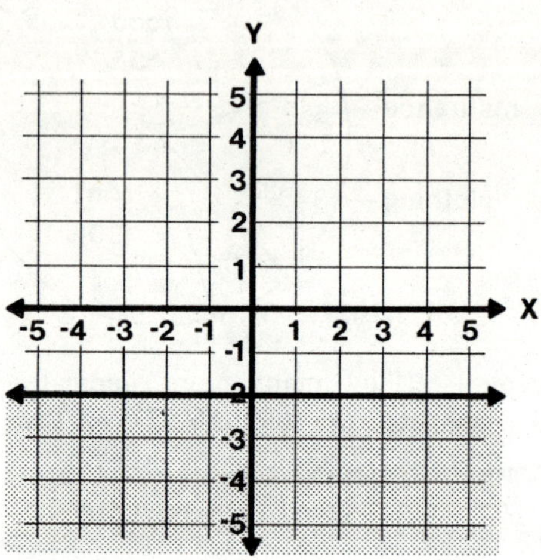

15. (B) First solve the equation for x:

$$5x + 9 = -16$$
$$5x = -16 - 9$$
$$5x = -25$$
$$x = -5$$

Now plug in -5 for x:

$$\tfrac{1}{5}x - 2 =$$
$$\tfrac{1}{5}(-5) - 2 =$$
$$(-1) - 2 = -3$$

16. (D) To solve simultaneous equations, multiply one of the equations so that the number in front of one of the letters (unknowns) is the same in each equation. In this problem, multiply the bottom equation by 3:

$$5x + 6y = 9$$
$$3x - 2y = 11$$

$$5x + 6y = 9$$
$$3(3x - 2y) = 3(11)$$

$$5x + 6y = 9$$
$$9x - 6y = 33$$

Now, adding both equations together cancels the y's:

$$5x + 6y = 9$$
$$+ \ 9x - 6y = 33$$
$$\overline{14x = 42}$$

And solve:

$$14x = 42$$

$$\frac{14x}{14} = \frac{42}{14}$$

$$x = 3$$

17. (D) To find the slope of a line from an equation, first make sure that the equation is in the form

$$y = mx + b$$

In this form, m (the number in front of the x) is the slope. Therefore, in the equation $y = 3x - 9$, the slope is 3.

18. (D) Notice that this problem does not give you answers in the simplest form. So you could solve for m, then quickly simplify each of the answer choices:

$$5m + 9 = -8m - 4$$

Bring $-8m$ from the right side of the equation to the left side by changing its sign:

$$5m + 9 = -8m - 4$$
$$5m + 8m + 9 = -4$$

Combine m's: $13m + 9 = -4$

Bring $+9$ to the other side in the same way:

$$13m = -4 - 9$$
$$13m = 13$$

Dividing by 13: $\dfrac{13m}{13} = \dfrac{-13}{13}$

$$m = -1$$

Answer (D)

$$\frac{-4-9}{5+8} = \frac{-13}{13} \quad \text{simplifies to } -1$$

You may have spotted the fact that each answer choice actually shows possible steps you would use to solve for x. First add 5m + 8m. Then add −9 to −4. Then divide by 5 + 8.

$$m = \frac{-4-9}{5+8} \text{ shows these steps.}$$

19. **(B)** If Tina's age now is T, Tina's age three years ago was T − 3. Now plug these quantities into the sentence:

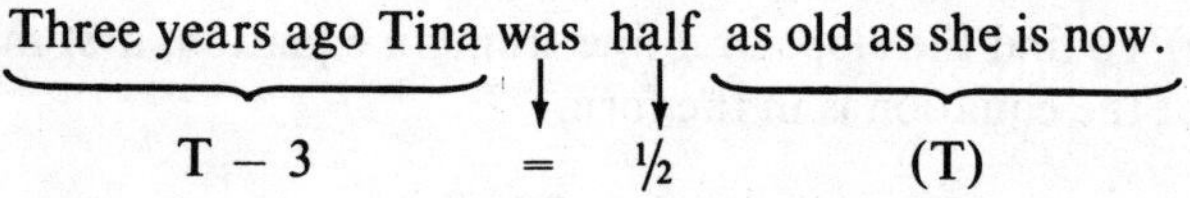

20. **(C)** To solve for c, first move 12c to the left side of the equation by changing its sign:

$$3c = 12c - 8$$
$$3c - 12c = -8$$
$$-9c = -8$$

Divide both sides by −9:

$$\frac{-9c}{-9} = \frac{-8}{-9}$$

$$c = \frac{8}{9}$$

21. **(A)** Represent the smallest angle as n. Since the largest angle is said to be 60 degees greater than the smallest angle, the largest angle is therefore n + 60. If each of the middle angles is twice the smallest angle, each of the middle angles can be represented as 2n. Now that all the angles are labeled, their total equals 360 degrees:

$$n + 2n + 2n + (n + 60) = 360$$

22. (C) This is a good problem to work from the answers. Since the question asks for the *greatest* number of 22¢ stamps, start from the largest answer, 75 (D). Since $75 \times .22 = \$16.50$, that's too many stamps, as Sara has only $16.20 to buy the stamps. The next largest answer, 60 (C), yields $60 \times .22 = \$13.20$ leaving $3.00 left from $16.20 to purchase six 50¢ stamps without receiving change.

23. (B) Since this quadratic equation is not factorable, you must either complete the square or use the quadratic formula. Using the quadratic formula would give the following:

Quadratic formula:

If $ax^2 + bx + c = 0$ and $a \neq 0$, then $x = \dfrac{-b \pm \sqrt{b^2 - 4ac}}{2a}$

Substituting 1 for a, 3 for b, and 1 for c

$$x = \frac{-3 \pm \sqrt{3^2 - 4(1)(1)}}{2(1)} = \frac{-3 \pm \sqrt{9 - 4}}{2} = \frac{-3 \pm \sqrt{5}}{2}$$

24. (D) Subtract common terms, remembering that subtracting a negative quantity is equivalent to adding its positive. For example, $10 - (-7) = 17$.

$$(6x^3y^2 - 3x^3y - 5x^2y^3 + xy) - (-7x^3y^2 + 2x^3y - 3x^2y^3 + 4xy)$$

$$6x^3y^2 - 3x^3y - 5x^2y^3 + xy + 7x^3y^2 - 2x^3y + 3x^2y^3 - 4xy$$

Combining like terms gives

$$13x^3y^2 - 5x^3y - 2x^2y^3 - 3xy$$

25. (A) use the F.O.I.L. method (multiply First terms, Outside terms, Inside terms, Last terms):

$$(5z^2 + 8)(6z^2 + 9)$$

Multiplying first terms $\quad 5z^2 \times 6z^2 = 30z^4$
Multiplying outside terms $\quad 5z^2 \times 9 = 45z^2$
Multiplying inside terms $\quad 8 \times 6z^2 = 48z^2$
Multiplying last terms $\quad 8 \times 9 = 72$

$$30z^4 + 45z^2 + 48z^2 + 72 = 30z^4 + 93z^2 + 72$$

or
$$
\begin{array}{r}
5z^2 +\ \ 8 \\
\times\ 6z^2 +\ \ 9 \\
\hline
45z^2 + 72 \\
30z^4 + 48z^2 \\
\hline
30z^4 + 93z^2 + 72
\end{array}
$$

26. (B) Since the broker earns a salary of \$800 per month, for the year that salary will total 12 times \$800, or \$9600. To have a total income of \$40,000 requires \$30,400 more in commissions. Working from the answers shows that 2% of answer (C) equals the additional \$30,400 more:

$$(.02)(\$1,520,000) = \$30,400$$

27. (C) Notice that everything is divisible by 5.

$$\frac{15}{45x + 25}$$

Therefore, dividing both the numerator and denominator by 5 yields

$$\frac{3}{9x + 5}$$

28. (C) From the graph, you can use the three points $(2, 2)$, $(-2, 2)$, and $(0, -2)$. Now, plugging each of these into each of the answer choices will give the right equation:

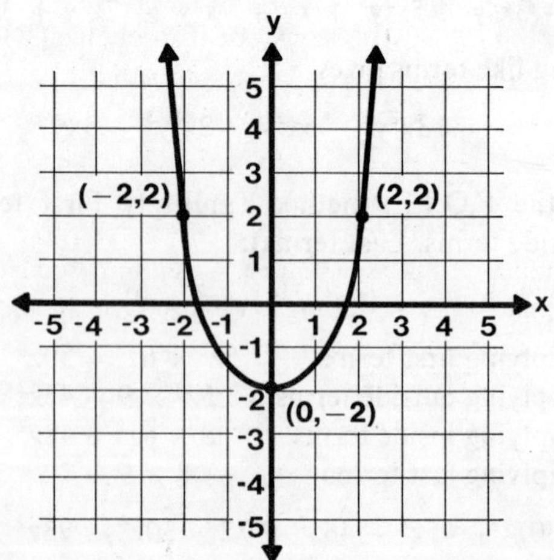

(A) $y = x^2 + 2$ $2 = 2^2 + 2$ (not true)
$$2 \neq 4 + 2$$

(B) $y = -x^2 + 2$ $2 = -(2)^2 + 2$ (not true)
$$2 \neq -4 + 2$$

(C) $y = x^2 - 2$ $2 = 2^2 - 2$ (true)
$$2 = 4 - 2$$

$$. \ 2 = (-2)^2 - 2 \quad \text{(true)}$$
$$2 = 4 - 2$$

$$-2 = 0^2 - 2 \quad \text{(true)}$$
$$-2 = 0 - 2$$

(D) $y = -x^2 - 2$ $2 = -(2)^2 - 2$ (not true)
$$2 \neq -4 - 6$$

29. (B) If $(x + 7)(x - 6) = 0$, at least one of the quantities in parentheses must equal 0. Therefore, setting each quantity equal to 0:

$$(x + 7) = 0$$
$$x = -7$$

$$(x - 6) = 0$$
$$x = 6$$

The greatest root of the equation is therefore $x = 6$.

30. (B) Keeping the cost, c, constant if in choice (B) p were to, say, double, n must be halved. In all the other choices, if p were to increase, n also would increase, to keep c constant. Therefore, only choice (B) is in inverse proportion.

31. (D) Notice that the semicircles at each end can be combined to form a complete circle. Therefore, the figure consists of one circle with radius r plus a rectangle with length 2r and width 2r. The total area is therefore $4r^2 + \pi r^2$.

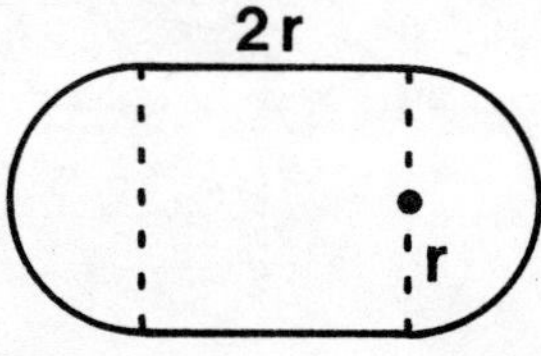

32. **(B)** Since the answer choices are not close in value, you should estimate this problem. The equation for the circumference of a circle is $2\pi r$. Approximate π as 3:

$$(2)(3)(9 \text{ yards}) = 54 \text{ yards}$$

33. **(B)** Use the given equation in two simple steps:

$$B = 20w^2 - 6w$$

For the first week, 5 workers were used:

$$B = 20(5)^2 - 6(5) = 20(25) - 30 = 500 - 30 = 470$$

This total is also the same for the second week.

For the third week, 7 workers were used:

$$B = 20(7)^2 - 6(7) = 20(49) - 42 = 980 - 42 = 938$$

This total is also the same for the fourth week. So the total for four weeks is

$$470 + 470 + 938 + 938 = 2816$$

34. **(C)** In any triangle, if two angles are equal, the sides opposite those angles are equal. So if $\angle EBD = \angle EFD$, in triangle BDF, $\overline{DF} = \overline{BD}$. In the small triangle EFD, it is given in the problem that $\angle FDE = \angle FED$; therefore, $\overline{DF} = \overline{EF}$. Since we know from the larger triangle that $\overline{DF}$ also equals $\overline{BD}$, all those sides are equal: $\overline{BD} = \overline{DF} = \overline{EF}$.

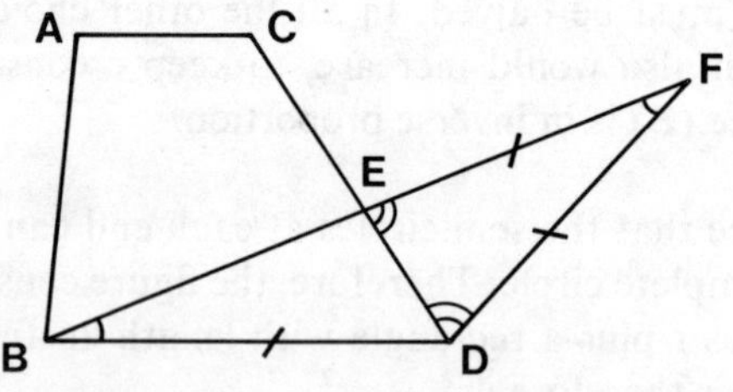

35. (C) If the front face of the open-topped box is a square, the dimensions of that face are 4″ by 4″. Since all the angles of a square measure 90°, using the Pythagorean theorem would give the length of the diagonal.

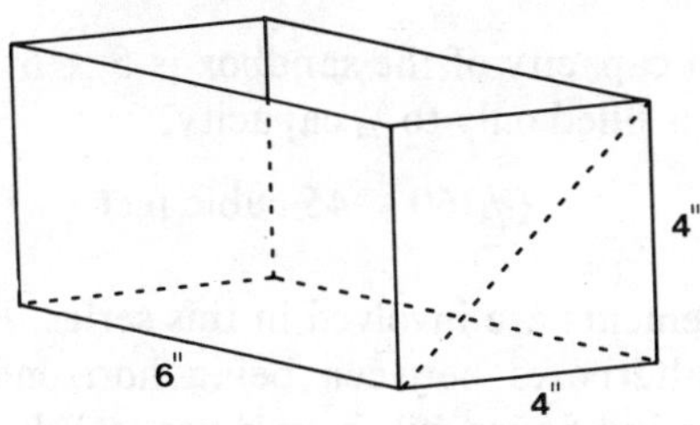

$$a^2 + b^2 = c^2$$
$$4^2 + 4^2 = c^2$$
$$16 + 16 = c^2$$
$$32 = c^2$$
$$\sqrt{32} = c$$

Simplifying $4\sqrt{2} = c$

If you realized that the triangle formed is an isosceles right triangle, the problem is more easily solved using the ratio of the sides

$$1\text{-}1\text{-}\sqrt{2} \quad \text{gives} \quad 4\text{-}4\text{-}4\sqrt{2}$$

36. (C) Whenever two lines are parallel, a line crossing those parallel lines forms equal opposite interior angles.

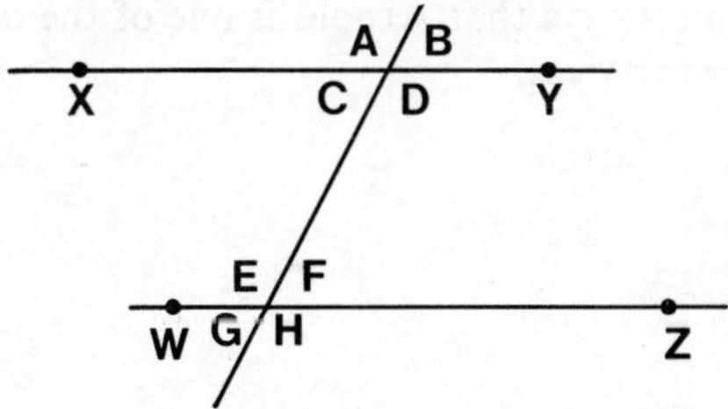

Therefore, in this diagram, $\angle C = \angle F$ and $\angle D = \angle E$. Since vertical angles are equal, $\angle A = \angle D$ and $\angle B = \angle C$. Notice that $\angle A$ equals $\angle E$. Therefore, since $\angle E + \angle F$ equal a straight line, $\angle A$ and $\angle F$ are supplementary (that is, their sum is 180 degrees).

37. **(B)** The total capacity of the sandbox is $5 \times 6 \times 2$, or 60 cubic feet. Since it is filled only to ¾ capacity,

$$(¾)60 = 45 \text{ cubic feet}$$

38. **(B)** Three elements are involved in this series. First, the outside "diamond" alternates between being horizontal and vertical. Thus, the missing figure will have a vertical diamond, eliminating choice (C). Second, note how the two shapes inside the diamond alternate with each other: first the triangle is the innermost shape, then the middle shape, then back to innermost. So the missing figure will again have the triangle being the middle shape, which eliminates choice (A). Finally, note how the shape that is rounded on one end turns clockwise with each figure: first its rounded side is right, then down, then left. So the missing figure will have this shape with its rounded side up.

39. **(A)** Since Fred and Ella live a mile away from the stamp collector, neither of them is the stamp collector. Since Sue and the friend who knits visited the stamp collector, neither is Sue the stamp collector. That leaves Tom as the stamp collector.

40. **(B)** Since statement 2 tells us that all children have brown eyes and statement 4 says that Arnold is one of the children, Arnold must have brown eyes.

WRITING

1. **(C)** The error here is the use of an adjective for an adverb. The adverb modifies the adjective *rooted*. The correct comparative form of the adverb is *more deeply*. If the adjective in its comparative form were needed, the correct word would be *deeper* without the *more*.

2. **(B)** The subject of the paragraph is stated in the first sentence, the relation of poverty to improper diet. This concern is also the issue in sentences 7 and 8. Sentence 6, though it is about diet, is not about the diet of the poor.

3. **(D)** The change corrects an error in the tense of the verb. The phrase *fourteen years ago* places the action in the past, and the verbs (*brutalized, behaved*) are in the past tense. The main verb in this sentence (*responded*) is also in the past tense, and *faced with* makes the tenses consistent.

4. **(D)** The logical sequence of the events described in the paragraph moves from sentence 8 to sentence 10 to sentence 9. By reversing the order of sentences 9 and 10, the sequence of events is clearer.

5. **(C)** The passage does present both *fight* (the attack of the bigoted neighbors) and *flight* (the Eastern Europeans leaving the neighborhood). When the author wrote the first sentence, he or she probably did not anticipate the application of *flight,* since the passage is sharply critical of the animalistic behavior of the neighbors but is sympathetic to the innocent victims.

6. **(B)** The error here is of agreement. With the singular subject *scarcity,* the verb must be the singular *has confined*. The tense and number of the other verbs in the parargraph are correct.

7. **(D)** Sentences 7, 8, and 9 all deal with the increased demand and competition for water. Though sentence 10 does tell us the West is dry (a fact the passage has already made clear), it is chiefly concerned with geographical information.

8. **(D)** The phrase *economic precepts* is a diction error. The writer probably wished to say *prospects,* that is, something likely to happen, a probable outcome; the word *precepts* means rules of conduct.

9. (A) The style of the passage is informal, relaxed. It is written using the first person pronoun (*I*). Choice (B) would change the personal pronoun from *I* to *you*. Choices (C) and (D) are written with a more formal diction. Choice (A) continues the series of questions begun in sentence 3 and answered in sentence 6, and its language level is consistent with the rest of the passage.

10. (B) The comma error in the paragraph is the omission of the punctuation after *afraid of*. The comma emphasizes the pause between the opposed *not the country* and *but myself*.

11. (B) The first clause presents a success (*was hailed*), but the second presents an opposite response (*viewed with suspicion and misgiving*). The second conjunction introducing the contrast must be a word or phrase like *on the other hand* or *nevertheless*. The first conjunction, *Although,* fits logically into the sentence.

12. (D) The subject of the paragraph is the agrarian and debtor classes' dissatisfaction with the Constitution. Unlike sentences 6, 7, and 8, sentence 9 deals with an approved section rather than with their objections.

13. (B) The series of four verbs which begins with *debated* should have commas after each of the first three verbs.

14. (C) Sentence 4 repeats what has already been said in sentence 3. The second half of the sentence repeats for a third time what is already clear.

15. (D) Despite its length and despite its having a subject and a verb, sentence 6 is not complete. It is a dependent clause introduced by *When*. Either the *When* must be deleted or a second clause that is independent must be added to make the sentence complete.

16. (B) There is no reason not to list the examples in chronological order. Thus, sentence 4, dealing with the thirteenth century, should come first, followed by sentence 2 (the fifteenth century) and sentence 3 (the nineteenth century).

17. (B) This sentence introduces the *field of futuristics,* the subject of the paragraph and the logical antecedent of the *subject* in sentence 8.

18. (D) The apostrophe is necessary in *today's* to indicate that the word is possessive singular, not a plural noun.

19. (D) The paragraph is concerned with hunting animals, and all of the first five sentences are on this topic. But the sixth sentence moves to a different subject, the gathering of edible plants.

20. (B) Sentence 2 is actually two sentences, but they have not been joined by a conjunction or separated by a semicolon. The sentence can be corrected either by adding a comma and *and* after *game* or by placing a semicolon after *game*.

21. (C) Choices (A), (B), or (D) are possible as final sentences for the first paragraph, but none of them prepares for the shift from the subject of speech to the subject of writing. Choice (C) logically concludes the first paragraph and prepares the reader for the new subject to be introduced in the second paragraph.

22. (D) Sentence 11 does nothing but restate sentence 10 and does so using more words. The paragraph is better if sentence 11 is omitted.

23. (C) The present infinitive form of the verb, *to become,* is correct here.

24. (B) The style of the letter is highly informal, even slangy. The level of diction in choices (A), (C), and (D) is much more formal, and the assertion of choice (A) is counter to the letter's argument. Choice (B), with its conversational, comic tone, is the most consistent with the rest of the paragraph.

25. (B) Again, the conversational tone of the passage is the key to finding the right answer. Choices (A) and (D) are, in fact, inappropriate words in this context, though *rise* not *rising* would be acceptable. The down-to-earth *hike* is much more in keeping with the speaker's tone than the over-formal *elevation*.

26. (B) Here *It's* is a contraction for *It is* and must have the apostrophe.

27. (D) The first sentence speaks of *public officials* and *public figures,* while the second cites *a movie star or a senator.* Clearly, the

second sentence is giving examples of what the first sentence spoke of. Of the four choices, only *For example* fits this context. The third sentence, which refers to a situation where the requirements do *not* apply, requires a phrase to introduce a contradiction such as *On the other hand*.

28. (B) The participle, *Writing,* which begins sentence 4, dangles. Who did this writing? It must have been a Supreme Court justice, but the participle modifies *it*.

29. (A) The verb should be in the third person, singular, present tense to agree with the singular subject, *Southern Clay*.

30. (A) Choice (B) is irrelevant in content, while choices (C) and (D) are far more serious in tone and content than the rest of the passage. The article is comic in tone, mocking the inappropriate application of government rules. The tone of the question in choice (A), as well as its use of *we,* is consistent with the rest of the paragraph.

31. (D) The last sentence is an unnecessary explanation of what is already clear. And *folly* and *foolishness* are redundant.

32. (D) The real subject of the paragraph is the network's intention to edit the film, not incidental facts about Beatty or about ABC's schedule.

33. (C) It would be possible to use either a singular or a plural— *timeslot* or *timeslots*—in a sentence like this one, but the use of the singular *it* makes the singular *timeslot* necessary here.

34. (A) Since sentence 1 refers to *the two nations* without identifying them, a sentence referring to the United States and Russia should precede sentence 1. The chronological references of the paragraph also begin with sentence 4 and progress to sentence 5 and sentence 1. Any of the other changes would produce added confusion.

35. (B) The sentence does have a verb (*hears*) but as part of a dependent clause.

36. (C) Choices (A) and (B) are in a more informal style than the rest of the passage, while choice (D) is more pompously phrased. The use of *eye to eye* prepares for the metaphorical *blink* in sentence 11.

37. (C) Of the four choices, only (A) or (C) could fit in sentence 5, introducing a positive assertion. But (A) cannot be right for sentence 6, which is also positive.

38. (C) The correct comparative form is either *heavier* or *more heavy*.

39. (A) Though we can make sense of the passage, it would be clearer immediately if we knew when the writer wrote this passage in relation to the events it describes. The addition of the sentence placing the events ten years earlier makes it clear.

40. (B) The sentence requires a main verb—*left* not *leaving*.

PRACTICE TEST 2

Section I:	Reading—40 Questions
Section II:	Mathematics—40 Questions
Section III:	Writing—Multiple-Choice—40 Questions
	Essay—1 300 to 600 word essay

The total time allowed for the test is four hours (with one additional hour allowed if necessary). You may work on any section of the test during this time period.

READING

DIRECTIONS

Several questions follow each of the passages in this section. Using only the stated or implied information given in the passage, answer the questions by choosing the best answer from among the four choices given.

Questions 1 through 5 are based on the following passage.

THE USES OF PHILOSOPHY

1   The statement that "philosophy bakes no bread" has sometimes been used to indicate that it has no practical value at all. Whether there is any truth in this statement depends on what one means by the word "practical." If one has in mind simply its usefulness as a direct means of making money, the production of material goods, or the achievement of financial success in the business world, philosophy is not practical in the same sense as would be true of other disciplines. If, however, one means by practical that which will increase the value and significance of life as a whole, then philosophy is one of the most practical studies that can be pursued. It should also be noted in this connection that philosophy, or love of wisdom, is something that is a value in itself even when it is not used as a means of achieving something else. Among the more specific values or uses of philosophy the following may be mentioned.

2   The pursuit of philosophy adds to an individual's knowledge about himself and the world in which he lives. Since the desire to know is one of the essential characteristics of human nature, any knowledge which a person obtains through the study of philosophy will contribute to a satisfaction of this desire. While it is true that knowledge is a source of both pleasure and pain, we are warranted in assuming that knowledge is better than ignorance, even though its consequences at times may be more painful than pleasant.

3   Philosophy has been and still remains one of the major influences on human conduct. To be sure, it is not the only influence on conduct, for it is true that people in general usually

follow their desires more than they do their intellects. Nevertheless, what a person believes to be true about himself in relation to the world about him will have its effect on what he does. An individual's life is, in one sense, an expression of his philosophy, for it indicates what he believes to be most worthful. The same is true for groups of people such as communities, nations, and public institutions.

4   Philosophy has to do with the realm of values as well as with the sciences and the factual information which they provide. Values have to do with the worth of things, and this is something that is outside the sphere of the physical sciences. The sciences can report what is, but they do not tell us what ought to be. They describe what actually exists, but they do not evaluate and they cannot tell us anything about what is good or bad in the moral sense in which those words are used. Philosophy cannot impart the final or absolute truth about values, but it can and does explore various theories concerning values, and it provides the means for criticizing and evaluating them. In this way it serves as a guide toward a more adequate understanding of what constitutes the meaning and value of human life.

5   Closely related to the above is the fact that philosophy encourages a person to think for himself rather than to accept blindly what he has learned from others. It brings to light the fact than an idea can be a person's own, provided that he has gone through the mental process of making it his own but in no other way. Otherwise it is merely a copy or reflection of another person's idea. It is in this connection that philosophy tends to develop a critical attitude of mind. The student is encouraged to refrain from accepting an idea just because it has been advocated by some other person. He is taught to examine the reasons on which it has been based and to accept it only when these reasons appear to be adequate.

6   Humans are not only thinking animals but religious ones as well. Religious questions are not scientific ones, and therefore they cannot be answered by means of experiment and observation. Philosophy, by exploring the various conceptions that have been held concerning the nature of religion, can point out many of the implications involved in each of them, and in the light of these implications, a person can select a view that will avoid self-

contradictions and inconsistencies with known facts and at the same time provide a meaningful interpretation of human experiences.

1. Which of the following best defines the phrase *critical attitude of mind* as it is used in paragraph 5?
   (A) a fault-finding attitude
   (B) a way of thinking that is sober and serious
   (C) carefully analytical approach
   (D) a necessary way of thinking

2. The main idea of the passage is expressed by which of the following?
   (A) Philosophy helps a person overcome a narrow-minded perspective.
   (B) Philosophy has a number of uses which add value and significance to life.
   (C) How a person acts is greatly influenced by his or her personal philosophy.
   (D) Philosophy is eminently practical because it can even supply answers to financial dilemmas.

3. Which of the following assumptions most probably influences the views expressed by the author?
   (A) Knowledge is better than ignorance so long as its consequence is pleasure.
   (B) Philosophy attempts to find self-contradictions and logical inconsistencies in religious views.
   (C) Philosophy and science are in conflict with each other.
   (D) The philosopher, though never arriving at complete truth, does progress toward answering life's ultimate questions.

4. The author's main purpose in this selection is to
   (A) contrast the methods of philosophic, scientific, and religious study.
   (B) discuss reasons that the study of philosophy would be worthwhile in itself, even if it were not useful.
   (C) outline some uses of philosophy.
   (D) argue that a person's desire to know can be satisfied through philosophic study.

5. According to the passage, the results of scientific research have no bearing on
    (A) questions whose answers depend upon experimental evidence.
    (B) questions dealing with moral value or purpose in life.
    (C) questions whose answers depend upon facts.
    (D) hypotheses which can be tested by means of observation.

Questions 6 through 10 are based on the following passage.

PROFESSOR ON TRIAL

1   There seems to be a trend in universities these days to have college students rate their professors. Some schools are even setting up student boards to decide whether a teacher should get tenure or not. If it continues, we can well imagine the following scene.

2   A board room with three somber students studying a dossier. There is a timid knock on the door. "Come in," one of the students shouts.

3   Enter Professor Higgins, nervously biting his lip. The three students study him for almost a minute. Then the chairman speaks: "You can smoke if you want. Professor, this report does not look very good. It says you slur your words, have a very annoying habit of clearing your throat, and your handwriting on the blackboard leaves much to be desired."

4   "All I'm asking is another chance," Professor Higgins pleads.

5   One of the other students says, "Higgins, I would like to remind you that your parents went to a great deal of trouble to make you a professor. Is this how you repay them?"

6   "I'm sorry, gentlemen. It's just that I've been writing my book on Antarctic philosophy and I haven't had enough time to work on my lectures."

7   "A likely story," another student says. "If you ask me, you're spending too much time thinking about your wife and children. This is not a country club, Higgins, and the sooner you discover this, the better off you're going to be."

8   The chairman says, "The report also states you give too many exams and rely too much on outside references. What do you have to say to this?"

9   "I don't want to complain, but the students are always picking on me. I just can't seem to do anything right."

10   "Higgins, I'd like to ask you this question. How many hours of television do you watch at night?"

11   "Two hours, maybe two and a half."

12   "Why don't you cut it down and shape up to your responsibilities? Decide what you want out of life, Higgins. We're here to

help you, but we can't do it if you don't help yourself."

13   "I'm trying to," Higgins says, "but it isn't easy. There's so much pressure on a professor these days that I seem to lose sight of my goal."

14   "Don't you think it's a simple matter of discipline, Higgins? You've got to identify with your subject matter. Here in the report it says you are constantly quoting from your own books. Do you call that teaching?"

15   "Higgins," the chairman says, "I don't want to get off the subject, but it also says in the report you seem to concentrate on the coeds in the first row when you're lecturing. Do you have any excuse for this?"

16   "No, sir."

17   "What are we going to do with you, Higgins? What are we going to do with you?"

18   "Maybe I could take an aptitude test. Perhaps I'm teaching in the wrong subject?"

19   "If we let every professor teach the subject he was most qualified for, Higgins, where would the university be?"

20   "Higgins, we're going to put you on probation. We are going to assign a student to tutor you, and you will report back in two months. If you don't show any improvement, we're going to have to ask you to leave."

21   "Thank you, gentlemen. I'll prove your faith in me. You won't regret it."

22   "We like your spirit, Higgins. Now let's see you measure up. Good day."

23   The chairman takes out a new dossier. "Who is next? Oh, no. Not the Dean of the Law School again?"

6. Which of these phrases best defines the word *dossier* as it is used in paragraph 2?
   (A) a set of documents relating to one person
   (B) the recorded minutes of a board meeting
   (C) completed teacher evaluation form
   (D) a university's rules for academic tenure

7. The main idea of the passage is best expressed by which of the following?
   (A) Students should be given a greater role in evaluating faculty members.
   (B) Many professors would conduct more interesting research if students were given the authority to advance or to fire a professor.
   (C) The trend of having students rate their professors may lead to a time when faculty are at the mercy of student boards.
   (D) Some professors are capable of carrying out serious research but not of teaching effectively.

8. The material presented in this passage is most suitable for
   (A) inspiring readers with a vision of the not-so-distant future.
   (B) satirizing a trend that gives students undue authority.
   (C) dramatizing what currently goes on in some student board room meetings.
   (D) analyzing the effects of ineffective teaching on the attitudes of law school students.

9. One of the points made in the report on Professor Higgins is that he
   (A) watches at least two hours of television a night.
   (B) is writing a book on Antarctic philosophy.
   (C) smokes.
   (D) gives too many exams.

10. For what purpose does the student say *This is not a country club, Higgins* in paragraph 7?
    (A) to state a fact for no other purpose than clarification
    (B) to imply that the university is not supported by rich country club members
    (C) to criticize Higgins's attitude toward his work by means of sarcasm
    (D) to suggest that Higgins spends time at a country club with his wife and children when he should be working

Questions 11 through 15 are based on the following passage.

ROMEO AND JULIET

1   The theme of *Romeo and Juliet* is a consuming love. It is a story of hatred overcome by that love, old hate versus young love, taking no thought for the past or the future, and this love ends in "love-devouring."

2   The atmosphere is one of passion and swiftness, full-blooded passion and rash swiftness. Consuming love calls for haste— "Gallop apace, you fiery-footed steeds." "From nine till twelve is three long hours." The whole play is in a hurry—speed into marriage, speed into banishment, speed back to Juliet, speed in another quarter to get Juliet married to Paris, speed to kill whoever steps in the way, and speed to commit suicide when life suddenly seems not worth living. Romeo's haste makes him happy in his marriage, and immediately thereafter unhappy in his banishment. *Romeo and Juliet* is a play of whirlwind and storm, full of angry feud, tremendous passion, and sudden death.

3   Even when things are going well, there is a sense of impending tragedy in the air, a grim foreboding that makes happy folk mistrust their happiness. The first Prologue speaks of "A pair of star-cross'd lovers" before the play proper starts. The first scene of the play shows how affairs are like powder waiting for a match, and there are those only too glad to bring one. There is a nameless dread before Romeo has ever set eyes on Juliet, and after they have met, both have a presentiment that their love will end in disaster. Romeo comes to marry Juliet with a challenge to fate on his lips—"Then love-devouring death do what he dare." And Juliet, as she looks on Romeo (alive) for the last time, admits:

> O God, I have an ill-divining soul!
> Methinks I see thee, now thou art so low.
> As one dead in the bottom of a tomb.

4   Most of Shakespeare's tragedies end on a note of hope, and this, the first, strikes the pattern of the rest. The lives of these lovers are burnt up, but the final effect of the play is not wholly pessimistic. It would have been had their deaths increased the hatred of the Montagues and Capulets. But at the end, the heads

of these two houses shake hands over the "poor sacrifices of their enmity." The tragedy has left things better than they were at the start of the play.

11. Which of the following phrases defines the word *presentiment* as used in paragraph 3?
    (A) justified belief
    (B) resistance to a parent's wishes
    (C) feeling about the future
    (D) refusal to accept

12. The main idea of the passage is best expressed by which of the following?
    (A) *Romeo and Juliet,* a play about the way love clouds the reason, has characters who hasten to quick, but often false, conclusions.
    (B) Romeo and Juliet, as young lovers rushing toward their tragic fate, reveal how passion without maturity leads to disaster.
    (C) The events in *Romeo and Juliet* happen with great speed because "three long hours" would be too much for an audience to sit through.
    (D) Befitting a play about consuming love, *Romeo and Juliet* is fast moving, driven by impulsive and passionate action and speech.

13. The material presented in this passage is most suitable for
    (A) relating the theme and atmosphere of *Romeo and Juliet.*
    (B) criticizing the rapid pace of Shakespeare's play.
    (C) provoking sympathy for the parents of Romeo and Juliet.
    (D) building suspense in readers who are about to read the play.

14. Romeo is quoted as saying, *Then love-devouring death do what he dare.* In this quotation, death is
    (A) the symbolic name Romeo gives to Paris.
    (B) devoured by love.
    (C) personified.
    (D) a fate Romeo fears.

15. Just prior to Juliet's quotation in paragraph 3, the author states that she *looks on Romeo (alive) for the last time*. What is the most likely explanation for why the author adds the word *alive* in parentheses?

(A) to suggest that Romeo is physically with her, not only "alive" to her in the vision she has of him

(B) to let readers know that Romeo is alive at the moment she admits to having a vision of him dead "in the bottom of a tomb"

(C) to emphasize that Juliet's love for Romeo is so intense that he seems fully alive to her

(D) to imply that Juliet will look on Romeo again, but he will not be alive

Questions 16 through 20 are based on the following passage.

CASSEROLES: BACK AGAIN

1   Remember casseroles? Remember when they faded away never to return, or so it seemed? Nostalgia for the '50s has brought casseroles back.

2   Casseroles may not last as part of the hip culinary scene beyond the next season, but they are classically American enough to warrant your attention, especially if you are planning a nostalgic '50s evening or trying your hand at the stuff that became a rage with the advent of canned foods. A better reason might simply be that you are interested in easy, low-cost, and nutritious cooking.

3   Casseroles, after all, are generally loaded with carbohydrates, which, say health experts, should be increased in our diets. Carbohydrates should make up 60% of the total calories we ingest. Protein should provide 10% of total calories consumed each day, and fat (inherent in food or consumed separately) 30%.

4   So meet *the* casserole—the all-American meal-in-a-dish that lured skilled cooks of the early 1900s away from the art of scratch recipes to the mechanics of convenience cooking, thus launching a new category in American-style cuisine.

5   Casseroles could, conversely, lure today's convenience cooks back into the kitchen, if only to open a can of Campbell's mushroom soup and throw a handful of noodles, cashews, and celery stubs into a dish that would become that evening's—and maybe even tomorrow's—supper.

6   There is really nothing to making a casserole, and the taste often belies its humble origins, low cost, and minimal effort. The only planning needed is for baking time, which usually is from 20 minutes to one hour, depending on the type of casserole.

7   American-style casserole cooking reached its peak of popularity in the 1950s when food companies, whose marketing research allowed them to estimate the kitchen skills of their customers, promoted their products by offering recipes with simple instructions. These dishes were based on good old one-two-three-ingredient recipes that convenience food cooks could easily master.

8   Many recipe favorites appeared on the labels of canned or boxed soups, vegetables, macaroni, meats, fish, and poultry. Innovative American cooks, however, improvised, giving breath and richness to dishes that often originated in the cold, clinical setting of a food company laboratory kitchen. The roster of American casseroles is endless with many variations on a single theme.

16. Which of these phrases best defines the word *belies* as it is used in paragraph 6?
    (A) reminds one of
    (B) contradicts
    (C) is the result of
    (D) lies underneath

17. According to paragraphs 4 and 5, the casserole *lured skilled cooks of the early 1900s away,* yet now *could, conversely, lure today's convenience cooks back* . . . Which of the following statements best expresses the main idea of these paragraphs about the "lure" of casseroles?
    (A) Cooks in the early part of the century were attracted to casserole recipes that relied only on fresh ingredients; the cooks of today are drawn to the convenience of casseroles made from boxed or canned ingredients.
    (B) Cooks both of today and of the past are drawn to making casserole recipes that depend exclusively on prepackaged ingredients.
    (C) The casserole led cooks of the early 1900s away from artistic cooking toward convenience cooking; on the other hand, the casserole could lead today's convenience cooks toward doing a little more cooking.
    (D) Cooks of the early 1900s were attracted to the idea that they were creating a new category of American-style cuisine; modern cooks, on the other hand, are attracted to the idea that casseroles are fun for a nostalgic '50s evening.

18. The author would most likely agree with which of the following statements?
    (A) Because casseroles are often easy to make, inexpensive, and nutritious, they will return as popular meals at various times again in the future.
    (B) Americans of the '50s enjoyed casseroles primarily because these meals introduced them to what eating was like in the early 1900s.
    (C) European casseroles are generally prepared from recipes calling for fresh (not canned or boxed) ingredients.
    (D) A casserole that requires less than eight or nine ingredients to make is probably not based on an American-style recipe advertised in the 1950s.

19. The author's plausibility is best assessed by which of the following statements?
    (A) Despite the selection's portrayal of casseroles as easy-to-prepare meals, the writer lacks plausibility because no effort is made to describe how complicated a casserole recipe can be.
    (B) Although the selection sketches the history of casserole making since the 1900s, the writer's plausibility is weakened because of a failure to provide enough information about advertising strategies used to sell casserole ingredients in the 1950s.
    (C) Although the passage might leave the impression that all casseroles are nutritious, the author nevertheless effectively presents the merits of preparing casserole meals.
    (D) The author's plausibility is questionable because insufficient emphasis is placed on how the average casserole provides a person with the amount of protein and fat required for a healthy diet.

20. Which of the following groups of topics best shows the content
organization of the passage?
(A)   I. The return of the casserole
       II. Reasons for making casseroles
       III. Promoting the casserole of the 1950s
(B)   I. Nostalgia for the 1900s
       II. Classic casserole recipes
       III. Variations on the casserole
(C)   I. Boxed recipes versus scratch recipes
       II. Marketing the casserole today
       III. Recipes created in a food laboratory
(D)   I. Casseroles and protein
       II. The drawbacks of convenience cooking
       III. A new category of cooking

Questions 21 through 25 are based on the following passage.

EXCERPT FROM *OUR MUTUAL FRIEND* BY CHARLES DICKENS

1   In these times of ours, a boat of dirty and disreputable appearance, with two figures in it, floated on the Thames between Southwark Bridge, which is of iron, and London Bridge, which is of stone, as an autumn evening was closing in.

2   The figures in this boat were those of a strong man with ragged, grizzled hair and a sun-browned face, and a dark girl of nineteen or twenty, sufficiently like him to be recognizable as his daughter. The girl rowed, pulling a pair of sculls very easily; the man kept an eager look-out. He had no net, hook, or line, and he could not be a fisherman; his boat had no cushion for a sitter, no paint, no inscription, no appliance beyond a rusty boat-hook and a coil of rope, and he could not be a waterman; his boat was too small to take in a cargo for delivery, and he could not be a lighterman or river-carrier; there was no clue to what he looked for, but he looked for something, with a most intent and searching gaze. His eyes watched every little race and eddy as he directed his daughter by a movement of his head. She watched his face as earnestly as she watched the river. But in the intensity of her look there was a touch of dread or horror.

3   This boat and the two figures in it obviously were doing something that they often did, and were seeking what they often sought. Half savage as the man showed, still there was business-like usage in his steady gaze. So with every lithe action of the girl, with every turn of her wrist, perhaps most of all with her look of dread and horror; they were things of usage.

4   It happened now that a slant of light from the setting sun glanced into the bottom of the boat, and, touching a rotten stain there which bore some resemblance to the outline of a muffled human form, coloured it as though with diluted blood. This caught the girl's eye, and she shivered.

5   The boat swung round, quivered as from a sudden jerk, and the upper half of the man was stretched out over the stern. . . . Now the upper half of the man came back into the boat. His arms were wet and dirty, and he washed them over the side. In his right hand he held something, and he washed that in the river too. It was money. He chinked it once, and he blew upon it once,

and he spat upon it once—"for luck," he hoarsely said—before he put it in his pocket.

6   "Here! Give me hold of the sculls. I'll take the rest of the spell."

7   "No, no, Father! No! I can't indeed. Father! I cannot sit so near it!"

8   He was moving towards her to change places, but her terrified expostulation stopped him, and he resumed his seat.

9   "What hurt can it do you?"

10   "None, none. But I cannot bear it."

11   "It's my belief you hate the sight of the very river."

12   "I—I do like it, Father."

13   "As if it wasn't your living! As if it wasn't meat and drink to you!"

14   At these later words the girl shivered again, and for a moment, paused in her rowing, seeming to turn deadly faint. It escaped his attention, for he was glancing over the stern at something the boat had in tow.

21. Which of the following best defines the word *sculls* as it is used in paragraph 2?
    (A) light racing boats
    (B) heads
    (C) oars
    (D) sails

22. Although the passage never explicitly identifies what the boat has in tow in the last paragraph, which of the following is most likely?
    (A) another boat
    (B) a body
    (C) a fish
    (D) wreckage of a ship

23. The writer's main purpose in writing the passage is to
    (A) establish a mood of horror and mystery.
    (B) persuade readers of the injustices suffered by women.
    (C) attack the inequities of the social system.
    (D) describe the river and its environs.

24. Which of the following quotations from the passage expresses an opinion of one of the characters?
    (A) . . . a boat of dirty and direputable appearance, with two figures in it, floated on the Thames . . .
    (B) This boat and the two figures in it obviously were doing something that they often did, and were seeking what they often sought.
    (C) "Here! Give me hold of the sculls. I'll take the rest of the spell."
    (D) "As if it wasn't your living! As if it wasn't meat and drink to you!"

25. Which of the following details of the passage suggests what the boat is towing?
    (A) Southwark Bridge, which is of iron
    (B) a strong man with ragged, grizzled hair and a sun-browned face
    (C) a slant of light from the setting sun glanced into the bottom of the boat
    (D) a rotten stain there which bore some resemblance to the outline of a muffled human form

Questions 26 through 30 are based on the following passage.

ISLAM AND ITS INFLUENCE

1   Mohammed was a prophet in the same way that Jesus had been. After Mohammed felt he had received divine messages, he decided to spread his new faith, which accepted only one god, Allah. Mohammed's first campaign was against the pagan beliefs of his home town Mecca in Arabia. Because he alienated the people there in 622 he fled to Medina (the Hegira), where he succeeded in converting the population to his new religion, Islam. The new adherents (Moslems) felt they had to convert the pagans and to use force if necessary in doing so; Christians and Jews, however, were tolerated because they were "People of the Book" (the Bible). Islam was such a militant faith that within ten years (Mohammed died in 632) most of Arabia had been conquered.

2   Because the Arab conquerors were tolerant of monotheistic peoples and imposed relatively low taxes, they successfully conquered the Near East. The Byzantine provinces had been suffering under a heavy tax burden since the time of Constantine; therefore, they were not completely adverse to Arab rule. Within 100 years of Mohammed's death, an Arab Empire extended from Persia to Spain. The Moslems were stopped at Tours, France, in 732.

3   Moslem Spain, which lasted from 711 to 1492, served as the transmission point of ideas between the Arab world and western Europe. The Spanish Moslems, as well as those of North Africa and the Near East, translated, studied, and added to the Greek classics. This was particularly true in philosophy, where Averroës (ibn-Rushd, 1126–1198) interpreted Aristotle in such a way that religious beliefs could be checked against his philosophy. Although Averroës was condemned by the Roman Catholic Church, his ideas influenced thinkers in the twelfth and thirteenth centuries. Avicenna (ibn-Sina, 980–1037) combined the medical ideas of Hippocrates and Galen with his own precepts in his book *Canon of Medicine*. His work made inroads against the accepted medical superstitions of medieval Europe. The Arabic impact on the sciences, such as chemistry, can be seen in words of Arabic derivation, for example, *alcohol* and *alkali*. The mathe-

matical genius of the Moslem world also affected the West. Roman numerals, used in Europe during the Middle Ages, were quite cumbersome and made higher mathematics impossible. After they learned of the zero from India, the Arabs devised a numeral system that was later transmitted to the West. It consisted of a system of units that could be multiplied by ten, for example, 1, 10, 100. The Arabic system made algebra (itself an Arabic word) and calculus possible.

26. Which of the following best defines the word *monotheistic* as it is used in paragraph 2?
    (A) believing there is only one God
    (B) non-Moslem
    (C) religious
    (D) believing in the principles of religious freedom

27. According to the passage, which of the following devised the numbering system we have now?
    (A) the Romans
    (B) the Indians
    (C) the Arabs
    (D) the Greeks

28. Which of the following is the only word that is *not* identified in the passage as being derived from Arabic?
    (A) algebra
    (B) alcohol
    (C) alkali
    (D) calculus

ᴉn of the following groups of topics best shows the content
organization of the passage?

(A) I. Mohammed and Islam
     II. The Islamic Empire
     III. Moslem Spain
(B) I. Mohammed and Jesus
     II. The Byzantine Empire
     III. Islamic Influences on Western Europe
(C) I. Mohammed and Islam
     II. The Empire of Islam
     III. Islamic Influence on Western Europe
(D) I. Mohammed's Influence on Islam
     II. The Arab Empire
     III. Spain in the Middle Ages

30. The author's main purpose in paragraph 3 is to
(A) discuss the role of Spain in the Middle Ages.
(B) present the range of Arab contributions to civilization.
(C) argue for the superiority of Moslem culture to that of the
    West.
(D) demonstrate how the Middle Ages have influenced the
    modern world.

Questions 31 through 35 are based on the following passage.

COURSE OUTLINE FOR CHEMISTRY
Professor J. P. Brewster

1   *Chemistry 100: Introduction to Chemistry* is a course designed to familiarize students with eight topics of chemistry. The topics are Atoms, Formulas, Chemical States, Solutions, Ionization Theory, Weight and Volume Relations, Reaction Rates and Chemical Equilibriums, and Oxidation and Reduction.

2   As I am sure you are aware, Chemistry 100 is a foundational course for all further study in the Chemistry major. The Chem 100 laboratory may be completed in a future semester, yet frankly I do not encourage you to wait. The labs explore course topics in a spirit of inquiry that your textbook study of them cannot duplicate. The textbook you should purchase is *The Enterprise of Chemistry* by Euland Boyle. By the end of the term, you will have read approximately half of the text. A schedule of your weekly readings is attached. Note that you are to have read Chapters 1 and 2 by next class period. I suggest that it is a good policy always to have read the assigned chapters before I go over them in lecture. You will be surprised at how much this simple study technique will improve your comprehension of what I present in class. Also, as you come across example problems in your reading, work them out fully for yourself on paper. You won't understand a worked-out answer as you should until you pick up a pencil and work it out for yourself. (Note: If you plan to take Chem 200, keep your text. We cover the second half of the book in that course.)

3   Purchase of the workbook that accompanies *The Enterprise of Chemistry* is not required but is highly recommended. Not only does the workbook provide you with numerous practice questions to aid your study, it contains a pool of potential test questions from which your professor has been known to dip around exam time.

4   Attendance is not mandatory, but if you make a habit out of missing class, I can almost guarantee that your test scores will suffer. There are two reasons for this: I cover topics in lecture that are not included in your reading; I make a special effort to explain difficult material from your reading.

5   I will calculate a course grade for you based on three midterm examinations, eight sets of homework, and a final exam. Each midterm (always to be administered on a Friday) is worth 15% of your grade. The final exam is worth 25% of your grade. The test is cumulative, so I would advise you to use your returned midterms as a study tool. The total of your homework grades make up the remaining 30%. A homework set is composed of problems from the back of each chapter. To get full credit for a homework problem, you must have both the correct answer and a valid set-up. In other words, show your work!

6   Intro to Chemistry is a problem-solver's course. The best grades generally go to those students who spend the majority of their study time working sample problems, homework problems, and workbook problems. It's time to pick up your pencil!

31. Which of the following phrases best defines the word *cumulative* as it is used in paragraph 5?
    (A) testing students only on topics included in the three midterms
    (B) evaluating the sum total of a semester's work
    (C) three times as long as each of the midterms
    (D) the most difficult because each each exceeds the previous one in difficulty

32. For what purpose does the author use the sentence *It's time to pick up your pencil!* as the last sentence of the passage?
    (A) to introduce a writing task
    (B) to convey a feeling of impatience toward laziness
    (C) to emphasize the need for active learning
    (D) to joke about being prepared

33. Which of the following is given as a possible hazard for a student who misses two Chemistry classes in a row?
    (A) The student may earn two unexcused absences in Professor Brewster's grade book.
    (B) The student would miss out on essential lab time.
    (C) The student may miss a lecture on material not covered in the text.
    (D) The student may lose participation points which figure into the calculation of a final grade.

34. Which of the following quotations from the passage expresses an opinion held by the author rather than a fact?
    (A) *Chemistry 100: Introduction to Chemistry* is a course designed to familiarize students with eight topics of chemistry.
    (B) The textbook you should purchase is *The Enterprise of Chemistry* by Euland Boyle.
    (C) I will calculate a course grade for you based on three midterm examinations, eight sets of homework, and a final exam.
    (D) You will be surprised at how much this simple study technique will improve your comprehension of what I present in class.

35. How many chapters will students in Chem 100 be assigned to read if each chapter covers one topic?
    (A) 4
    (B) 6
    (C) 8
    (D) 10

Questions 36 through 40 are based on the following passage.

HOW DICTIONARIES ARE MADE

1   It is an almost universal belief that every word has a correct meaning, that we learn those meanings principally from teachers and grammarians (except that most of the time we don't bother to, so that we ordinarily speak "sloppy English"), and that dictionaries and grammars are the supreme authority in matters of meaning and usage. Few people ask by what authority the writers of dictionaries and grammars say what they say. The docility with which most people bow down to the dictionary is amazing, and the person who says, "Well the dictionary is wrong!" is looked upon as out of his mind.

2   Let us see how dictionaries are made and how the editors arrive at definitions. What follows, applies, incidentally, only to those dictionary offices where first-hand, original research goes on— not those in which editors simply copy existing dictionaries. The task of writing a dictionary begins with the reading of vast amounts of the literature of the period or subject that it is intended to cover. As the editors read, they copy on cards every interesting or rare word, every unusual or peculiar occurrence of a common word, a large number of common words in their ordinary uses, and also the sentences in which each of these words appears, thus:

pail
The dairy *pails* bring home increase of milk

Keats, *Endymion*
I, 44–45

3   That is to say, the context of each word is collected, along with the word itself. For a really big job of dictionary writing, such as the *Oxford English Dictionary* (usually bound in about 25 volumes), millions of such cards are collected, and the task of editing occupies decades. As the cards are collected, they are alphabetized and sorted. When the sorting is completed, there will be for each word anywhere from two to three to several hundred illustrative quotations, each on its card.

4   To define a word, then, the dictionary editor places before him the stack of cards illustrating that word; each of the cards represents an actual use of the word by a writer of some literary or historical importance. He reads the cards carefully, discards some, rereads the rest, and divides up the stack according to what he thinks are the several senses of the word. Finally, he writes his definitions, following the hard-and-fast rule that each definition *must* be based on what the quotations in front of him reveal about the meaning of the word. The editor cannot be influenced by what *he* thinks a given word *ought* to mean. He must work according to the cards or not at all.

5   The writing of a dictionary, therefore, is not a task of setting up authoritative statements about the "true meanings" of words, but a task of *recording,* to the best of one's ability, what various words *have meant* to authors in the distant or immediate past. *The writer of a dictionary is a historian, not a lawgiver.* If, for example, we had been writing a dictionary in 1890, or even as late as 1919, we could have said that the word *broadcast* means "to scatter" (seed and so on) but we could not have decreed that from 1921 on, the commonest meaning of the word should become "to disseminate audible messages, etc., by wireless telephony." To regard the dictionary as an "authority," therefore, is to credit the dictionary writer with gifts of prophecy which neither he nor anyone else possesses. In choosing our words when we speak or write, we can be *guided* by the historical record afforded us by the dictionary, but we cannot be *bound* by it, because new situations, new experiences, new inventions, new feelings, are always compelling us to give new uses to old words. Looking under a "hood," we should ordinarily have found, five hundred years ago, a monk; today, we find a motorcar engine.

36. Which of the following best defines the word *docility* as it is used in paragraph 1?
    (A) tame, accepting manner
    (B) reluctance
    (C) bending at the waist
    (D) sudden movement

37. The main idea of the passage is best expressed by which of the
    following?
    (A) By learning how a dictionary is made, people find out why it
        deserves to be the ultimate authority for what words mean.
    (B) To see how a dictionary is made is to see that it can guide,
        but not enforce, how one should use words.
    (C) A dictionary writer defines a word by analyzing how it has
        been used in the past, then deciding how it ought to be used
        in the future.
    (D) The writing of a dictionary is a task of revising an existing
        dictionary so that old or seldom used words are replaced
        with new and popular words.

38. At the end of paragraph 2, the author includes a sentence using
    the word *pails*. The author most likely includes this information
    to help readers understand that
    (A) *pails* is the plural form of the word *pail*.
    (B) Keats, in his poem *Endymion,* uses the word *pail* in an
        unusual or peculiar way.
    (C) collected with each word is a sentence illustrating how it has
        been used.
    (D) the correct meaning of *pail* can be determined by analyzing
        how an intelligent poet like Keats uses the word.

39. Which of the following, according to the passage, should *never*
    occur in the process of writing definitions?
    (A) reading a vast amount of literature
    (B) defining words strictly according to the cards
    (C) legislating how words should be used
    (D) recording what words have meant

40. Which of the following groups of topics best shows the content organization of the passage?
   (A)   I. Collection of words in context
           II. Steps in defining the word *pail*
         III. The future of selected words
   (B)   I. Dictionaries as final authority
           II. The making of a dictionary
         III. The dictionary's value as a historical record
   (C)   I. The correct meanings of words
           II. The making of the *Oxford English Dictionary*
         III. New uses for old words
   (D)   I. A rebel against the dictionary's authority
           II. Collecting definitions
         III. Choosing words to fit new experiences and aims

MATHEMATICS

DIRECTIONS

Solve each problem in this section by using the information given and your own mathematical calculations. Then select the one correct answer of the four choices given.

Following are some mathematical symbols and formulas for reference during your exam.

Common Math Symbols

Symbol References:

$=$ is equal to	$\geq$ is greater than or equal to
$\neq$ is not equal to	$\leq$ is less than or equal to
$>$ is greater than	$\parallel$ is parallel to
$<$ is less than	$\perp$ is perpendicular to

Math Formulas

Triangle
Perimeter $= s_1 + s_2 + s_3$
Area $= \frac{1}{2}bh$

Square
Perimeter $= 4s$
Area $= s \cdot s$, or s^2

Rectangle
Perimeter $= 2(b + h)$, or $2b + 2h$
Area $= bh$, or lw

Parallelogram
Perimeter $= 2(l + w)$, or $2l + 2w$
Area $= bh$

Trapezoid
Perimeter $= b_1 + b_2 + s_1 + s_2$
Area $= \frac{1}{2}h(b_1 + b_2)$, or $h\left(\dfrac{b_1 + b_2}{2}\right)$

Circle
Circumference $= 2\pi r$, or πd
Area $= \pi r^2$

Pythagorean theorem (for right triangles) $a^2 + b^2 = c^2$
 The sum of the squares of the legs of a right triangle equals the square of the hypotenuse.

Cube
Volume $= s \cdot s \cdot s = s^3$
Surface area $= s \cdot s \cdot 6$

Rectangular Prism
Volume $= l \cdot w \cdot h$
Surface area $= 2(lw) + 2(lh) + 2(wh)$

1. 45 is what percent of 300?
   - (A)   6⅔%
   - (B)   15%
   - (C)   45%
   - (D)   355%

2. Simplify.

$$\frac{3 \times 1.8}{0.03}$$

   - (A)   54
   - (B)   180
   - (C)   600
   - (D)   1800

3. Give the closest approximation for $23\tfrac{1}{5} \times 3\tfrac{4}{5}$.
   - (A)   69
   - (B)   72
   - (C)   92
   - (D)   96

4. Of the following, which is the largest?
   - (A)   20% of 30
   - (B)   30% of 20
   - (C)   40% of 15
   - (D)   13% of 50

5. Do the following operations.

$$-3(2 - 1) + 6(-2 + 1)$$

   - (A)   3
   - (B)   −3
   - (C)   −9
   - (D)   −27

6. Which of the following is the scientific notation for 37×10^7?
   - (A) $.37 \times 10^9$
   - (B) 3.7×10^8
   - (C) 37×10^8
   - (D) 3.7×10^9

7. A house is on the market for a selling price of $64,000. The buyer made a $1500 deposit, but fifteeen percent of the selling price is needed for the down payment. How much more money does the buyer need for the down payment?
   (A) $3200
   (B) $6400
   (C) $8100
   (D) $9600

8. In a public library, the librarian is trying to fill a bookshelf that is marked "science fiction" with only science fiction books. The bookshelf has 7 shelves, and each shelf holds 25 books. If the librarian places all of the books and has 21 books left over, how many science fiction books does he have?
   (A) 196
   (B) 175
   (C) 147
   (D) .53

9. On a map of the state of Texas, 1.5 cm represents 5 miles. On the same map, how far would 6 cm represent?
   (A) 6.5 miles
   (B) 7.5 miles
   (C) 9 miles
   (D) 20 miles

10. Use this line graph to answer the following question.

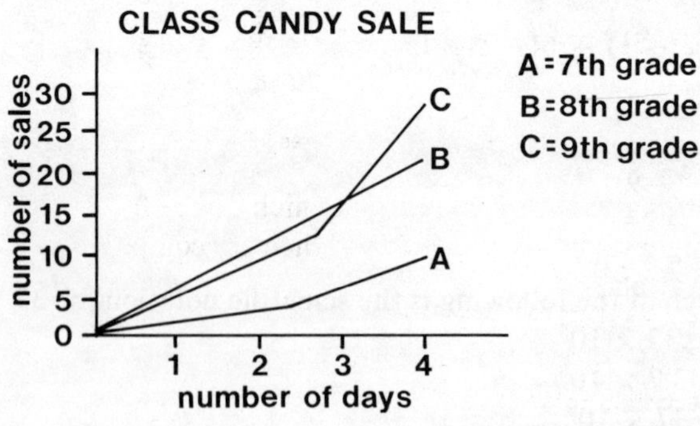

According to the graph, which of the following is true?
(A) The 7th grade sold more candy than did the 8th grade.
(B) By day 3, the 9th and 8th grades sold equal amounts.
(C) The 9th grade sold less than did the 7th grade.
(D) After 2 days, the 7th grade made 10 sales.

11. Use this graph to answer the following question.

ATTENDANCE: SELECTED MAJOR LEAGUE BALL PARKS

Highest Annual, 1948–1985

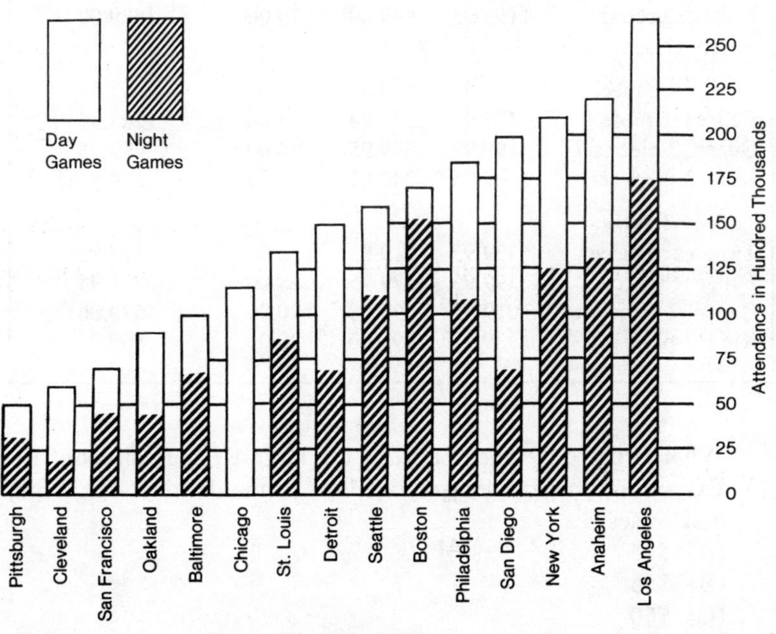

According to the graph above, which of the following cities had the highest night game attendance as compared with its day game attendance?
(A) Los Angeles
(B) New York
(C) Cleveland
(D) Boston

12. Use this table to answer the following question.

SUPER SALE ON MATTRESSES

	Original Price	Sale Price	Bonus Discount	Your Final Cost With Bonus
Regal				
Twin, each piece	299.95	249.00	15.00	234.00
Full, each piece	399.95	299.00	20.00	279.00
Queen, 2-piece set	949.95	499.00	50.00	449.00
King, 3-piece set	1199.95	699.00	70.00	629.00
Extra Firm				
Twin, each piece	329.95	179.95	18.00	161.95
Full, each piece	429.95	249.94	25.00	224.95
Queen, 2-piece set	999.95	549.95	55.00	494.95
King, 3-piece set	1249.95	749.95	75.00	674.95
Royal Satin				
Twin, each piece	329.95	219.95	22.00	197.95
Full, each piece	399.95	279.95	28.00	251.95
Queen, 2-piece set	1019.95	699.00	70.00	629.00
King, 3-piece set	1339.95	899.00	90.00	809.95

What is the difference between the largest bonus discount for Extra Firm mattresses and smallest bonus discount for Regal mattresses?

(A) $75

(B) $65

(C) $60

(D) $57

13. Use this coordinate graph to answer the following question.

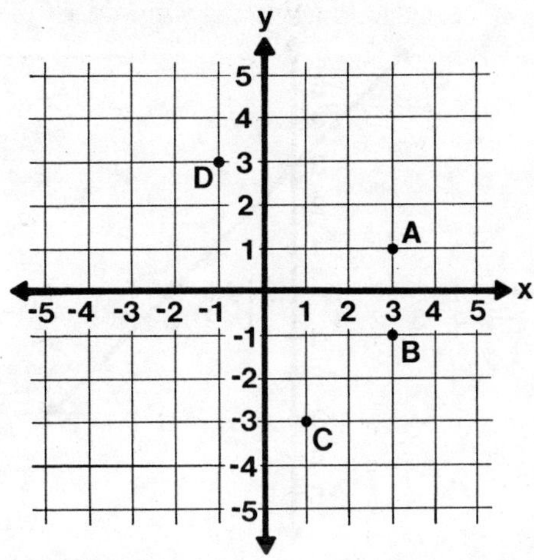

In the coordinate graph above, the points $(-1, 3)$ are represented by

(A) A
(B) B
(C) C
(D) D

14. Use this coordinate graph to answer the following question.

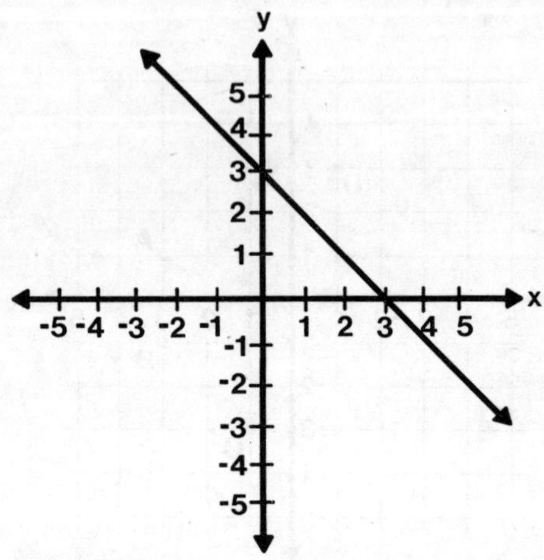

The line in the coordinate graph above represents which of the following equations?

(A) $x = 3$
(B) $y = 3$
(C) $x + y = 3$
(D) $x - y = 3$

15. Given the equation $\frac{3}{4}x - 2 = 7$, find the value of $3x - 1$.
    (A) 12
    (B) 20
    (C) 35
    (D) 36

16. What is the value of x?

    $2x + 4y = 10$
    $3x + 2y = 3$

    (A) -1
    (B)   0
    (C)   1
    (D)   3

17. Find the slope of the line for the equation $6x + y = 3$.
    (A)   6
    (B)   3
    (C) −2
    (D) −6

18. If Shirley rides her bicycle to Martha's house by going 2 miles due north, 3 miles due west, and 2 more miles due north, how may miles is it from Shirley's house to Martha's house in a straight line (as the crow flies)?
    (A) 4 miles
    (B) 4½ miles
    (C) 5 miles
    (D) 6 miles

19. Last year Jorge was three years less than twice Teresa's present age. If Jorge is 10 years old now, which equation will enable Jorge to correctly find Teresa's present age, T?
    (A) $10 + 1 = 2T − 3$
    (B) $9 − 3 = 2T$
    (C) $9 = 2T − 3$
    (D) $11 = 2T − 3$

20. What is the value of d if $8g = 3d + 5$?

    (A) $d = \dfrac{8g + 5}{3}$

    (B) $d = \dfrac{8g − 5}{3}$

    (C) $d = \dfrac{8g}{3} − 5$

    (D) $d = \dfrac{8g}{3} + 5$

21. To find the total surface area in square meters of a rectangular
    solid whose length is 7 meters, width is 6 meters, and depth is 3
    meters, one would use which of the following calculations?
    (A) 7m × 6 m × 3m
    (B) 2(7m × 6m) + 2(6m × 3m) + 2(7m × 3m)
    (C) 7m × 6m + 6m × 3m + 3m × 7m
    (D) 7m × 6m × 3m × 2

22. Donations for a charity were received from five organizations, A,
    B, C, D, and E. Organization A donated ⅕ the total amount
    received; B donated ⅙ the total amount received; C donated
    twice A's donation; D donated half B's donation. What fraction
    was E's donation of the total amount donated?
    (A) $\frac{9}{60}$
    (B) $\frac{7}{30}$
    (C) $\frac{23}{30}$
    (D) $\frac{51}{60}$

23. If the quadratic equation $30x^2 - 19x - 4$ is factored into two
    terms, one of the factors is
    (A) $(4x + 5)$
    (B) $(5x + 4)$
    (C) $(4x - 5)$
    (D) $(5x - 4)$

24. Put the following into its simplest form.

    $$(12r^4s^2 - 3r^3s + 2r) - (7r^4s^2 - 4r^3s - 2rs^2 + 2r)$$

    (A) $5r^4s^2 - 7r^3s - 2rs^2 + 4r$
    (B) $5r^4s^2 + r^3s + 2rs^2$
    (C) $5r^4s^2 + r^3s + 2rs^2 + 4r$
    (D) $19r^4s^2 - r^3s + 4r$

25. Dad's wallet contains 18 bills totaling $134. There are at least
    one each of $1 bills and $5 bills and at least a dozen $10 bills.
    How many $5 bills does the wallet contain?
    (A) 1
    (B) 2
    (C) 3
    (D) 4

26. A plumber charges $45 for the first hour of work and $20 per hour for each additional hour of work after the first. What would be the total bill for labor if the plumber works for 6 consecutive hours?

    (A) $ 65
    (B) $120
    (C) $145
    (D) $165

27. $\dfrac{3a + 4}{a} + \dfrac{2b + 5}{b} =$

    (A) $\dfrac{5ab + 9a}{ab}$

    (B) $\dfrac{5ab + 4b + 5a}{ab}$

    (C) $\dfrac{9 + 3a + 2b}{ab}$

    (D) 14

28. Use this graph to answer the following question.

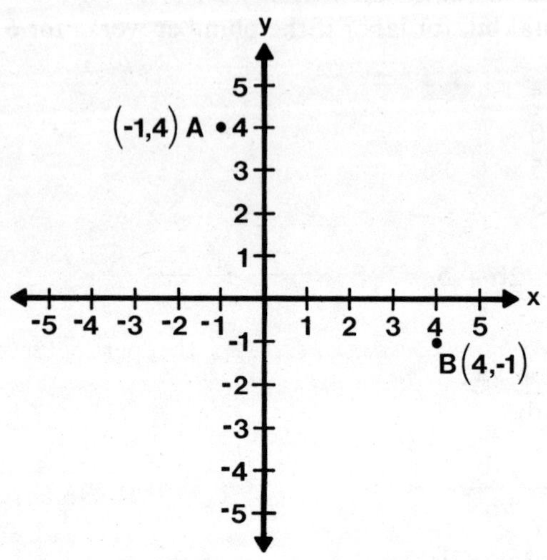

What is the length of line segment AB?
(A) 5
(B) $4\sqrt{2}$
(C) 6
(D) $5\sqrt{2}$

29. What is the product of the roots of the equation
$(3x - 1)(x + 3) = 0$?
(A)   3
(B) $\frac{1}{3}$
(C) $-\frac{1}{3}$
(D) -1

30. If Suzanne first traveled h hours at a speed of m miles per hour
and then traveled an additional q hours at t miles per hour, which
of the following expresses her total distance traveled?
(A) hmtq
(B) (h/m) + (t/q)
(C) (ht)/(mq)
(D) hm + tq

31. Use this diagram to answer the following question.

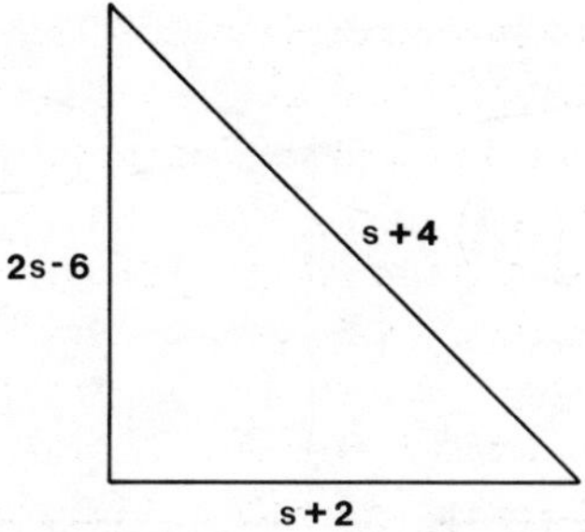

Which of the following expresses the perimeter of the above triangle?
(A) $(2s - 6)(s + 4)$
(B) $\frac{1}{2}(2s - 6)(s + 4)$
(C) $4s$
(D) $4s + 12$

32. What is the approximate area of a circle with diameter of 6 feet?
(A)   18 square feet
(B)   27 square feet
(C)   54 square feet
(D) 108 square feet

33. If the edge of a cube is 5 inches, which of the following is a valid conclusion about the relationship between the units of volume and surface area of that cube?
(A) The volume is equal to the surface area.
(B) The volume is greater than the surface area.
(C) The surface area is greater than the volume.
(D) The surface area and volume differ by 50.

34. Use this diagram to answer the following question.

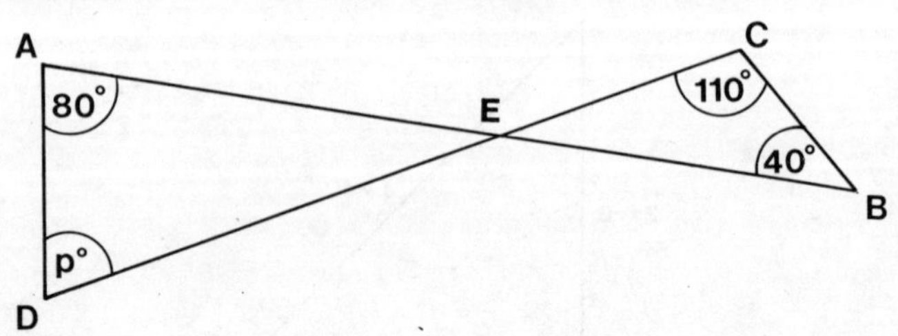

If $\overline{AB}$ intersects $\overline{DC}$ at point E, which of the following must be true?
(A) ∠p must be greater than 50° but less than 70°.
(B) ∠p must equal 90°.
(C) ∠p must be greater than 70° but less than 90°.
(D) ∠p must equal 70°.

35. Use this diagram to answer the following question.

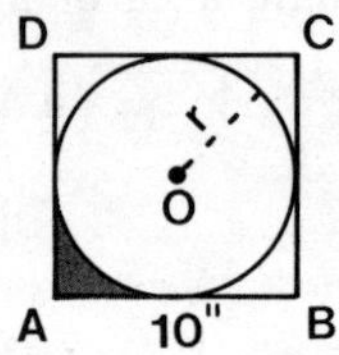

Circle O is inscribed in square ABCD as shown above. The area of the shaded region is approximately
(A)   6 square inches
(B) 25 square inches
(C) 30 square inches
(D) 75 square inches

36. Use this diagram to answer the following question.

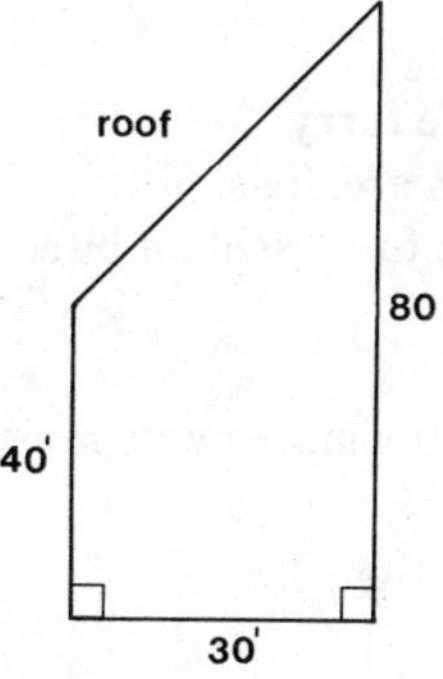

The cross-sectional diagram of a downtown office building shows dimensions as above. What is the length along the roof?
(A) 40 feet
(B) $30\sqrt{2}$ feet
(C) 50 feet
(D) $40\sqrt{3}$ feet

37. The distance traveled by an object in a free fall without any wind resistance is represented by the equation $S = (\frac{1}{2})at^2$, where S is the distance traveled measured in meters, a is the acceleration of gravity measured in meters per second^2, and t is the time measured in seconds. If the falling object has a wind resistance, w, measured in meters per second, the equation becomes $S = (\frac{1}{2})at^2 - w^2$. If the acceleration of gravity is always 16m/sec^2, then what is the difference between the distances traveled of two objects, each falling for 2 minutes, if one of them has a wind resistance of 3 m/sec?
(A)   4 meters
(B)   6 meters
(C)   9 meters
(D) 32 meters

38. Answer the following question by using the statements below.

    1. All cats have tails.
    2. Some animals are furry.
    3. All furry animals are dogs.
    4. Animals that are furry seldom bite.
    5. Chico is a cat.

    Which of the following statements must be true?
    (A) Chico has a tail.
    (B) Chico seldom bites.
    (C) Chico is furry.
    (D) Chico is a dog.

39. The sequence below follows a certain pattern. Answer the
    question that follows by finding the pattern.

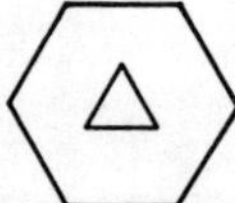 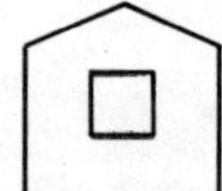 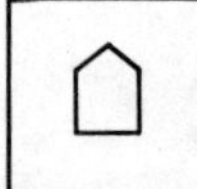 **?**

    Which of the following is the missing design in this sequence?

(A) 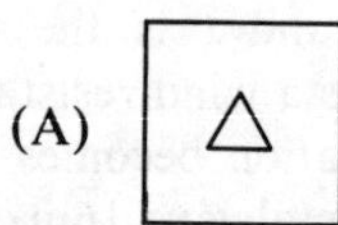

(B) 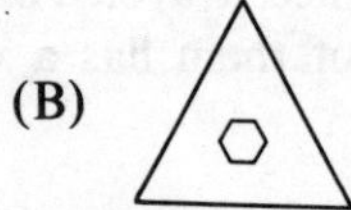

(C) 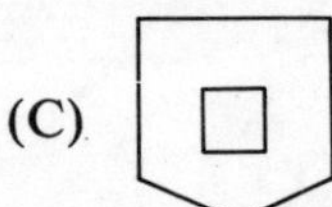

(D) 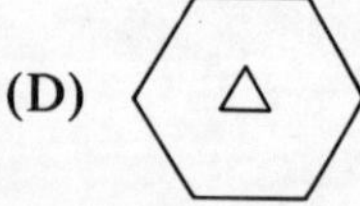

40. Five flagpoles are in a line from left to right. Each flies one flag and each flag is a different color—red, yellow, blue, green, or brown. Answer the following questions by using the statements below.

   I. The red flag is at one end of the line.
  II. The yellow flag flies on the middle flagpole.
III. The blue and green flags are adjacent.

Which of the following must be true?
(A) The blue flag is at one end.
(B) The brown flag is between the red and yellow flags.
(C) The green flag is at one end.
(D) The green flag is next to the red flag.

WRITING—MULTIPLE CHOICE

DIRECTIONS

Each of the passages is followed by questions based on the writing in the passage. Read each passage and answer each of the questions that follow. Each of the small raised numbers identifies the sentence or sentence fragment which follows it.

Questions 1 and 2 are based on the following excerpt from an anthropology text.

[1]The earliest tools which archeologists have a record of are made of stone. [2]Because stone is durable material. [3]But it is likely that the first man-made tools were made of wood or other perishable materials which are easy to work with. [4]These tools, of course, have not survived the passage of time. [5]No doubt early man also made use of ready-made objects which required no modification. [6]Many eoliths are of questionable origin.

[7]The first man-made stone tools are called eoliths. [8]They are often hard to recognize because of their similarity to stones shaped into tool-like forms by the action of natural forces. [9]The earliest eoliths known were found in Africa in the Olduvai Gorge. [10]They may be more than two million years old.

1. Which of the following sentences is nonstandard?
   (A) Sentence 1
   (B) Sentence 2
   (C) Sentence 3
   (D) Sentence 6

2. Which of the following sentences, if moved from the first paragraph to the second, would improve the clarity of both paragraphs?
   (A) Sentence 2
   (B) Sentence 4
   (C) Sentence 5
   (D) Sentence 6

Questions 3, 4, and 5 are based on the following fine arts article.

¹The plastic and graphic arts can be divided into two main categories. ²The first (and most popular) is figurative, or representational, or naturalistic art. ³The second is the abstract, or geometric, art. ⁴Paintings like those of Mondrian which seem to be merely blocks of color are examples of abstract, or geometric, art. ⁵To distinguish between the two kinds is not always easy. ⁶Some painting are both representational and abstract.

⁷Why is representational art so much more popular? ⁸For one thing, it is, at least on the surface, easier to understand. ⁹Seeing a tree on a mountainside or a mother and her baby, the obvious meaning of a picture is at once clear. ¹⁰But when we are faced with three red cubes and one green triangle and the title "Circus," we are confused and disconcerted.

3. Which of the these editorial changes would make the main idea of the first paragraph clearer?
   (A) Omit sentence 1.
   (B) Reverse the order of sentences 2 and 3.
   (C) Add a sentence after sentence 3 that gives an example of a representational artist.
   (D) Omit sentence 6.

4. Which of these changes is needed?
   (A) Sentence 2: Change "is" to "was."
   (B) Sentence 3: Change "is" to "are."
   (C) Sentence 5: Change "kinds" to "kind."
   (D) Sentence 6: Change "painting" to "paintings."

5. Which of the following sentences uses nonstandard placement of a modifier?
   (A) Sentence 5
   (B) Sentence 8
   (C) Sentence 9
   (D) Sentence 10

Questions 6, 7, and 8 are based on the following excerpt from a college writing text.

[1]One good way to approach a question which asks you to explain, analyze, or evaluate is to use a format built around a thesis sentence. [2]The thesis sentence begins with your opinion, followed by the word "because," followed by a list of the most important reasons the opinion is valid reasonable, or well founded. [3]In an essay on the Back to Basics movement in education, for example, you might use the following as a thesis sentence: ____

[4]The thesis statement should conclude <u>your</u> introductory paragraph. [5]Each of the following paragraphs <u>will</u> explain the reasons cited in your thesis sentence. [6]They should give evidence or examples to support your reasons. [7]A concluding paragraph summarizes <u>one's</u> reasons and may repeat your thesis statement in a <u>slightly</u> different form.

6. Which of the following sentences, if inserted in the blank in sentence 3, would best support the main idea of the first paragraph?
   (A) I am a strong supporter of the Back to Basics movement in education which will improve the education of students throughout the nation.
   (B) I am against the Back to Basics movement because it inhibits creativity, fails to recognize the importance of the arts, and restricts the curriculum.
   (C) Back to Basics won't work because what are we going to do with all the teachers who teach subjects that are not Back to Basics subjects, such as music.
   (D) The only way to get our schools and school children to compete with students all over the world is to make sure they know reading, writing, and arithmetic well.

7. Which of these changes in needed?
   (A) Sentence 1: Remove the comma after "explain."
   (B) Sentence 2: Add a comma after "valid."
   (C) Sentence 3: Remove the comma after "education."
   (D) Sentence 3: Change the colon after "sentence" to a comma.

8. Which of the underlined words in the second paragraph should be replaced by a word more consistent with the rest of the passage?
    (A) your
    (B) will
    (C) one's
    (D) slightly

Questions 9 and 10 are based on the following letter to a college newpaper.

[1]The new Menlo Park Street parking lot saves commuters from the half-hour-long search for a parking space on campus. [2]But what good it is if the shuttle buses which are supposed to run every ten minutes run only every half hour? [3]At best. [4]Last week, I waited forty minutes. [5]Friends of mine claim they've had to wait over an hour if they come very early in the morning or after eight at night. [6]If it weren't so far, I'd rather walk than ride the shuttle.

[7]The answer to the problem is to reserve two new on-campus parking structures for the exclusive use of commuter students. [8]The University promised to restrict the Third Street structure for commuter use, but eighty percent of it's spaces go to the faculty. [9]Let's get together and boycott the Menlo Park Street lots. [10]Let the faculty ride the shuttles for a week, and see what happens.

9. Which of the following sentences, if added between sentences 5 and 6, would be most consistent with the style and intent of the passage?
    (A) It is inconvenient for one to have to wait this length of time.
    (B) The shuttle buses are frequently late, and they are unpleasant and uncomfortable to ride in, because they are not clean and carry too many passengers.
    (C) When they do run, the shuttles are overcrowded, smoke filled, and filthy.
    (D) It was the responsibility of the University to see to it that students had a safe place to park.

10. Which of the following changes is needed?
    (A) Sentence 5: Change "they've" to "they have."
    (B) Sentence 6: Change "I'd" to "I have."
    (C) Sentence 8: Change "it's" to "its."
    (D) Sentence 9: Change "Let's" to "Lets."

Questions 11, 12, and 13 are based on the following student English paper.

[1]Some parents, teachers, and educators have tried to spoil the centennial celebration of one of America's greatest novels, *The Adventures of Huckleberry Finn,* by claiming that it and the author Mark Twain were racist. [2]In addition to being a critic of slavery, Mark Twain was fascinated with the subject of transmogrification. [3]Most readers over the years have viewed this masterpiece as anything but offensive to blacks. [4]Beneath the surface of a darn good yarn, it is one of several major writings by Twain that condemn the brutality of slavery. [5]For some who suddenly find the novel offensive, the misunderstanding may lie in Twain's unmatched use of irony and the crude vernacular of river folk to tell the story of the friendship between a runaway Negro slave and young Huck—through the eyes of the uneducated boy.

[6]Any doubts about Twain's views on slavery should have been dispelled by an even later work published in 1894, *Pudd'nhead Wilson.* [7]The famous murder trial story also shows how slavery damages the human personality. [8]It reveals the harm that slavery can do.

[9]But silly detractors apparently need more than the unspoiled and color-blind innocence of Huck or the eccentric but clever lawyer Wilson. [10]For they, we have a letter from Mr. Twain himself, or rather Samuel L. Clemens, the writer's real name. [11]Written the same year as *The Adventures of Huckleberry Finn,* the letter details Twain's offer to pay the expenses of one of the first black students at the Yale Law School. [12]The student Twain befriended and financially assisted, Warner T. McGuinn, was the commencement orator at his graduation and went on to a distinguished legal and political career in Baltimore.

11. Which of these sentences is *least* relevant to the main idea of the first paragraph?
    (A) Sentence 2
    (B) Sentence 3
    (C) Sentence 4
    (D) Sentence 5

12. Which of these sentences should be omitted to avoid unnecessary repetition?
    (A) Sentence 5
    (B) Sentence 6
    (C) Sentence 7
    (D) Sentence 8

13. Which of the following changes is needed?
    (A) Sentence 9: Change "need" to "needs."
    (B) Sentence 10: Change "they" to "them."
    (C) Sentence 11: Change "Twain's" to "Twain."
    (D) Sentence 12: Change "was" to "is."

Questions 14 and 15 are based on the following excerpt from an education text.

[1]The elementary school teacher is reponsible for making all children aware, early in their school careers, that there are two important types of writing. [2]The first, practical writing, which answers practical needs, requires a quality of honesty, clearness, and expression in acceptable form. [3]Such writing may take the form of reports, listings, captions, and plans made by a large group or individual student. [4]______________ personal writing, includes those experiences in which children are free to express their thoughts and ideas in unique ways. [5]______________ such writing may be trivial at the outset, children may realize that the writing experience offers a secret weapon for expressing their innermost feelings.

[6]Beautiful flourishes and creative appendages will no doubt be added as individual students experiment with a unique style, but these must be channeled into the creative realm. [7]Regardless of grade level taught, the elementary school teacher is responsible

for careful and consistent guidance of each child toward improved legibility. [8]Children must become cognizant of the fact that handwriting must be pleasing both to oneself and to the reader. [9]Like music or drawing, handwriting can become a subject students look forward to, especially when they discover their talent. [10]It should never be drudgery to them.

14. Which of the following words or phrases would most logically fit in order into the blanks in the first paragraph?
    (A) The second,—Because
    (B) The second,—Even though
    (C) In addition—Although
    (D) However,—Due to the fact that

15. Which of the these changes would make the sequence of ideas in the second paragraph clearer?
    (A) Move sentence 6 to follow sentence 8.
    (B) Omit sentence 7.
    (C) Omit sentence 9.
    (D) Move sentence 9 to follow sentence 10.

Questions 16, 17, and 18 are based on the following excerpt from an American history text.

[1]Herbert Hoover's life story reads like something taken from the pages of Horatio Alger. [2]Born in West Branch, Iowa, Hoover was orphaned at an early age and taken to Oregon to be cared for by an uncle. [3]He worked his way through the newly established Stanford University and became a mining engineer. [4]After a slow start, achieving great success and becoming a millionaire by the age of forty.

[5]When Calvin Coolidge decided not to seek the nomination in 1928 (although there is some evidence that he wanted to be drafted), Hoover was the logical Republican choice. [6]The nation was enjoying considerable prosperity, and the American people were conditioned to accept the Republican claim that Herbert Hoover as Secretary of Commerce was the "architect of prosperity." [7]The 1928 campaign was, of course, marred by the vicious outburst of religious bigotry directed against the Catholicism of

Al Smith, the Democratic candidate, but Hoover was not responsible for this combat. [8]In fact, Hoover tried to combat and attempted to fight against this prejudice and intolerance. [9]Throughout the 1930's, the Democratic party successfully ran against the image of Hoover as a cold, heartless Republican president who was not only responsible for the Great Depression but also too inhumane to alleviate the sufferings of his fellow Americans.

16. Which of the following sentences is nonstandard?
    (A) Sentence 1
    (B) Sentence 2
    (C) Sentence 3
    (D) Sentence 4

17. Which of the sentences should be changed to reduce its repetition?
    (A) Sentence 5
    (B) Sentence 7
    (C) Sentence 8
    (D) Sentence 9

18. Which of these changes would make the sequence of ideas in the second paragraph clearer?
    (A) Reverse the order of sentences 6 and 7.
    (B) Omit sentence 7.
    (C) Place sentence 9 before sentence 5.
    (D) Omit sentence 9.

Questions 19 and 20 are based on the following student essay.

[1]By the time I was a junior in college, I had developed criteria for good teaching and bad teaching, criteria based on my experiences during those first two college years. [2]The good teachers were always models of enthusiasm and curiosity about their subject. [3]_______________, they were interested in students' fulfilling their own potential and not trying to please the instructor. [4]_______________, they were friendly as well as scholarly. [5]Of the few good teachers I enjoyed, Bob Lincoln (a

professor of English) was the best. [6]Four times a week, sluggish and yawning from listening to my classics professor drone endlessly in a muffled monotone about Zeus and the Olympians, I slumped into Dr. Lincoln's class on the Victorian novel. [7]And always he would lift my spirits with his own spirited approach. [8]He never imposed his viewpoints on <u>us</u>. [9]The importance of the literature was <u>ours</u> to decide. [10]We kept journals in which <u>I</u> wrote about how instances in the novels were like those in our own experience. And by sharing those responses in class, we learned how many different viewpoints a novel can provoke and learned to respect each other's differences. [11]All this came about because Dr. Lincoln was more interested in what the subject meant to us than what it meant to <u>him</u>.

19. Which of the following words or phrases would most logically fit in order into the blanks in the first paragraph?
    (A) In addition— Finally
    (B) Yet—Because
    (C) Because—Because
    (D) Second—On the contrary

20. Which of the underlined words in the second paragraph should be replaced by a different pronoun?
    (A) Sentence 8: us
    (B) Sentence 9: ours
    (C) Sentence 10: I
    (D) Sentence 11: him

Questions 21, 22, and 23 are based on the following excerpt from a college history text.

[1]Thomas Jefferson's dream of a nation of independent self-sufficient farmers was lost forever in the post-Civil War years as Alexander Hamilton's more pragmatic vision of a nation of manufacturers and workers unfolded on a vaster scale than even he could have ever imagined. [2]The reasons for this great industrial boom are not difficult to grasp. [3]The United States was blessed with a bountiful supply of natural resources such as iron ore, gold, silver, and copper. [4]It possessed a magnificent trans-

portation system of rivers, canals, and railroads; a large domestic market; and an unlimited supply of low-cost labor as a result of immigration. [5]Another important factor was the scientific advances that led to a large number of inventions.

[6] ____

[7]Sometimes known as "the robber barons," the majority of these men came from humble backgrounds, built great industrial empires, and amassed huge personal fortunes. [8]The three best known are John D. Rockefeller, whose wealth, earned chiefly in oil, was estimated at over $815 million in 1982; Andrew Carnegie, the steel magnate, who averaged $7.5 million in profits for several years and then sold his holdings in 1900 for over $400 million; and J. Pierpont Morgan, _______________________

____ .

[9]For many years it was the fashion to condemn these industrial giants of the Gilded Age as ruthless, greedy individuals who clawed their way to the top by fair means or foul. [10]A revisionist trend in recent years is trying to rewrite the history of the Gilded Age in order to place the business leaders in a more favorable perspective. [11]While there is no doubt that these titans of business and finance helped to make America a powerful industrial nation; the fact remains that they also exploited their workers, bribed politicians, cheated customers, and ruthlessly crushed their competitors.

21. Which of the following sentences, if inserted in the blank labeled sentence 6, would *best* make the transition from the first to the second paragraph and appropriately introduce the subject of the second paragraph?
    (A) The skill and shrewdness of many of the business tycoons of the period also contributed to the rapid industrialization.
    (B) It was Hamilton, not Jefferson, who saw more clearly what the future would bring.
    (C) The period known as the Gilded Age was famous for its very rich men.
    (D) The tycoons of the period were very successful despite their poor beginnings.

22. Which of the following clauses could most logically be inserted in the blank in sentence 8?
    (A) who was the third
    (B) the banker, who accumulated immense wealth while becoming the most powerful figure in the history of American finance
    (C) whose wealth was enormous, and who lived a very reclusive private life
    (D) who was New York's leading socialite, and whose houses were lavishly decorated by the finest artists

23. Which of these changes is needed in the second paragraph?
    (A) Sentence 9: Place a comma after the word "individuals."
    (B) Sentence 10: Place a semicolon after the word "Age."
    (C) Sentence 11: Change the semicolon after the word "nation" to a comma.
    (D) Sentence 11: Change the comma after the word "customers" to a semicolon.

Questions 24 and 25 are based on the following excerpt from an economics text.

[1]The vicious cycle of poverty makes it extremely difficult for an underdeveloped nation to achieve a significant level of economic growth through its own efforts. [2]This is so because a disproportionate amount of a poor nation's productive capacity (60%–70%) has to be used to produce goods for current consumption (food, clothing, shelter) leaving very little to be set aside for the production of investment or capital goods (tools, factories, machinery). [3]Thus the cycle. [4]A country that has little capital is poor. [5]A country is poor because it has little capital. [6]With little capital it must concentrate on consumer goods. [7]Concentration on consumer goods prevents an increase in capital goods. [8]With little capital, production levels cannot be increased. [9]With constant production and increasing population, the country remains poor.

[10]The cumulative nature of economic growth <u>makes</u> it clear that if one country is growing at a faster rate than another, the

result <u>will be</u> an increasing gap between their standards of living.
[11]For example, if two countries have the same income level now,
but one is <u>growing</u> at a 3% rate and the other at a 2% rate, in just
72 years the income level of the 3% country <u>is</u> double that of the
2% country.

24. Which of the following sentences should be omitted to eliminate
    repetition?
    (A) Sentence 5
    (B) Sentence 6
    (C) Sentence 7
    (D) Sentence 8

25 Which of the underlined verbs in the second paragraph shows an
   error in tense?
   (A) Sentence 10: makes
   (B) Sentence 10: will be
   (C) Sentence 11: is growing
   (D) Sentence 11: is

*Questions 26 and 27 are based on the following excerpt from a social
science text.*

   Laws controlling the conduct of elections vary widely from
one state to another. [2]While encouraging citizens to register and
vote, many states have erected formidable barriers to effective
voting in the form of difficult registration procedures, incompre-
hensible, long ballots, and other technical requirements. [3]And
convincing statistics are advanced which indicate that a smaller
proportion of Americans vote than citizens of most European
countries. [4]Some discriminatory state barriers to voting, such as
the poll tax and literacy tests, have been ruled out by the national
government. [5]In addition, recent federal court decisions indicate
that lengthy residence requirements for voter registration are on
the way out.
   [6]The U.S. Census Bureau has estimated that Americans are
<u>contested</u> with more than 100,000 elections each year, consider-
ing all offices within the 50 states. [7]Within the outlines of the
United States Constitution, state legislatures are responsible for

setting the ground rules regulating the electoral process. [8]States must comply with the fifteenth amendment's enfranchisement of blacks, the nineteenth amendment's enfranchisement of eighteen-year-olds, and federal statutes relating to voting in elections. [9]Otherwise the prerogative remains with state legislatures.

26. Which of these changes would make the sequence in the first paragraph clearer?
    (A) Reverse the order of sentences 1 and 2.
    (B) Place sentence 3 before sentence 1.
    (C) Omit sentence 3.
    (D) Reverse the order of sentences 3 and 4.

27. Which of the following should be used in place of the underlined word in sentence 6?
    (A) confronted
    (B) complied
    (C) subjected
    (D) compliant

Questions 28, 29, and 30 are based on the following magazine article.

[1]During my first week at the hospital, I was assigned to the children's wards. [2]One of the first patients I encountered was a four-year-old child pinned tightly with the label of "autistic." [3]His name was Gregory, and in him I saw immediately all that I had previously only read about. [4]He had all of the usual behaviors of a child who was autistic. [5]He would not respond to touch or affection, engaged in constant finger flicking and hand gazing, and seemed to withdraw into his own world.

[6]In the days that passed, I spent much time with Gregory, involving him in whatever I was doing, always maintaining some physical contact with him. [7]It was not until the fourteenth day that I dropped the label I had pinned upon him.

[8]Gregory and I frequently engaged in games, but his favorite game was entitled "Up." [9]In this game, I was to lift Gregory into the air as he gleefully shouted, "up, up!" [10]After several times

my arms grew wearily, and instead of putting him down, Gregory remained in my arms. [11]There we stood in an embrace of trust—an opening to a place beyond his label. [12]Tears flowed freely from my eyes as he calmly touched each one with his fingers, smiling as their wetness served to cement our relationship. [13]Somehow, in that moment, all of what I had read mattered little compared to what I knew. [14]As my teacher had warned us in class, "The labels only serve to make things easy—it is up to you to discover the truth."

28. Which of the following sentences, if added after sentence 5 at the end of the first paragraph, would be most consistent with the style and intent of the passage?
    (A) "Same old story," I thought; "the kid is beyond me."
    (B) By definition, autism is a state of mind characterized by daydreaming, hallucinations, and disregard of external reality.
    (C) He seemed to fit exactly everything I could remember from my textbooks about autism.
    (D) In the work of the most respected psychologists, one reads that the autistic child is extremely unreachable.

29. Which of the following sentences uses nonstandard placement of a modifier?
    (A) Sentence 10
    (B) Sentence 11
    (C) Sentence 12
    (D) Sentence 13

30. Which of these changes is needed?
    (A) Sentence 8: Change "frequently" to "frequent."
    (B) Sentence 9: Change "gleefully" to "gleeful."
    (C) Sentence 10: Change "wearily" to "weary."
    (D) Sentence 12: Change "freely" to "free."

Questions 31 and 32 are based on the following magazine article.

[1]Those teenagers and young adults who accounted for talk-show host Dave Considine's high ratings years ago are precisely the viewers who are his audience of today. [2]The twenty-year-old radical of 1969 is now the middle-aged, middle-class viewer who loves late-night television. [3]Eighty-five percent of the viewers of daytime television are women, according to polls take in California and New England. [4]Although these viewers no longer fight for controversial issues, they recall with happy nostalgia those days of political rebellion and "dangerous" comedy and identify with the heroes of their youth. [5]Considine is one of those heroes, as the popularity of his "Remember the Sixties" special demonstrates.

[6]Dave has lost none of the comedic talent, ability to be funny, and skill in raising laughs that brought him tremendous early popularity. [7]He continues to be in demand internationally, and he is invited back again and again for appearances on other networks. [8]His talent as a sketch comedian was remarkable in his first series and has matured since then.

31. Which of these changes would help focus atention on the main idea of the first paragraph?
    (A) Omit sentence 3.
    (B) Remove the phrase "and identify with the heroes of their youth" from sentence 4.
    (C) Change the period at the end of sentence 4 to a comma followed by "and."
    (D) Omit sentence 5.

32. Which of these sentences should be changed to avoid its repetition?
    (A) Sentence 5
    (B) Sentence 6
    (C) Sentence 7
    (D) Sentence 8

Questions 33, 34, and 35 are based on the following student essay.

[1]A unicorn is a mythical beast, you say. [2]Oh, no, it isn't. [3]There's one on display right now in New York, during the Madison Square Garden appearance of the Ringling Brothers and Barnum & Bailey Circus. [4]This circus unicorn is a billy goat with a black polished horn growing straight from the center of his forehead. [5]It appears the goat's horns were fused together in infancy. [6]The operation <u>is told</u> to be painless.

[7]This unicorn is really getting the goat of officials from the American Society for the Prevention of Cruelty to Animals. [8]They want to know where he came from so they can stop any future "creations." [9]Actually, the ASPCA comes to the rescue rather late. Unicorns have been in the news for several years, appearing at carnivals and festivals. [10]In ancient days, hunters were convinced that unicorns were suckers for purity and beauty. [11]One of the first of the modern-day unicorns was created by Dr. W. Franklin Dove at the University of Maine in 1933. [12]Dr. Dove transplanted the horn buds of a day-old Ayrshire bull calf from the side of it's head to the center. [13]In the bull's later life, the horn proved to be a great weapon, and he became the leader of the herd.

33. Which of the following should replace the underlined words in sentence 6?
    (A) are said
    (B) is saying
    (C) was told
    (D) is said

34. Which of these sentences is *least* relevant to the main ideas of the second paragraph?
    (A) Sentence 9
    (B) Sentence 10
    (C) Sentence 11
    (D) Sentence 13

35. Which of the these changes is needed?
    (A) Sentence 1: Change "you say" to "says you."
    (B) Sentence 3: Change "There's" to "Theirs."
    (C) Sentence 8: Remove the quotation marks from "creations."
    (D) Sentence 12: Change "it's" to "its."

Questions 36, 37, and 38 are based on the following student paper.

[1]Some people argue that a poem can mean whatever the reader thinks it means. [2]Every reader, they argue, is different and brings to every poem a unique background and experience, which is different from everyone else's. [3]For instance, when I read Jarrel's poem about the dead World War II gunner, I think the poem is all about the horror of war. [4]But you may think the poem praises courage in the face of annihilation. [5]Whose to say which of us is right or wrong?

[6]People usually see poems as support for what they already believe. [7]Someone who is a pacifist before reading the Jarrell poem will probably see the poem as an attack on war. [8]But someone who is in the army will be more likely to see the poem as glorifying military sacrifice. [9]In short, how one reads a poem depends on the beliefs and attitudes you bring to it.

36. Which of the these sentences should be changed to avoid its repetition?
    (A) Sentence 2
    (B) Sentence 3
    (C) Sentence 4
    (D) Sentence 5

37. Which of the following changes is needed?
    (A) Sentence 3: Insert a comma after "think."
    (B) Sentence 5: Change "Whose" to "Who's."
    (C) Sentence 7: Insert a comma after "Someone."
    (D) Sentence 9: Remove the comma after "short."

38. Which of these sentences includes nonstandard use of a pronoun?
    (A) Sentence 6
    (B) Sentence 7
    (C) Sentence 8
    (D) Sentence 9

Questions 39 and 40 are based on this excerpt from a geology text.

[1]The history of the changes in the life forms of the planet is the story of evolution. [2]Life seems to have originated in the primeval waters. [3]The first organisms were structurally similar to viruses, consisting of chains of protein molecules. [4]Progressive differentiation led to the first cellular organisms. [5]Eventually, minute invertebrate forms evolved into the first known vertebrate animals, the fishes. [6]The single-celled animals, mircoscopic in size, are called protozoans. [7]The planet's vertebrate fauna was strictly aquatic until Devonian times.

[8]Amphibians were the first vertebrates to occupy a <u>dry environment</u>. [9]Sometime in the <u>mysterious abyss</u> of the past a transitional form between fish and amphibian appeared which had developed limbs and a respiratory system capable of <u>utilizing oxygen</u> directly from the atmosphere. [10]But the amphibians were destined to remain a <u>transitional form</u>. [11]In fact, many modern forms have returned to the water permanently.

39. Which of these changes would make the sequence of ideas in the first paragraph clearer?
    (A) Omit sentence 2.
    (B) Reverse the order of sentences 4 and 5.
    (C) Reverse the order of sentences 5 and 6.
    (D) Omit sentence 7.

40. Which of the underlined phrases in the second paragaph is different in style from the rest of the passage?
    (A) dry environment
    (B) mysterious abyss
    (C) utilizing oxygen
    (D) transitional form

WRITING SAMPLE

DIRECTIONS

For this section, you should spend approximately 60 minutes to plan and write your essay. You may use the bottom of your directions page to organize and plan before you begin writing. You should plan your time wisely, using enough time to understand the question, plan and outline, write, and finally reread your essay and revise if necessary.

You must write on the specified topic. An essay on another topic will not be acceptable.

Your essay must be written on the lined pages provided. (For this simulation test, use three sides of an 8½″ by 11″ page.) No other paper may be used. Your writing should be neat and legible. Do not skip lines, do not write excessively large, and do not leave large margins.

Your essay will be judged for its

- being on topic

- clarity

- support and development

- organization

- use of correct standard written English

No reference materials (dictionary, thesaurus, etc.) may be used.

Topic

The Chamber of Commerce of your community each year makes a contribution to a worthy cause. This year the Chamber is prepared to donate $50,000 but is undecided whether that amount should be given to the Parks Department to renovate its deteriorating community recreational facility (consisting of tennis courts, ballfields, playgrounds, picnic area, and swimming pool) or to the town library, which has had to shorten its hours and restrict its services due to low funding. Two facts are certain: (1) The donation will solve the problems of only one facility, either the park *or* the library, but not both. (2) The Chamber has decided not to split its donation but to give the full $50,000 to only one of the two facilities. Decide which facility (the park or the library) you believe is the more deserving of the grant. Write an essay persuading the members of the Chamber of Commerce to vote for your choice. Support your position using examples from your own experience, reading, and/or observations.

Essay Checklist

Use the following checklist to evaluate your finished essay:

A well-written essay will

☐ be on topic: Does your essay address the assignment? Does it complete all the tasks set by the topic?

☐ be written clearly: Is your essay consistent in its tone and its arguments? Is it carefully focused on the assignment?

☐ be well developed: Does your essay use lots of specific examples and details to support its points?

☐ use language correctly and skillfully: Is your essay written in standard written English, with only minor flaws, if any, in grammar, sentence structure, and punctuation?

☐ be well organized: Is each paragraph one main idea? Are there smooth transitions between paragraphs? Is the entire essay unified?

☐ be legible: Is your handwriting neat enough to be read and understood?

ANSWER KEY FOR PRACTICE TEST 2

Reading		Mathematics		Writing Multiple Choice	
1. C	21. C	1. B	21. B	1. B	21. A
2. B	22. B	2. B	22. A	2. D	22. B
3. D	23. A	3. C	23. D	3. C	23. C
4. C	24. D	4. D	24. D	4. D	24. A
5. B	25. D	5. C	25. B	5. C	25. D
6. A	26. A	6. B	26. C	6. B	26. C
7. C	27. C	7. C	27. B	7. B	27. A
8. B	28. D	8. A	28. D	8. C	28. C
9. D	29. C	9. D	29. D	9. C	29. A
10. C	30. B	10. B	30. D	10. C	30. C
11. C	31. B	11. D	31. C	11. A	31. A
12. D	32. C	12. C	32. B	12. D	32. B
13. A	33. C	13. D	33. C	13. B	33. D
14. C	34. D	14. C	34. D	14. B	34. B
15. D	35. C	15. C	35. A	15. A	35. D
16. B	36. A	16. A	36. C	16. D	36. A
17. C	37. B	17. D	37. C	17. C	37. B
18. A	38. C	18. C	38. A	18. D	38. D
19. C	39. C	19. C	39. B	19. A	39. C
20. A	40. B	20. A	40. B	20. C	40. B

ANALYZING YOUR TEST RESULTS

The following charts should be used to carefully analyze your results and spot your strengths and weaknesses. The complete process of analyzing each subject area and each individual question should be completed for this Practice Test. These results should be reexamined for trends in types of error (repeated errors) or poor results in specific subject areas. THIS REEXAMINATION AND ANALYSIS IS OF TREMENDOUS IMPORTANCE FOR EFFECTIVE TEST PREPARATION.

PRACTICE TEST 2: SUBJECT AREA ANALYSIS SHEET

	Possible	Completed	Right	Wrong
Reading	40			
Mathematics	40			
Writing—Multiple Choice	40			
TOTAL	120			

ANALYSIS—TALLY SHEET FOR QUESTIONS MISSED

One of the most important parts of test preparation is analyzing why you missed a question so that you can reduce the number of future mistakes. Now that you have taken Practice Test 2 and corrected your answers, carefully tally your mistakes by marking them in the proper column.

	REASON FOR MISTAKE			
	Total Missed	Simple Mistake	Misread Problem	Lack of Knowledge
Reading				
Mathematics				
Writing—Multiple Choice				
TOTAL				

Reviewing the above data should help you determine WHY you are missing certain questions. Now that you have pinpointed the type of error, focus on avoiding your most common type.

ANSWERS AND COMPLETE EXPLANATIONS
FOR PRACTICE TEST 2

READING

1. (C) As it is used in this paragraph, a *critical attitude of mind* is one that is independent and based upon reasons that *appear to be adequate*. The word *critical* can have several meanings. Choice (A) assumes *critical* means *tending to find fault,* but the context makes it clear that choice (C), which defines *critical* as characterized by careful analysis is the correct answer.

2. (B) Choice (D) makes a claim for philosophy which is not supported by the passage. The ideas of choices (A) and (C) are parts of the passage, but only choice (B) makes clear that the passage offers a number of points to support an argument for the usefulness of philosophy.

3. (D) Choices (A), (B), and (C) distort specific points made in the passage. Only (D) is an assumption that could motivate the writer to claim that philosophy has many uses and specific values.

4. (C) Choice (A) overstates what are only occasional references (in paragraphs 4 and 6) to how philosophy differs from science and religion. Choice (B) states a subordinate point noted only in the first paragraph. Choice (D) also states a subordinate point.

5. (B) Paragraphs 4 and 6 indicate that the results of scientific research have bearing on choices (A), (C), and (D). Paragraph 4 discusses how sciences *report what is* and provide *factual information.* Paragraph 6 indicates that science is able to answer only questions which allow for *experiment and observation.* Paragraph 4 also makes it clear that questions of value are *outside the sphere of the physical sciences.*

6. (A) The context makes it clear that a *dossier* is something the students are studying before the meeting. Paragraph 3 refers to this *report,* and the last paragraph refers to a *new dossier* on the Dean of the Law School.

7. (C) Because the passage pokes fun at student evaluators, choice (A) is false. The selection does not focus specifically on research as is suggested by choices (B) and (D). Only choice (C) identifies how the satirical story points to a possible time when students have control over professors.

8. **(B)** Choice (C) states that the selection dramatizes *what currently goes on;* the author introduces the scene as something that could go on in the future. Choice (A) mistakenly suggests that the passage uplifts or invigorates the imaginations of readers. Only choice (B) indicates that the passage is satirical.

9. **(D)** This point from the report is stated explicitly in paragraph 8. Points made by choices (A), (B), and (C) are not acknowledged as being in the report. Higgins states how much television he watches and that he is writing a book on Antarctic philosophy. Higgins is given the opportunity to smoke.

10. **(C)** In paragraph 7, one of the students ridicules Professor Higgins for taking his work much too lightly, as if he were enjoying the freedom and pleasures available at a country club. The comic point is that a remark like this is normally made by a professor to a student. Choice (A) is incorrect because it would be nonsense for the student simply to clarify something so obvious during his stern lecture. The student is clearly not referring to a literal country club; thus choices (B) and (D) are improbable.

11. **(C)** The parts of the word *presentiment* offer the best clue to its meaning. The prefix *pre-* means *before* or *earlier than.* The root *sentiment* refers to a feeling or emotion. Taken together the word parts carry the idea of an advance feeling, or a feeling about the future. Also supporting choice (C) is much of the language in paragraph 3—*there is a sense of tragedy in the air, a grim foreboding; a nameless dread.* Choice (B) speaks of resistance to a parent's wishes. Although Romeo and Juliet are in love against their parent's wishes, no direct reference is made to the Montagues and Capulets in paragraph 3.

12. **(D)** Choice (D) makes clear that the speed and passion of the play reflect the idea that *Consuming love calls for haste.* Choice (A) inaccurately represents what the author says the play is about. Choice (C) twists the meaning of the phrase *three long hours,* which in fact indicates not how an audience feels about the length of the play, but how an impatient character experiences the time from *nine till twelve.*

13. **(A)** Best supporting choice (A) are the topic sentences of paragraphs 1 (which explains the play's theme) and 2 (which

explains one aspect of its atmosphere). Choice (B) is incorrect in asserting that the writer is critical; the discussion of the pace is intended only to clarify its role in expressing the theme of consuming love.

14. (C) Death is personified when Romeo refers to death as *he*. Choice (B) reverses the meaning of *love-devouring death;* actually, death devours love. Choice (D) runs counter to Romeo's challenge, which expresses his defiance, not fear, of death.

15. (D) Choice (D) is the most probable explanation. The entire context of paragraph 3 points to a soon-approaching death. To say that Juliet looks on Romeo alive for the last time is to suggest that soon she will look on him again, dead, as in her vision. Choices (A) and (C) suggest that the author uses the word *alive* in a figurative or metaphorical sense, but there is nothing to indicate that *alive* should not be taken literally.

16. (B) Paragraph 6 emphasizes how ordinary the casserole is. It's inexpensive and easy to prepare; it has simple, healthy ingredients. Yet, the delicious taste of a casserole often *belies* or *contradicts* one's expectations. Because the selection seeks to interest readers in casserole-making, one would imagine that the taste of a casserole would rise higher than its humble origins and easy preparation. However, choices (A) and (C) seem to suggest that the taste is on the same level. Choice (D) seems to suggest that it might, in fact, be lower.

17. (C) Choice (A) distorts the fact that cooks of the early 1900s moved away from the art of scratch cooking. Choice (B) makes far too extreme a claim in saying that past and present-day cooks are interested only in making casseroles from prepackaged ingredients. Choice (D) is incorrect, in part, as it states that the lure of casseroles for contemporary cooks is a nostalgic '50s evening. Choice (C) is the best answer because it asserts that the old-time casserole cooks were led toward convenience, while present-day cooks are led toward a little more time spent cooking.

18. (A) The writer would most likely agree with choice (A) because the attractions of the casserole are great enough for one to expect it to reemerge periodically as a popular dish. Choices (B), (C), and (D) all make assertions that are not supported by evidence in the passage.

19. (C) Despite the fact that a dish is only as healthy as the ingredients that go into it, the author gives readers good reason to believe that casseroles are easy to prepare, inexpensive, and nutritious. The concern in choice (B) over the absence of information on advertising strategies is irrelevant to the author's purpose. Choice (D) makes a highly doubtful assertion about the levels of protein and fat in the average casserole.

20. (A) Choice (A) offers the most accurate and complete outline of the information in the passage. Topic I in choice (B) would better read *Nostalgia for the 1950s*. Topic I in choice (C) suggests an opposition that is not dealt with in the passage. Choice (D) introduces the topic of *Casseroles and protein*, but this relationship is not covered in the passage.

21. (C) The word *sculls* can refer to either the light racing boats used in competitive rowing or to the oars which propel a boat. The context makes it clear that the second meaning is used here. The word for the head sounds the same but is spelled *skull*.

22. (B) We have several clues that suggest the something in tow is a human body. The girl's look of dread or horror, the man's having coins after leaning into the river, the girl's being afraid of the cargo, and the stain on the boat associated with blood and a human form all suggest that the boat plies the river seeking the bodies of dead persons.

23. (A) Of the four choices, only (A) can be well supported by the passage. Though the passage does give a few descriptive details of the river, these are only incidental. Though the book might go on to make a social statement like that in choices (B) or (C), this passage is more concerned with introducing the two characters and their grim business while powerfully suggesting the horror of the scene.

24. (D) Choices (A) and (B) are assertions of the narrator of the passage and not opinions of the characters. Choice (C) is an order of one character, while (D) is the father's opinion of the role the river plays in his daughter's life.

25. (D) The reference to the human-shaped stain on the bottom of the boat, with the added detail of its color, like diluted blood, points to the identification of what is towed as a corpse.

26. (A) One root of the word *monotheistic* is *mono-,* the prefix meaning *one.* The same root is the basis of words like *monoplane, monologue, monocle, or monotony.* The first paragraph refers to the Moslem tolerance of Christians and Jews, two other monotheistic religions.

27. (C) The final paragraph speaks of the Arabs' learning of the zero from the Indians and devising the system (Arabic numerals) transmitted to the West.

28. (D) The word *calculus* has a Latin root. The passage does not identify the word *calculus* as being of Arabic origin. The *al* prefix of the three Arabic-derived words means *the.*

29. (C) Choice (C) gives an accurate summary of the content of each of the three paragraphs. Though the first sentence of the third paragraph refers to Spain, the real topic of the paragraph is Moslem influence in the sciences and philosophy. The first paragraph discusses Mohammed and the founding of Islam; the second paragraph is about the rapid rise of the Islamic Empire.

30. (B) The role of Spain is a minor issue, and choice (C) misrepresents the content of the paragraph. Though the paragraph does discuss the Middle Ages, its specific focus is on Islamic contributions, not on the period in general.

31. (B) The word *cumulative* as the instructor uses it means that the final exam will evaluate knowledge of the material *accumulated* over the entire semester. Using the three midterms as a study tool will help prepare students on material that was covered up to the third midterm; but students are also responsible for material after the third midterm and until the last day of instruction. Choice (D) should be considered incorrect because each midterm exam is worth the same percentage of the course grade.

32. (C) In paragraphs 2 and 3, and in the second-to-last sentence of the syllabus, the instructor stresses that the best way to learn chemistry is through working as many practice problems as possible. Choice (B) attributes a critical attitude to the instructor; however the overall tone in the syllabus is positive, not negative. For example, he or she says, *The labs explore course topics in a spirit of inquiry that your textbook study of them cannot duplicate.* This speaks to students as if they want to get the most from the course, not just to get by.

33. (C) Choice (C) is supported by the instructor's statement *I cover topics in lecture that are not included in your reading.* Attendance and participation, the concerns of choices (A) and (D), do not figure into Professor Brewster's grading system; so they are not hazards. Choice (B) does not state a hazard because Chem 100 is not the lab course.

34. (D) Choices (A), (B), and (C) are facts, not open to dispute. Choice (D), however, is an opinion. One could easily argue that some students would not be surprised at how the study technique improves comprehension.

35. (C) Since there are eight topics to be covered in the course, students will be assigned to read eight chapters.

36. (A) The context in which *docility* is used makes it clear that it refers to meaningful movement of the body. Choices (C) and (D) speak only to physical movements, not significant ones. The context also suggests that *docility* refers to a willing, not reluctant, action.

37. (B) Choices (A) and (C) are contradicted by the statements in paragraph 5 that *The writing of a dictionary, therefore, is not a task of setting up authoritative statements about the "true meanings" of words* and that *The writer of a dictionary is a historian, not a law-giver.* That choice (B) is the best statement of the main idea is made clear at the end of paragraph 5.

38. (C) Because the author discourages any authoritative view that words have *true meanings,* choice (D) is eliminated because it speaks of a *correct* meaning. Just prior to the *pail* sentence is an account of an editor's process of copying words and their uses on cards. The word *thus* signals that what follows is an illustration of the process.

39. (C) Choices (A), (B), and (D) are all identified as part of the process of writing definitions. The correctness of choice (C) is revealed when the writer of a dictionary is said *not* to be a *law-giver.*

40. (B) Topic II in choice (A) is not covered in the passage. Topic II in choice (C) is too narrow; the larger topic is the making of any dictionary. Topic I in choice (D) inaccurately implies that there is a specific individual who is a rebel against the dictionary's authority. Only choice (B) identifies the major topics covered in the passage.

MATHEMATICS

1. (B) Since the answer choices are far apart in value, the fastest technique is to quickly estimate. Round 45 to 50, so the problem now is "50 is what percent of 300?" Since 50 goes into 300 six times, 50 is one sixth of 300, which is slightly less than one fifth (20%). The closest answer slightly less than 20% is 15% (choice B).

Mathematically, you could work to the exact answer by dividing the "part" (45) by the "whole" (300):

$$45 \div 300 = .15 \text{ or } 15\%$$

2. (B) First multiply both the top and bottom of the fraction by 100 to clear the decimals:

$$\frac{3 \times 1.8}{0.03}$$

$$\frac{3 \times 1.8 \times 100}{0.03 \times 100} = \frac{3 \times 180}{3} = \frac{180}{1} = 180$$

3. (C) To estimate, round to whole numbers. In this problem, round $23\frac{1}{5}$ down to 23, and round $3\frac{4}{5}$ up to 4. So the problem is now 23×4, which equals 92.

4. (D) Since "of" means multiply, you would get

(A) 20% of 30 = .20 × 30 = 6
(B) 30% of 20 = .30 × 20 = 6
(C) 40% of 15 = .40 × 15 = 6
(D) 13% of 50 = .13 × 50 = 6.5

Therefore, (D) is the largest.

5. (C) If multiplication, addition, parentheses, etc., are all contained in one problem, the order of operations is as follows: (1) parentheses, (2) powers and square roots, (3) multiplication and division, whichever comes first, left to right, and (4) addition and subtraction, whichever comes first, left to right. Therefore,

$$-3(2 - 1) + 6(-2 + 1) =$$
$$-3(1) + 6(-1) =$$
$$-3 + (-6) = -9$$

6. (B) To change 37×10^7 to scientific notation, simply move the decimal point one place to the left and add one more power to the exponent of 10^7.

$$37. \times 10^7 = 3.7 \times 10^8$$

7. (C) Fifteen percent of the selling price is needed for a down payment. Since the selling price of the house is $64,000, 15% of the selling price equals

$$(.15)(\$64,000) = \$9600$$

The buyer has already paid $1500 towards the deposit, so to figure how much *more* money is needed for the down payment, subtract $1500 from $9600:

$$\$9600 - \$1500 = \$8100$$

8. (A) The librarian has completely filled 7 shelves with 25 books each (7×25), which equals 175 books, and still has 21 *more* books that haven't been shelved. The total number of science fiction books is therefore 175 shelved *plus* 21 left over, or a total of 196 books.

9. (D) On a map, each 1.5 cm represents 5 miles. Notice that 6 cm is 4 times 1.5. So it represents 4 times 5, or 20, miles. You could also set up a proportion, "centimeters is to miles," as follows:

$$\frac{cm}{mi} \qquad \frac{1.5}{5} = \frac{6}{x}$$

Cross multiplying yields
$$1.5x = 30$$

$$\frac{1.5x}{1.5} = \frac{30}{1.5}$$

$$x = 20$$

10. (B) Notice that lines B and C (the 8th and 9th grades) intersect at the third day. This indicates that by day 3 the 9th and 8th grades had the same number of sales. In other words, by that day they sold equal amounts.

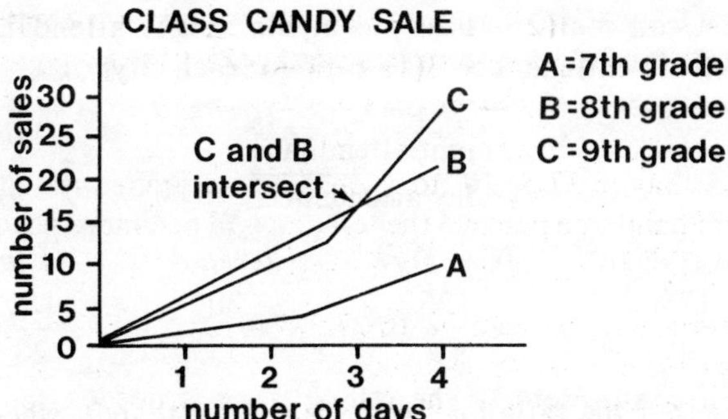

11. **(D)** You can visually determine that the bar representing Boston has far greater percentage night attendance (the shaded part of the bar) compared to its day attendance (the white portion of the bar) than do the bars representing the other cities.

ATTENDANCE: SELECTED MAJOR LEAGUE BALL PARKS

Highest Annual, 1948–1985

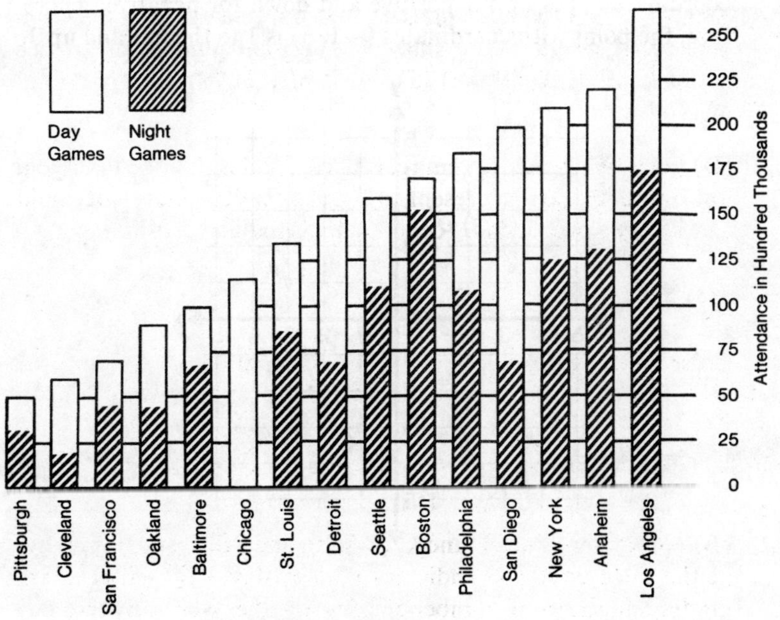

Or you can mathematically compute "night attendance compared to day attendance" as a ratio for each city:

$$\frac{\text{night attendance}}{\text{day attendance}}$$

Los Angeles	*New York*	*Cleveland*	*Boston*
$\dfrac{175}{90}$	$\dfrac{125}{80}$	$\dfrac{20}{35}$	$\dfrac{150}{20}$

Notice that the ratio for Boston is greater than 7, whereas Los Angeles, New York, and Cleveland are each less than 2.

12. (C) The largest bonus discount for Extra Firm mattresses is $75 for the King. The smallest bonus discount for the Regal mattresses is $15 for the Twin. So the difference between the two is $75 − $15, which equals $60.

13. (D) Starting at the origin ("cross hairs"), the first coordinate (x) is across, right for positive and left for negative. The second coordinate (y) is up for positive and down for negative. Therefore, the point with coordinates $(-1, 3)$ is 1 to the left and up 3.

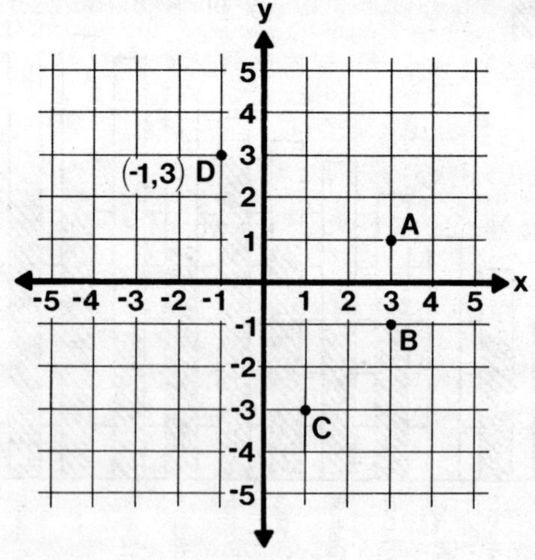

14. (C) From the graph, you can see that the line passes through the points (3, 0) and (0, 3).

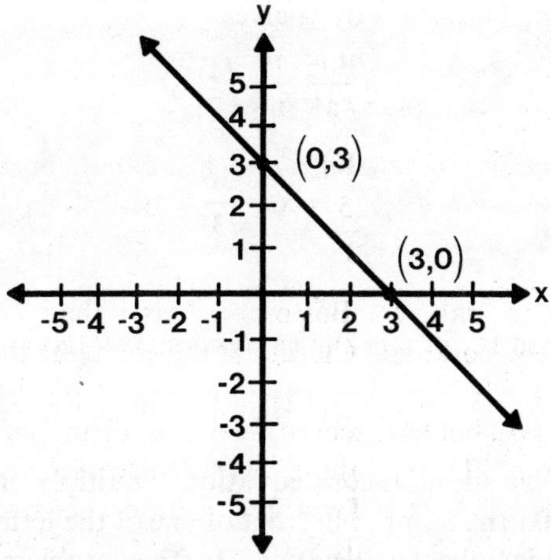

Now simply work from the choices and check which equation has those points. Choice (A) x = 3 has only one of these points, (3, 0). Choice (B) y = 3 has only one of these points, (0, 3). You should also notice that (A) would be a vertical line and (B) would be a horizontal line and eliminate them immediately. Choice (C) x + y = 3 has both points. Simply plug in each set of points to check:

$$x + y = 3$$
$$(3) + (0) = 3$$
and
$$(0) + (3) = 3$$

Notice that choice (D) would not work:

$$x - y = 3$$
$$(3) - (0) = 3$$
but
$$(0) - (3) \neq 3$$

15. (C) First solve the equation for x:

$$\frac{3}{4}x - 2 = 7$$

so
$$\frac{3}{4}x = 9$$

Multiplying both sides by ⁴⁄₃ gives

$$\left(\frac{4}{3}\right)\frac{3}{4}x = \left(\frac{4}{3}\right)9$$

$$x = \frac{36}{3}$$

$$x = 12$$

Now plug in 12 for x in the expression $3x - 1$:

$$3x - 1 = 3(12) - 1 = 36 - 1 = 35$$

16. (A) To solve simultaneous equations, multiply one of the equations so that the number in front of one of the letters (unknowns) is the same in each equation. In this problem, multiply the bottom equation by 2:

$$2x + 4y = 10$$
$$3x + 2y = 3$$

$$2x + 4y = 10$$
$$2(3x + 2y) = 2(3)$$

$$2x + 4y = 10$$
$$6x + 4y = 6$$

Now subtract the equations from each other:

$$\begin{array}{r} 2x + 4y = 10 \\ -6x + 4y = 6 \\ \hline -4x = 4 \end{array}$$

And solve:
$$-4x = 4$$

$$\frac{-4x}{-4} = \frac{4}{-4}$$

$$x = -1$$

17. (D) First change the equation to slope-intercept form $y = mx + b$, where m is the slope and b is the y intercept:

$$6x + y = 3$$
$$\underline{-6x \qquad\qquad -6x}$$
$$y = 3 - 6x \qquad \text{or} \qquad -6x + 3$$

Next, you can see that in the equation $y = -6x + 3$, -6 is in the m position and is therefore the slope.

18. (C) If you draw the bicycle route it would look like this:

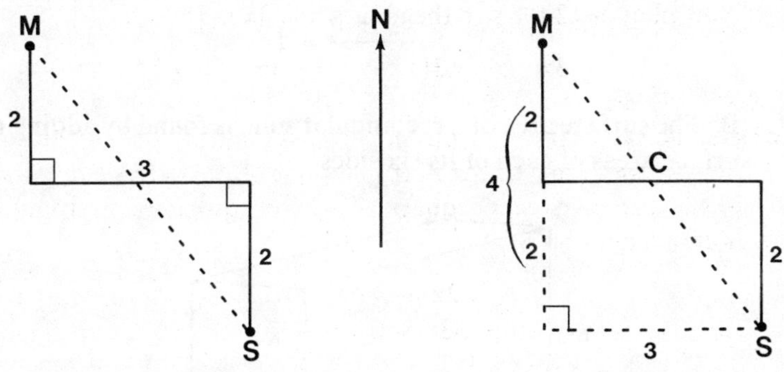

Now, making a right triangle would allow you to use the Pythagorean theorem as follows:

$$a^2 + b^2 = c^2$$
$$(4)^2 + (3)^2 = c^2$$
$$16 + 9 = c^2$$
$$25 = c^2$$
$$5 = c$$

You may have noticed that this is a 3-4-5 right triangle.

19. (C) If Teresa's present age is T, twice Teresa's age equals 2T. Three years less than twice Teresa's age is $2T - 3$. If Jorge is 10 years old now, last year he was 9. So

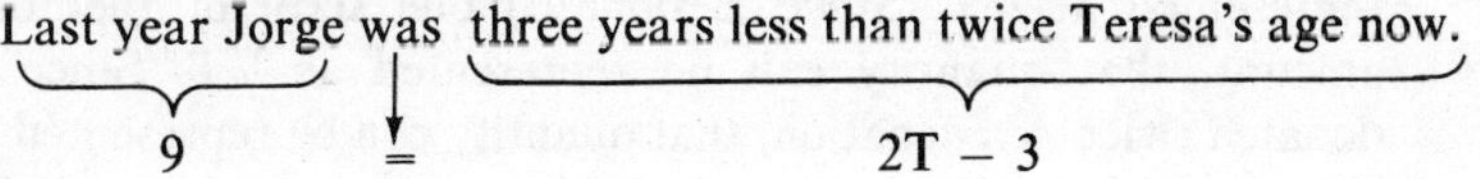

Last year Jorge was   three years less than twice Teresa's age now.

$$9 \qquad = \qquad 2T - 3$$

20. (A) To solve for d, first move $+5$ to the other side by changing its sign:

$$-8g = -3d + 5$$
$$-8g - 5 = -3d$$

Multiply both sides by -1 to eliminate minus signs:

$$8g + 5 = 3d$$

Divide both sides by 3: $$\frac{8g + 5}{3} = \frac{3d}{3}$$

$$\frac{8g + 5}{3} = d$$

21. (B) The surface area of a rectangular solid is found by adding the surface areas of each of its six sides.

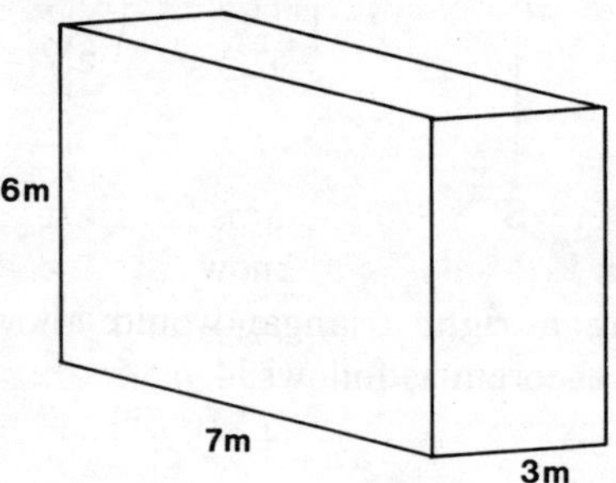

Notice that a rectangular box has three pairs of rectangular sides. In this instance, two sides are 7m by 6m, two sides are 6m by 3m, and two sides are 7m by 3m. So the total surface area equals

$$2(7m \times 6m) + 2(6m \times 3m) + 2(7m \times 3m)$$

22. (A) Let T represent the total amount of donations. Since A donated one fifth of the total amount, that quantity can be represented at $\frac{1}{5}T$. Since B donated one sixth of the total amount, that quantity can be represented as $\frac{1}{6}T$. Since C donated twice A's donation, that quantity can be represented as twice one fifth of the total, or $\frac{2}{5}T$. Since D donated one half B's

donation, that quantity can be represented as $(\frac{1}{2})\frac{1}{6}T = \frac{1}{12}T$. Total the donations:

$$\frac{1}{5}T + \frac{1}{6}T + \frac{2}{5}T + \frac{1}{12}T = \frac{12}{60}T + \frac{10}{60}T + \frac{24}{60}T + \frac{5}{60}T = \frac{51}{60}T$$

Subtract from the total, T, to determine E's donation:

$$T - \frac{51}{60}T = \frac{9}{60}T$$

23. (D) $30x^2 - 19x - 4 = (5x - 4)(6x + 1)$. Therefore, $(5x - 4)$ and $(6x + 1)$ are each factors.

24. (D) Subtract and combine common terms, remembering that subtracting a negative quantity is equivalent to adding its positive.

$$(12r^4s^2 - 3r^3s + 2r) - (7r^4s^2 - 4r^3s - 2rs^2 + 2r)$$
$$12r^4s^2 - 3r^3s + 2r - 7r^4s^2 + 4r^3s + 2rs^2 - 2r$$
$$5r^4s^2 + r^3s + 2rs^2$$

25. (B) If a wallet with \$134 contains "at least one \$5 bill . . . and at least a dozen \$10 bills," you know that it cannot contain 13 \$10 bills, since that equals \$130 and therefore at least one \$5 bill would amount to more than \$134. Therefore, you know that the wallet contains exactly a dozen \$10 bills. Subtracting:

$$\$134 - \$120 = \$14$$

The only way to reach exactly 18 bills with the \$14 containing just \$5 bills and \$1 bills is with two \$5 bills and four \$1 bills.

26. (C) If the plumber works for 6 consecutive hours, he charges \$45 for the first hour, plus \$20 for each of the five additional hours:

$$\$45 + 5(\$20) = \$45 + \$100 = \$145$$

27. (B) You could solve this problem algebraically by first getting a common denominator of ab and then changing each fraction to that common denominator as follows:

$$\frac{3a + 4}{a} \times \frac{b}{b} = \frac{3ab + 4b}{ab}$$

$$\frac{2b + 5}{b} \times \frac{a}{a} = \frac{2ab + 5a}{ab}$$

Then combine the like terms and put over the common denominator.

$$\frac{3ab + 4b}{ab} + \frac{2ab + 5a}{ab} = \frac{3ab + 4b + 2ab + 5a}{ab} = \frac{5ab + 4b + 5a}{ab}$$

28. (D) One way to find the length of the line segment is to quickly construct a right triangle:

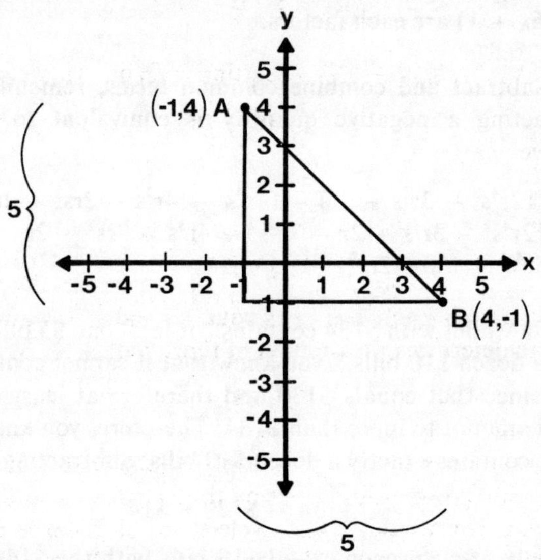

Notice that each leg of the right triangle equals 5. Thus, using the Pythagorean theorem:

$$a^2 + b^2 = c^2$$
$$(5)^2 + (5)^2 = c^2$$
$$25 + 25 = c^2$$
$$50 = c^2$$
$$\sqrt{50} = c$$
$$\sqrt{25 \cdot 2} = c$$
$$\sqrt{25} \cdot \sqrt{2} = c$$
$$5\sqrt{2} = c$$

You may have noticed that this is an isosceles right triangle with ratio 1-1-$\sqrt{2}$, so 5-5-5$\sqrt{2}$.

You could also use the distance formula:

$$\text{distance} = (x_2 - x_1)^2 + (y_2 - y_1)^2$$

And solve as follows:
$$d = \sqrt{(4 - -1)^2 + (-1 - 4)^2}$$
$$= \sqrt{(5)^2 + (-5)^2}$$
$$= \sqrt{25 + 25}$$
$$= \sqrt{50}$$
$$= 5\sqrt{2}$$

29. (D) If $(3x - 1)(x + 3) = 0$, setting each quantity equal to 0:

$$(3x - 1) = 0$$
$$3x = 1$$
$$x = \tfrac{1}{3}$$

and
$$x + 3 = 0$$
$$x = -3$$

Now that you know the roots equal $\tfrac{1}{3}$ and -3, simply multiply them to determine the product of those roots:

$$(\tfrac{1}{3})(-3) = -1$$

30. (D) Distance is found by multiplying the time traveled by the rate (speed). For example, if you traveled for 3 hours at 40 miles per hour, you would have traveled a total distance of $(3)(4) =$ 120 miles. So if Suzanne first traveled for h hours at m miles per hour, that distance equals h times m, or hm. But then she traveled an additional q hours at t miles per hour, so the second distance she went was tq. Adding the two yields her total distance traveled.

31. (C) To find the perimeter of a geometric shape, total the length of all its sides.

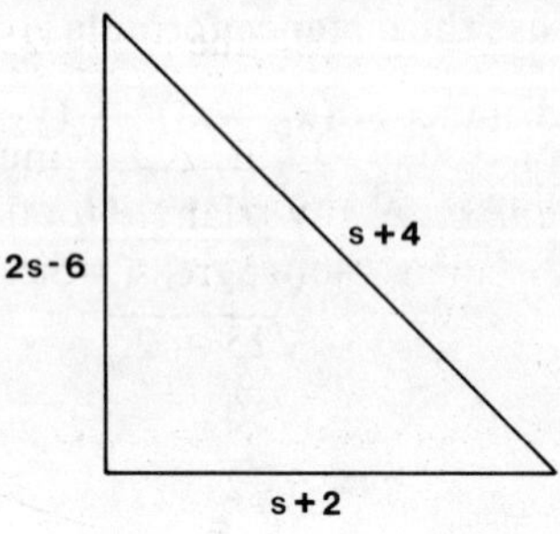

In this problem:

$$(s + 4) + (s + 2) + (2s - 6) = 4s$$

32. (B) The equation for the area of a circle is $A = \pi r^2$.

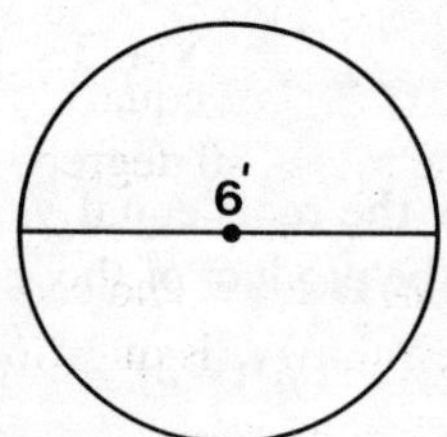

Since the problem asks for the *approximate* area, and since the answer choices are numerically widely spread, round π to 3. (Remember that the radius is half the diameter of a circle.)

$$A = 3(3)^2 = 3(9) = 27$$

33. (C) All edges of a cube are equal; the volume of a cube = edge^3. If the edge of a cube is 5 inches, its volume is $5 \times 5 \times 5$, or 125.

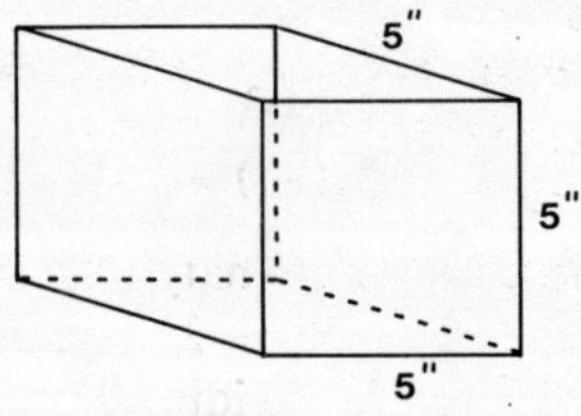

A cube consists of 6 equal squares, so the surface area of a cube is 6 times the area of one face. Since one face of this cube is 5 × 5, or 25, the surface area of this cube is 6 × 25 = 150.

34. (D) Note that in triangle ECB, ∠CEB must equal 30 degrees, since the three angles of any triangle total 180 degrees. Therefore, ∠AED also equals 30 degrees, since vertical angles are always equal.

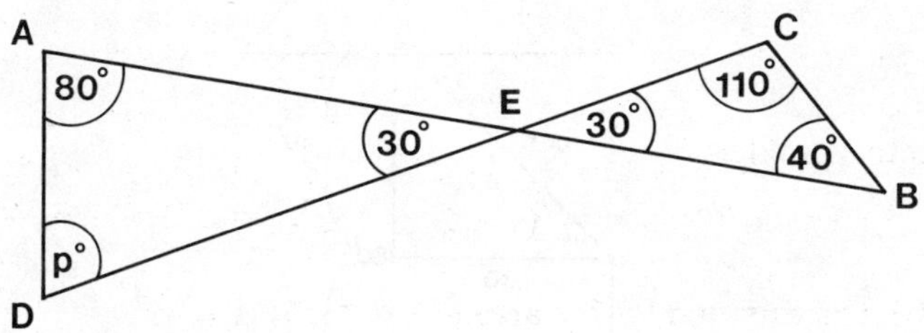

Thus, in triangle AED, ∠ADE equals 70 degrees, since the three angles of any triangle total 180 degrees.

35. (A) Noting that the answer choices are numerically widely spread, you should estimate this question.

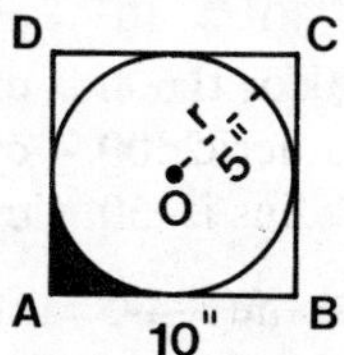

First find the area of the circle, realizing that its radius is half the side of the square, or 5. Using the equation A = πr² and rounding π to 3:

$$A = (3)(5)^2$$
$$A = (3)(25) = 75$$

The area of the circle is approximately 75. Subtracting from the area of the square: 100 − 75 = 25 square inches for all four "corner sections." Therefore, dividing 25 by 4 for just one of the corner sections (the shaded region) gives approximately 6 square inches. But perhaps the fastest way to answer this question is to realize first that the total area of the figure is 100 square inches and then that the shaded area is obviously well under one quarter of the figure. The only possible answer is therefore (A).

36. (C) Drawing a line parallel to the floor as shown below divides the figure into a lower rectangle (40 by 30) and a right triangle above whose legs are 30 and 40.

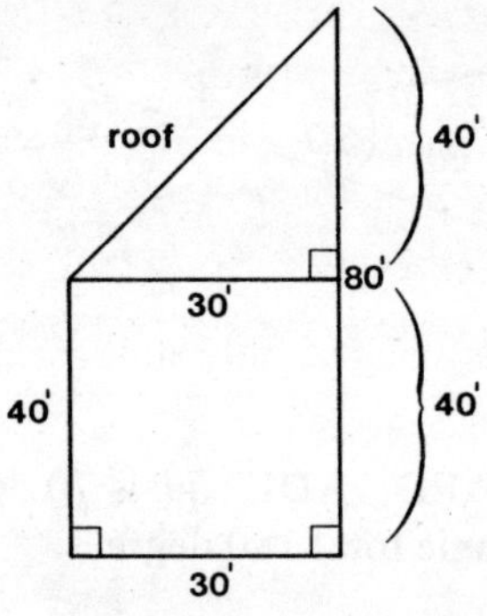

Using the Pythagorean theorem:

$$a^2 + b^2 = c^2$$
$$30^2 + 40^2 = c^2$$
$$900 + 1600 = c^2$$
$$2500 = c^2$$
$$50 = c$$

You might have spotted the 3-4-5 ratio, making it 30-40-50.

37. (C) Notice that the only difference between the two equations is w^2. Therefore, the difference between the two objects falling is $w^2 = 3^2 = 9$.

38. (A) Since statement 5 tells us that Chico is a cat and statement 1 that all cats have tails, it must be true that Chico has a tail.

39. (B) The number of sides of the inner figure increases by one as it moves to the right, whereas the outer figure's number of sides decreases by one each time.

40. (B) From statements I, II, and III, a simple chart can be constructed:

$$\underline{B1} \quad \underline{G}$$
$$\text{or}$$
$$\underline{R} \ \_ \ \underline{Y} \quad \underline{G} \quad \underline{B1}$$

OR

$$\underline{B1} \quad \underline{G}$$
$$\text{or}$$
$$\underline{G} \quad \underline{B1} \quad \underline{Y} \ \_ \ \underline{R}$$

Either chart is possible. The only statement that *must* be true is (B).

WRITING

1. (B) Though it has a subject and a verb (*stone is*), the sentence is a dependent clause and needs another independent clause to make it a complete sentence.

2. (D) We come to *eoliths* in this sentence before we know what they are. If the sentence were moved to follow sentence 7, both the first and second paragraphs would be improved.

3. (C) The addition of a sentence giving an example of a representational artist would make the paragraph clearer. As it is now, it defines two kinds of art but gives an example of only one of the two. None of the other choices would improve the clarity of the paragraph. In fact, they would make it harder to follow.

4. (D) The plural verb *are* requires a plural subject, so *painting* should be the plural *paintings*.

5. (C) The participle *Seeing* is a dangling modifier. The sentence should have a human agent who sees. As it is written, the participle modifies *meaning*. The corrected sentence might read *Seeing a tree on a mountainside or a mother and her baby, a viewer can easily understand the meaning*.

6. (B) Sentence 2 defines the thesis sentence as stating an opinion, followed by the word *because* and a list of reasons supporting the opinion. Choice (B) follows this pattern exactly. Choice (A) gives no reasons; choice (C) is ungrammatical and gives only one ill-considered reason; choice (D) gives no reasons.

7. (B) The series of adjectives, *valid, reasonable,* and *well founded,* requires a comma after *valid*.

8. (C) The passage has used the second person pronoun (*you, your*) to refer to the reader. The change to the third person (*one's*) here is inconsistent. The correct word here is *your*.

9. (C) The passage is written in an informal, direct prose and makes its critical points directly. Choice (C) is consistent with this style. Choice (A) changes from the first person (*I*) used in the passage to a third (*one*) and is bland in its criticism (*inconvenient*). Choice (B) is wordy and more formal in its word choice. Choice (D)

changes the tense of the passage to the past and introduces a slightly off-topic idea.

10. (C) The apostrophe in *it's* is used for the contraction of *it is*. The correct punctuation here for the possessive of *it* is *its*.

11. (A) The subject of the paragraph and the whole passage is Twain's alleged racism. Sentence 2 is about a wholly different interest of Twain's, and its idea is never developed in the paragraph. The paragraph is improved if the sentence is deleted.

12. (D) Having said that the book shows how slavery damages the personality in sentence 7, the writer repeats the point in sentence 8 (*reveals the harm*).

13. (B) Sentences 9, 11, and 12 are correct as written. Sentence 10 should read *For them*. The objective case, *them,* rather than the subjective case, *they,* is needed because the pronoun is the object of the preposition *For*.

14. (B) Sentence 1 states that there are two kinds of writing. Sentence 2 begins with *The first* and describes one kind of writing. Since sentence 4 describes the other, we should expect it to begin with *The second*. Sentence 5 is one in which the first clause contrasts with the second; the first half speaks of triviality, but the sentence concludes with an assertion of importance. An introductory phrase or word like *Even though,* or *Although,* or *Despite the fact that* would probably introduce this sentence.

15. (A) The second paragraph moves on from the discussion of writing of the first paragraph to the discussion of handwriting. But sentence 6 with its references to *flourishes* and *style* could refer to either handwriting or to prose style. If the paragraph begins with sentence 7, the new subject is made clear at once. And sentence 6 follows logically after sentence 8.

16. (D) Sentence 4 has no subject and no main verb, only participles. It can be corrected easily by changing *achieving* to *he achieved* and *becoming* to *became*.

17. (C) The phrase *tried to combat* means the same as *attempted to fight,* and only one of the two nouns *prejudice* and *intolerance* is needed.

18. (D) The first four sentences in the paragraph are about the period leading up to Hoover's election as President and follow a logical sequence. The last sentence jumps ahead to the period after Hoover's election and presidency. It has no real connection with the rest of the paragraph.

19. (A) The paragraph lists three qualities of good teachers in sentences 2, 3, and 4. Sentences 3 and 4 should begin with words that make clear this series, such as *in addition* and *finally*. The writer might also have used *Second* and *Third* or *Second* and *Finally*.

20. (C) The paragraph uses the first person plural (*we, us, ours*) to refer to the class. Later in this sentence, the pronoun *our* is used. Therefore, the *I* should be changed to *we*.

21. (A) The subject of the first paragraph is the causes of the industrial boom. This sentence gives a fourth cause to go with those at the end of the first paragraph. At the same time, it introduces the tycoons, referred to as *robber barons* in the next sentence, who are the central subject of the second paragraph. Choices (C) and (D) do refer to these men, but fail to link them to the subject of the first paragraph.

22. (B) The clauses describing the two other tycoons in this sentence have told us about the size of their wealth and its sources. Choice (B) is the most clearly parallel to these of the four choices

23. (C) The semicolon is used like a period to set off grammatically complete clauses. Here, the clause introduced by *While* is dependent, and if set off by a semicolon, would be a sentence fragment. The needed punctuation here is the comma.

24. (A) Sentence 5 simply repeats sentence 4 in slightly different form. The paragraph needs only one of the two sentences.

25. (D) The sentence looks ahead 72 years. The verb should be in the future tense, *will be* rather than *is*.

26. (C) The subject of the paragraph is state-erected barriers to voting. The comparison of European and American voting statistics has no real bearing on the rest of the paragraph, and without sentence 3, the paragraph is clearer.

27. (A) The correct word in this context is one that means *are faced with:* choice (A), *confronted.*

28. (C) The passage is an informal, personal account of an encounter between the writer and a four-year-old autistic child. It is written in the first person. Though the passage is informal, it is not slangy, and in choice (A), diction like *the kid* clashes with the style of the rest of the passage. Choices (B) and (D), on the other hand, are too formal, too stiff. The pronoun *one* is inconsitent with the *I* used throughout the passage. Both sentences move away from the specific child, who is the real subject, to discuss autism. Choice (C) is the most consistent with the rest of the paragraph and is relevant to the central idea of the passage, that is, going beyond textbooks.

29. (A) The phrase *putting him down* must refer to the speaker, the *I* of the passage, but as the sentence stands, the phrase seems to modify *Gregory.* The corrected sentence should read *and instead of putting him down, I held Gregory in my arms.*

30. (C) Three of the adverbs are correct. They modify the verbs *engaged* (sentence 8), *shouted* (sentence 9) and *flowed* (sentence 10). Though *wearily* appears to modify the verb *grew,* it really refers to *arms.* The arms are *weary* rather than *growing.* In this sentence, *grew* is a linking verb, like *became* or *were,* and the adjective is used with a linking verb, rather than the adverb—in this case, *weary* not *wearily.*

31. (A) The paragraph is about a late-night talk-show host and his audience. The watchers of daytime television are irrelevant, and the sentence about them should be omitted.

32. (B) *Comedic talent, ability to be funny,* and *skill in raising laughs* are three ways of saying the same thing. Any one of these three is sufficient.

33. (D) Since the subject of the sentence is the singular *operation,* the verb should be the singular *is.* The phrase *is said* is used to suggest that this is the opinion of others, not the author's own.

34. (B) Only sentence 10 is concerned with *ancient days.* All the rest of the paragraph is about modern beasts made to resemble the unicorn.

35. **(D)** Here *its* is the possessive of the pronoun *it* and should be written without the apostrophe.

36. **(A)** Sentence 2 could be reduced to *Every reader brings to every poem a unique background.* The first *is different* and certainly the phrase *which is different from everyone else's* are unnecessary.

37. **(B)** The correct form here is the contraction *Who's* for *Who is. Whose* is a possessive form meaning *of whom.*

38. **(D)** The sentence handles its pronouns inconsistently, moving from *how one reads* to *you bring.* Since the passage has been using *you* before, this sentence should be corrected to *how you read.*

39. **(C)** The paragraph describes the development of animals from the simplest and smallest forms. Since sentence 4 alludes to the first cellular organism, sentence 6, which describes one-celled animals, would follow logically. Sentence 5 then describes a higher form of life.

40. **(B)** This is a passage from a science textbook. Throughout the passage, the language is specific, literal, scientific. The romantic metaphor calling the past a *mysterious abyss* is noticeably different from the style of the rest of the passage.

Final Preparation: Putting It All Together

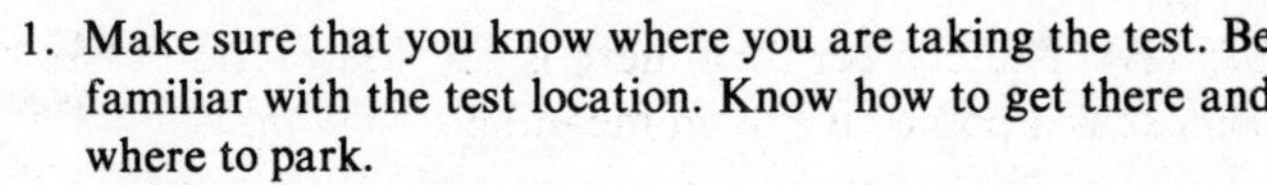

1. Make sure that you know where you are taking the test. Be familiar with the test location. Know how to get there and where to park.

2. Spend the week before the test on a general review of important concepts, test-taking strategies, and techniques.

3. Don't cram the night before the exam. It's a waste of time!

4. If you usually eat breakfast, eat a nourishing one before the exam.

5. Arrive in plenty of time at the testing center.

6. Remember to bring the proper materials: identification, admission ticket, three or four sharpened Number 2 pencils, an eraser, and a watch.

7. Dress comfortably. Wear layers of clothing so that you can adjust to the temperature of the room (taking off a sweater if it's too hot or putting one on if it's too cold).

8. Start off with confidence and with a plan. Answer the questions you know first, and then go back and try to answer the others.

9. Try to eliminate one or more answer choices before you guess, but make sure that you fill in an answer for each question. There is no penalty for guessing.

10. Make sure that you are answering "what is being asked."

11. Remember that working from the answers by eliminating choices is very helpful.

12. Use a Positive Approach, the key to getting the questions right that you should get right and the key to success on the TASP!